THE Adventurer

THE
Adventurer

Paul Zweig

PRINCETON UNIVERSITY PRESS
PRINCETON, NEW JERSEY

Illustration on page 53 used by permission of Macmillan Publishing Co., Inc. from *The Children's Homer* by Padraic Colum. Copyright 1918 by Macmillan Publishing Co., Inc., renewed 1946 by Padraic Colum.

Excerpts from *Beowulf* as translated by Burton Raffel, copyright © 1963 by Burton Raffel; and Dante, *The Inferno* translated by John Ciardi, reprinted by arrangement with The New American Library, Inc., New York.

Excerpts from *The Portable Nietzsche,* translated by Walter Kaufmann. Copyright 1954 by The Viking Press, Inc. Reprinted by permission of The Viking Press, Inc., and Chatto & Windus, London.

Excerpts from *The City in History,* © 1961 by Lewis Mumford. Reprinted by permission of Harcourt Brace Jovanovich, Inc.

Published by Princeton University Press, Princeton, New Jersey
In the U.K.: Princeton University Press, Guildford, Surrey

© 1974 by Paul Zweig
Library of Congress Catalog Card Number: 81-47798
ISBN 0-691-06451-2
ISBN 0-691-01387-X pbk.
Printed in the United States of America by
Princeton University Press, Princeton, New Jersey
TEXT DESIGNED BY VINCENT TORRE
First Princeton Paperback printing, 1981

For Francine

Preface

THE oldest, most widespread stories in the world are adventure stories, about human heroes who venture into the myth-countries at the risk of their lives, and bring back tales of the world beyond men. These tales bind together the fragile island of human needs and relationships by affirming the possibility that mere men can survive the storms of the demonic world. Even the shaman plunging mentally into his transe voyage to the spirit world is an adventurer of sorts.

The modern world's dismissal of adventure as an entertaining but minor experience is unprecedented. Few cultures have been so willing to tempt the gods. That we should do so says a great deal about the arrogance of our cultural values.

This book explores the archaic values of adventure and examines that demonic, half-human personage, the adventurer, who inhabits the folklore and the epic literature of Europe, Greece, and the ancient Middle East. It traces the overthrow of the adventurer in our own domestically inclined culture, as well as the isolated irruptions of a new adventure myth in the work of rare modern writers. The possibility of adventure lies within our grasp. Perhaps not the exploits of Odysseus in the magic countries, but the irruptive, dazzling intensities of risk and inner venture which flit by us in the margins of our lives. We need only value them and take them with high seriousness, to possess them, and to be possessed by them.

Portions of this book were presented as the Christian Gauss Seminars at Princeton University. I would like to thank the Christian Gauss committee for the opportunity to test some of the ideas in the book on an attentive, perceptive audience.

Contents

PART ONE

PART TWO

Contents

PART THREE

PART ONE

CHAPTER

1

Introduction

THERE is an extraordinary moment in Sergio Leone's movie, *Once Upon a Time in the West,* when two gunfighters who have been carried inexorably toward each other by the story meet for the shootout. The scene is filmed in surrealistic slow motion. It does not seem to be happening in a clearing behind a house, but in a silent space containing only these two men. The metallic pounding of the music articulates every movement as if, under its influence, the gunfighters were performing a grave ritual. At last the shooting takes place, and the dreamlike movement dissolves. With appalling suddenness the dying man and the victor are stranded in the peopled world where, for a moment, it seems strange that a man should be dying because of what happens there, in the dream.

My example of an adventurous encounter might have been taken from a novel, a television serial, a science-fiction story. It would have been harder to have taken it from my own life, because adventures are precisely what few of us know from experience. Our familiarity with them tends to be "literary." Adventures draw the reader into a strange distance which the story alone has made accessible.

Yet the distance is not wholly strange. Haven't all of us, now and then, experienced moments of abrupt intensity, when our lives seemed paralyzed by risk: a ball clicking around a roulette wheel; a car sliding across an icy road; the excruciating uncertainty of a lover's response; perhaps merely a walk through the streets of a strange city? The cat's paw of chance hovers tantalizingly, and suddenly the simplest outcome seems unpredictable. For a brief moment, we are like warriors, charged with the energies of survival, reading every detail of the scene as if it were a sign revealing what was to come. Ordinarily we don't endow these excursions of excitement with overmuch importance. They flit by us, and we reknit the interrupted links of time. We think of them as "vacations" from our actual selves; side steps to be indulged and pursued, but not too far.

Yet it is possible of think of these moments in another way. The gleams of intensity which invest them have an otherworldly quality, as if a man's duel with risk were not a "vacation" at all, but a plunge into essential experience. This is the view developed in adventure stories. They offer us heroes obsessed by risk and confrontation, who spell out a choice we glimpse only fleetingly in ourselves: the choice to pursue adventures, to interpret life itself as a series of solitary combats, with death as the adversary.

Adventure stories transpose our dalliance with risk into a sustained vision. That is why they are often accused of being "escapist." They remove us radically from ourselves, happening "out of this world," if this world is taken to mean the circle of relationships and responsibilities that we know. Thus Eric Ambler writes about the cloaked world of international espionage; Edgar Rice Burroughs about the African jungle; Conrad and Melville about the distant seas; T. E. Lawrence about the Arabian desert; science-fiction authors about imagined worlds and bizarre technologies.

The exotic quality of the adventure story is closely connected to another important element: the story must be charged with "action": episodes of flamboyant risk which become focal points for the narrative, as in old-style Western movies, where the plot is rarely more than an occasion for a number of enthralling climaxes: gunfights, chases, ordeals in the desert. The demands we

4

make on this kind of story are apparently different from those we make on "serious" literature. We are quite ready to forgive conventional setting and stereotyped characters, provided the "action" is abundant and well-executed; as if "action" were the real subject matter of the story, and the human involvement only a cursory background. When the gunfighters in Sergio Leone's movie confront each other across a mythic space, the plot with its sketchy moral attitudes vanishes. For a moment neither man is a hero or a villain. They are accomplices in risk, comrades in the dreamlike element of action.

According to prevailing literary, and moral, values, this defines the marginal character of adventure literature, as Graham Greene explains in his espionage novel, *The Ministry of Fear*, where the principal character experiences adventure as a sort of immature lark, wonderfully engrossing but irresponsible. As he careens through the English countryside, he reflects:

Over there among the unknown tribes a woman was giving birth, rats were nosing among sacks of meal, an old man was dying, two people were seeing each other for the first time by the light of a lamp: everything in that darkness was of such deep importance that their errand could not equal it—this violent superficial chase, this cardboard adventure hurtling at forty-five miles an hour along the edge of the profound natural common experiences of men. Rowe felt a longing to get back into that world: into the world of homes and children and quiet love and the ordinary unspecified fears and anxieties the neighbor shared. . . .[1]

Having escaped from the net of human cares and needs, the adventurer prowls in a limbo of cardboard intensities. According to Greene, the reader should know better than to be drawn into it with him. Yet, somehow he doesn't know better. His "childish" nature succumbs, tempting him to abandon the responsibility of plot, for the irresponsibility of action.

Our modern disregard for adventure reveals how thoroughly domesticated is the view we have come to take of our human, and cultural limits. Man, we have decided, is the laboring animal whose ability to create values depends upon his infinite capacity to buy and to sell: his time, his work, his very life. From this point of view, adventure is, at best, a recreation.

Yet other civilizations have thought differently about adventure, as becomes abundantly clear when we enlarge our perspective to include the literature of ancient Greece and the Middle East, the narrative tradition of tribal cultures in Africa and, in general, of any of the non-Western, non-Christian cultures we know. When we do so, we make an interesting discovery. For adventure then appears to be the oldest, most persistent subject matter in the world. The tales of Greek mythology, themselves transcribed from the oral, pre-Homeric culture of Mycenae, are filled with episodes of high adventure: Perseus confronting the snake-haired Gorgon; Herakles performing his interminable tasks for the sheer love of risk; Jason and his Argonauts questing for the Golden Fleece. The fullest literary treatment of adventure in Greece occurs in the *Odyssey*. Odysseus, "skilled in all ways of contending," wanders over the Aegean, displaying his indomitable cunning, ruthlessness, and courage, because the energy of his character exists only amidst the unpredictable turns of "action."

What is so obviously true of Greek mythology is no less true of stories in the *Upanishads* (especially those concerning Indra), of American Indian myths, of shamanic tales in Siberia. In fact, the raw material of mythologies throughout the world seems largely to be made up of perilous journeys, encounters with inhuman monsters, ordeals of loneliness and hunger, descents into the underworld. No matter how the myth is moralized and integrated into a system, the kernel of experience which makes it worth telling and listening to is adventure; precisely the sort of "action" which, in modern trappings, continues to enthrall millions of readers and moviegoers.

It could be further argued—as I will in a later chapter—that the narrative art itself arose from the need to tell an adventure; that man risking his life in perilous encounters constitutes the original definition of what is worth talking about.

6

Introduction

The ancient Middle Eastern *Epic of Gilgamesh* is perhaps the oldest written story in the world. It opens with a description of the hero, Gilgamesh, tormented by his "restless heart," unable to control his half-divine energies. Although he is king of the city of Uruk, he experiences the confinement of his own kingdom with bitterness and morbidity. The epic tells how Gilgamesh finally meets up with his heroic twin, Enkidu, and resolves to leave Uruk in search of adventure. Together the companions travel to the great cedar forest where they encounter the monster Humbaba, of whom it is written:

Humbaba is not like men who die, his weapons are such that none can stand against them; the forest stretches for ten thousand leagues in every direction; who would willingly go down to explore its depths? As for Humbaba, when he roars it is like the torrent of the storm, his breath is like fire and his jaws are death itself.[2]

In this encounter, and in the later episodes where Gilgamesh journeys to the land of Faraway to learn the secret of immortality, the poem creates a pattern of adventurous quest which reappears in strikingly similar form in the *Odyssey*, and the tales of Herakles; in Celtic mythology; in medieval romance; even in fairy tales.

Clearly adventure constitutes an ancient and widespread subject matter. Not an occasion for marginal escapist literature, as it has become for us since the seventeenth century, but an act claiming to be constitutive of culture itself, as in the Prometheus story and in other origin myths.

A great deal needs to be said about the "uses" of adventure in traditional cultures, and the first part of my study will attempt to describe some of these uses: in epic literature, in traditional storytelling, but also in the ecstatic techniques and tales of shamanism. There is, however, a question which must be raised. If adventure has been held in such high esteem, as the particular subject matter of so many narrative traditions in so many cultures, including our own until the Renaissance, then what has happened to change this? How have we come to have such a low opinion of an experience which was held to be central by "high" cultures which we ourselves continue to value.

Our modern disregard for adventure is peculiar, and unprecedented. Only in the Orient does one find a mood as hostile to the fascinations of adventure as our own. There too, the enthrallment of danger and physical risk is made subservient to other, "higher" values. In the Tibetan folk epic *Guesar of Ling*, for example, the hero, Guesar, rarely engages himself in "action" as we usually understand the word. Each encounter from which he emerges victorious is controlled by the intervention of superior magic, and divine force. Guezar himself is known to be the corporeal shadow of a god. He need only manipulate a magical stick, or mutter a formula, as he is instructed to do by messengers from above, for his enemies to vanish. Instead of plunging into epic adventures, Guesar is lifted above them, as in the following passage describing his assault against a monastery-fortress, where the voice of a divine protector instructs him:

To destroy the ramparts one of your magic arrows will suffice, but the way there is long and dangerous. You will have to go through narrow canyons filled with tigers, lions, and worse than that, certain cannibal demons. In your body of flesh, you could never succeed in passing. So transform your divine steed into the king of vultures. If you mount on him, and steer a course through space higher than that of the birds, you'll be in India in a few seconds.[*]

Here as elsewhere Guezar achieves glory by overcoming the merely human limitations which would have constrained him to adventure. He represents not the self-affirming individuality of the hero, but the pure instrumentality of the spirit which acts and speaks through him.

We are faced with an interesting paradox. Oriental traditions discourage adventure because they consider the vigorous individuality of the adventurer to be an illusion, a trick of the Maya. Modern traditions in the West have been even less hospitable to the adventurer. For the most part, our adventure stories constitute a second-rate literature, appropriate for pulp magazines and low-grade movies. Yet vigorous individuality is precisely what our culture has come to value most.

Perhaps the problem lies in the limitations we have come to place upon the concept of individuality. Consider the figure of the philosopher in Descartes's *Meditations*, arriving at knowledge of his selfhood not through any sort of "action," but by doing nothing at all, and less than nothing. Only when he has closed off all the avenues by which the world impinges on his sensibility —closing his eyes, mouth, nose, and ears—can he begin to know who he is, and if he is: he is precisely what is left—he is the inward traces which continue when the world has been excluded. Viewed by an observer, the act of establishing his identity resembles a sort of catatonia.

Descartes's *cogito* defines the self in terms of inward qualities, and since the seventeenth century we have continued to believe that a man's identity depends upon psychic patterns which operate invisibly within him. When a man talks or acts, he emits signals to be interpreted by anyone who knows how words and acts are translated back into psychology. Of all that a man does, we tend to be interested especially in those acts which tell his secrets. We are not curious about his great accomplishments, which belong to the world, but about the flow of his mannerisms, his tone of voice, and his daily gestures. It is said that no man is a hero for his valet, and that is the point of view we choose: we desire to know what the valet knows. In the modern world a man is never merely what he does; he is neither more nor less than the "miserable heap of his secrets," as André Malraux has written.

The principal innovations of the novel, since the eighteenth century, can be described as new and better ways of telling secrets: by making public what was meant only for private ears (early letter novels, like *Pamela*, or the *Liaisons Dangereuses*); or by creating the point of view of an ideal snooper, the narrator, who allows us to glean a character's net of secrecies, his individuality, from a reading of his ordinary habits. The best novel, therefore, is the one which tells the best, and the most, secrets, preferably those which the characters themselves are unaware of.

The fascination with secrets has of course been a crucial feature of modern psychoanalysis, which has provided us with a model for the fully disclosed individual: a man lying on a couch, revealing all of his psychic connections in an interminable discourse which, carried to its logical extreme, would leave him time or energy to do little else. The image, although exaggerated, is not unfamiliar. It has a startling resemblance to certain modernist heroes in literature: Joyce's Bloom, Beckett's monologuists, Proust's Marcel, Musil's man without qualities. Eventually one had to coin the term "antihero" to describe such resolutely inactive characters. Yet, from the novelistic view, if they had been busier, they would not have been as true; less elementary confession would have filtered past the surface of their acts. To become subject matter, they had to avoid interfering with their convolute identities. They had to avoid demanding, and therefore impersonal, situations, not to mention anything so extravagant as "action." According to the view expressed by the modern novel, "actions" and adventures hinder individuality, they do not reveal it.

This was true even for the classical novel. If a character was to be fully realized, he could not be too busy. It was better if he were imprisoned in a room, like Pamela, or in a provincial town, like Emma Bovary. Unless of course his busyness was portrayed ironically as a hindrance on the road to full adulthood, as with Julian Sorel in Stendhal's novel *The Red and the Black*. From the start, Julian is frantic with romantic ambitiousness, he is filled with the spirit of undertaking, and that is his ultimate ridicule. For he lives in a world in which nothing can, or should, be undertaken. When, at the end of the novel, he refuses an opportunity to escape from prison, he shows us that he has learned how to be a "man"; he has learned how to do nothing even to the death.

Introduction

The more thoroughly novelists grasped their subject matter (historically accurate and unique individuals), the less subject matter in the traditional sense there was to grasp. That, at least, is a conclusion that can be drawn from the progress of the Victorian novel, as Mario Praz has suggested.[4] The decline of "subject matter" in the nineteenth century is, of course, generally recognized. For Impressionist painters, matter was infinitely less significant than the sensuous manner by which the painter translated his unique vision. From there to Manet's color patterns, Seurat's pointillism, and eventually to complete abstraction, was a short, logical road. It was a road which was followed by the novel too. The full battery of narrative "techniques" could not be freed until subject matter in the old sense had dwindled away completely. Take as an example Conrad's novel, *Lord Jim*. Even as a young man, Jim dreams of becoming a hero. His imagination is filled with scenes out of boys' adventure books:

He saw himself saving people from sinking ships, cutting away masts in a hurricane, swimming through a surf with a line; or as a lonely castaway, barefooted and half-naked, walking on uncovered reefs in search of shellfish to stave off starvation. He confronted savages on tropical shores, quelled mutinies on the high seas, and in a small boat upon the ocean kept up the hearts of despairing men—always an example of devotion to duty, and as unflinching as a hero in a book.[5]

But Jim is recuperated for serious literature, and for the narrative modernism which Conrad applies to his case, because of one salient fact: Jim fails to live up to his dream. Where the hero of boys' literature would have leapt into action, Jim is immobilized. Where even the most ordinary sailor would have been busy at his duty, Jim sinks into passiveness, becomes nobody, like Descartes's philosopher. But that makes all the difference; for out of the enforced leisure (that is, failure) of his character pours his ineffable, complex individuality. Because the stereotype he dreamed of failed him, Jim pours out his heart in a stream of compulsive talk, thereby qualifying as an individual.

It should come as no surprise that the novel as a genre is devoted to leisure, and to a definition of individuality which depends upon leisure. The novel is, to all intents and purposes, a middle-class genre, written by and for people who had, at best, a distant connection to the prevailing modes of labor in the eighteenth and nineteenth centuries. Novelistic individuality depends upon social relationships, upon talking, upon a thousand minute and novelistically recorded gestures. It requires the framework of the ordinary if it is to be expressed and activated. Outside that framework, the individual is lost and must live with the fear that there is nothing for him to become. The individual, as the novel portrays him, is essentially conservative. He can tolerate only small doses of change, gradual involvements of "action," but not revolutions, and not the explosive energies of adventure. The conservatism of so many great novelists is not accidental: Balzac, Jane Austen, Henry James. All needed to believe in the essentialness of ordinary life, and all needed for their individuals to move, not too energetically, in a solid world of relationships.

It is significant to note, in this connection, that the popular literature of the eighteenth and nineteenth centuries—rogues' biographies, the Gothic novel, the *roman noir*—are in no sense merely subspecies of the novel. They are antinovels. They overturn the scale of novelistic values. Lower-class and lower-middle-class readers, for whom the ordinary was very much a prison, defined by relative poverty, demanding labor, insecurity, and large families, might well resent the individuality of leisure and talk. Novels were not written by or for them. Thus, as the spread of literacy made ever larger numbers of people into potential readers, it created the need for a literature which could appeal more realistically to the imagination of the new public. The rapid spread of popular literary forms from the late eighteenth century onward is evidence for this fact. It is evidence also for an understanding of what the popular imagination craved: Gothic horror, exotic tales of struggle and warfare, stories of crime and the underworld. Not "realistic" chronicles of polite behavior and budding individuality, but fantasies of risk and high adventure; tales about extraordinary characters like Melmoth, or the Monk, who defined themselves not socially, but demonically, in terms of their passions.

Such literature was in the profoundest sense escapist. Not only because it located fantastic events in unreal places, but because the subject matter itself was articulated around the experience of escape: innocent girls escaping from oppressive dungeons; outcast sons escaping from the evil society of monasteries; criminals escaping from the law. One might describe "imprisonment" and "escape" as the primary experience of most Gothic novels, of the *roman noir*, and of much popular literature since then. Is it an unreasonable step to interpret those massive dungeons, oppressive monasteries, and haunted castles which appear in the Gothic novel, as paradigms, admittedly oversimplified, of society itself? And the popular fascination with heroes like the Monk, Rocombole, or Vautrin, as a craving to share vicariously the sheer energy of characters for whom the ordinary was not a prison, but a limit they could destroy, or, conversely, put to their own use, as keepers of the deadly prison?

The popular literature of the late eighteenth and nineteenth centuries expresses an insight into the constraints and the psychic impoverishment of contemporary social reality which was, at the same time, being formulated theoretically by the new social criticism of the nineteenth century, in the work of Carlyle, Tocqueville, Proudhon, and Marx.

This leads us to recognize a curious historical paradox. The popular literature of which we speak is not novelistic. Its values are profoundly and precisely antinovelistic: instead of celebrating the patterns of social reality, and the corresponding patterns of individual experience, it celebrates the energies which disrupt the pattern, and the characters who uproot it in themselves. So doing, the Gothic novel and the *roman noir* adapt the prenovelistic conventions of romance, presenting idealized characters in exotic circumstances, and improbable stories filled with coincidence. The distinction Clara Reeve makes in the eighteenth century between romance and the novel holds true decades later for most popular literature:

The Romance is an heroic fable which treats of fabulous persons and things.—The Novel is a picture of real life and manners, and of the times in which it is written. The Romance in lofty and elevated language describes what never happened nor is likely to happen.—The Novel gives familiar relation of such things, as pass every day before our eyes. . . .[6]

Maturin pointedly calls *Melmoth* a romance, not a novel, and the same is true for most Gothic authors. Thus a literary genre which had previously expressed the idealized vision of an aristocratic class, is now transformed into a vehicle of mass literature, presenting an anarchic dream of heroic energies and escape. In the transformed shape of popular romance, "adventure" preserves itself from the corrosions of novelistic morality.

Thus, the very sociological changes which influenced the rise of the novel as a new "high" literary form[7] gave rise decades later to a new "low" literary form, the popular feuilleton novel, and its immediate predecessor, the Gothic novel; and this new "low" form became a repository for the archaic fascination with risk and struggle. Since the sixteenth century, and great works like Ariosto's *Orlando Furioso*, romance had become increasingly precious and frivolous. When the first novels appeared in the eighteenth century, they filled what essentially was an empty place. But the rise of the popular literature of the nineteenth century changed that. In its Gothic ramification, it gave a new energy to the very conception of romance, and a foothold for the almost extinct values of traditional storytelling.

When a countertradition of great adventure literature began once more to appear in the nineteenth century, it was largely the product of a bizarre cross-fertilization between novelistic narrative and popular fantasy. Balzac, for example, was exasperated by Eugene Sue's incredible popular success as a feuilletonist, and decided to use the formula for his own ends. He adopted the atmosphere of charged mystery, the rapid-fire succession of climaxes, the sense of demonic character, and created Vautrin, hero of *Splendeurs et Misères des Courtisanes*. Another briefer essay in the genre is his *Feragus ou l'Histoire des Treize*. The *Narrative of Arthur Gordon Pym* is obviously an outgrowth of Edgar Allan Poe's Gothic storytelling which, in turn, cast Poe, in his lifetime, as a writer of popular fiction, not a "serious" representative of "high" culture.

But probably the greatest tributes to the stylistic genius of Gothic come in Melville's *Moby Dick*, and in Conrad's early fiction, especially *Heart of Darkness* and *Lord Jim*. Here romance once more is raised to its preeminence as a high literary form. Above all, the charged style of the popular literature, its dramatization of dark emotions, its ability to evoke haunting mysteries against which the hero struggles: these baroque possibilities of the language itself are heightened, creating a difficult, and unprecedented, literary medium.

Poe, Melville, Conrad, T. E. Lawrence, Malraux, Genet, all found their subject matter in the margins of culture, where it had been flattened into a form of escapist entertainment. These writers could all be described as antinovelists. Their subject matter was not the ordinary, but the extraordinary; not the minute rhythm of common events, but the exaltation of bizarre circumstances. Their work implies a judgment on human experience which is radically different from that of the novel. For Melville, Malraux, T. E. Lawrence, or Genet, a man's essential moment comes in the midst of danger, when all of his life must be translated into action. While the modernist tradition created a language of radical privacy, these antinovelists attempted to reestablish action and adventure as the highest modes of personal definition. There exists in their work a profound sympathy for heroic experience. When the *Pequod* crosses the Pacific, it is gliding back through time toward the "first ages." Marlowe's journey to Africa in *Heart of Darkness* resembles a "voyage to the center of the earth." T. E. Lawrence longs to recreate the epic splendor of Saladin and the Arab Middle Ages. Malraux, flying through a storm over North Africa, feels that he has

15

"entered into the universe of Homer and the Ramayana." For Genet, the criminal underworld is radiant with the somber energies of the mythological underworld.

In his preface to *Le Temps du Mépris*, Malraux writes that the novel, with its texture of "individual antagonisms," was not an adequate model for his story. He needed to recreate the "antique world" of actions and destinies, thereby rejecting a sense of "vague individualism which was so general in the nineteenth century. . . . The individualism of artists, mainly interested in protecting the 'inner world'. . . ." [8]

Behind the elaborate fiction of writers such as Melville, Malraux, T. E. Lawrence, and Genet lies the splendor of ancient figures: Gilgamesh, Odysseus, Herakles, Beowulf, Sir Gawain: characters for whom life declared itself in the energy of their exploits, as they explored the margins of the human world, where men and gods, the known and the unknown, the human and the monstrous, were mingled.

The argument of my book falls essentially into three parts. In the first, I attempt to define the intrinsic qualities of adventure by considering several of the great adventure stories in the Western tradition. I approach these stories not as literature, but as cultural myths in which the adventurer appears as a darkly antisocial character, an escape artist from the confinements of the human situation. Writing about the *Odyssey*, I articulate the requirements of the adventure myth for the Greek sensibility. Writing about *Beowulf*, I distinguish between the moralized ideal of the hero, essentially a Roman creation, and the demonic ideal of the adventurer. I explore the connection between adventure and tragedy, in the character of Achilles, and what I call the "guest mentality," suggesting a profound sexual ambivalence in the adventurer: his fear of women, yet the surprising femininity of his character devoted to courting Lady Luck.

In the second part of the book, I describe the shift in cultural attitudes after the Renaissance, which demoted adventure from a high cultural myth to a sinful action to be exorcised by prayer, rather than emulated and admired. During the seventeenth and eighteenth centuries, labor and speculative thought replace adventure as the creators of essential value. The "Providence" literature of seventeenth-century England, and the work of Defoe, especially *Robinson Crusoe*, undermine the ideal of adventure, as does the Enlightenment, with its belief in natural law and in man's perfect sociability. Only the frivolous world of the aristocracy remained sheltered from the Protestant ethic. As adventure became frivolous, frivolity became a remarkable field for adventure in the life and memoirs of Casanova, the perfect adventurer of the eighteenth century.

In the third part of the book, I trace the origin of a new adventure myth in the Gothic novel and the writing of de Sade. Adventure becomes an act of revolt, an access to the underworld of romantic energies. I describe how Edgar Allan Poe's *Narrative of Arthur Gordon Pym* draws upon the new mythology of adventure. But the crowning development in the nineteenth century's rediscovery of adventure is the philosophy of Nietzsche, who presents his Overman as an adventurer, questing for an order of experience beyond domestic categories, "beyond good and evil." In the concluding chapter, I trace the fate of adventure in the modern world, exploring the contemporary fascination with episodic forms of experience. I describe in particular the modern ambivalence which blurs the distinction between inward and outward adventure, as the shamanistic stories once did. I try to suggest answers to some questions. Where is adventure to be found today? What sort of stories do we tell about it? What new forms of storytelling will it require?

In writing this book I have made assumptions which I ask the reader to share, if only tentatively. I have assumed that human experience falls into categories which survive particular social moments; that these categories find expression in works of literature which also survive the net of historical attitudes and relationships which gave rise to them. Literature in this sense becomes a sort of mythology, a language spoken not by individuals but by cultures. Pursuing this image, I assume that many, perhaps all cultures speak dialects of one "language"; that the experiences of risk, of domestic security, of authority, of death, of birth, give rise to a permanent vocabulary, adaptable to the social configurations of any time. Thus we read fragments of a Sumerian myth, and find that it is talking to us, and about us.

Adventure is a category of experience about which we know less than other cultures have known. It represents a portion of the "language" we no longer speak with skill. That is why I have felt it necessary to clarify the requirements of the adventure myth by examining stories from traditional cultures, before I approach the particular crises in our own culture which shunted adventure aside, until its resurrection in the underworld of popular literature.

CHAPTER

2

The Myth of Odysseus

ODYSSEUS is the perfect adventurer of Greek tradition. In Homer's epic poem he is mobile and cunning, a sort of trickster who is never caught short and never surprised. The Homeric language is an excellent medium for Odysseus. It is a language attuned to acts, not to feelings or motives. We never learn how Odysseus spent his years of idleness on Calypso's island, because those actionless years cannot exist in the story. We discover Odysseus only in his adventures. Perhaps that is simply another way of describing the aristocratic nature of Homer's world. The humble people have no place in the song because they have *done* nothing. They do not act, but merely work, offering no hold to Homer's words. This is generally true of myths and folktales. The characters are rudimentary, but they are not thin, because their deeds tell us everything we need to know. The pattern of their acts makes them as compelling as the complex characters in a novel, but they are compelling for different reasons.

For one thing, they move across a landscape of definite mysteries and meanings. "Mere" geography does not exist in the old stories. When the anger of the gods drives Odysseus across the Mediterranean, he is shipwrecked in a world of strangeness and magic. The familiar countries fall under the horizon, and new lands appear, which are only half human. To reach these magic countries, Odysseus has had merely to cross a great distance. Between Ithaca and the Land of the Lotus Eaters, between home and the farthest reaches of myth, there is only space, shading progressively from the known into the unknown. The magic countries are a crossroads between Olympus, where Zeus and Athena keep track of the wanderer, and the underworld, where the dead spirits will prophesy for him. Wherever he goes, Odysseus navigates across a map of spiritual realities. The adventures of Odysseus are real, not because he feels they are, but because they make a difference in the network of powers. When he acts, the gods are affected, which means that he is never alone. When a storm spills him into the ocean, a magic scarf is wrapped around his waist, given to him by the sea nymph Ino. The storm itself is not so much a "natural" phenomenon, as an expression of Poseidon's anger. There is no hint of existential darkness in Odysseus' plight: he is quite simply a man with enemies.

This sort of connection with the world is difficult for us to grasp. It implies that every place, person, or event belongs to a kind of language, that every action is a way of conversing with the world, a way of teaching and learning. Because Odysseus is an alert wanderer, he is also skilled in council; he is wise and cunning. In *Troilus and Cressida*, Shakespeare presents Odysseus as a philosopher, expressing his sense that the adventurer is essentially wise. Because Odysseus has been everywhere, contended with the half-human languages which the gods speak, he "knows." Odysseus has been schooled in the world. He has accomplished what we imagine today the philosopher must accomplish; and the way of Odysseus is not meditation or systematic reasoning, but action.

We too, in the modern world, believe that experience is a good teacher. But, on the whole, we mean something different by it. We mean that experience should teach us about ourselves. When we act, we discover traces of our inward life in the events we shape. By the light of our acts, we accumulate a view of our personal landscape. This modern attitude has greatly affected the

way we read the *Odyssey*. Our tendency has been to treat the poem as a novel, deciphering the hero's adventures in order to understand his evolution as a character, interpreting his relationships with other characters as evidence of his inward complexity. The trouble with such readings is that they are too wordy, like Talmudic glosses on a few sparse lines of text. Homer's world is wholly visible, as Erich Auerbach has pointed out. It is a world of surfaces. All of its secrets have been translated into brightly lit shapes, as in a dream whose language is wholly visual. Does Odysseus express latent hostility to his father, Laertes, in the recognition scene in Book XXIII? Are there Oedipal overtones in the scene in Hades, where Odysseus bars his mother from the sacrificial blood by holding out a bare sword? Should we speculate about Odysseus' overprotected childhood when we learn that his mother, Anticlea, died of grief at his departure for Troy? We may ask such questions, but the answers have little to do with the elaborate foreground of Homer's language.

In order to save the *Odyssey* from becoming a mere fairy tale of adventure, which would "remove it from serious consideration as one of the world's greatest poems,"[1] according to George deF. Lord, it has been necessary to discover a moral fable in the story, a progress, for example, from the brutal ethos of the heroic age to a "higher" order of domestic peace. In this view, Odysseus becomes a warrior who learns that war is hell, pays for his brutality through the misfortunes of his homecoming, and finally settles down, a peaceful aging husband. After having been "nobody" in the Cyclops' cave, he goes on to assume the fullness of his identity as king of Ithaca, upholder of morality and human values. But what if the *Odyssey* is precisely an adventure story and nothing more? What if C. S. Lewis is right in claiming that "As far as greatness of subject goes, [the *Odyssey*] is much closer to *Tom Jones* or *Ivanhoe* than to the *Aeneid* or the *Gerusalemme Liberata*."[2] If we define epic according to the stature of its subject matter, then Lewis has a point; the *Odyssey* simply does not fit. Unlike *Gilgamesh*, the *Iliad*, or the *Aeneid*, the story it tells has neither historical nor mythical importance. A famous soldier gets lost on his way home from war, has adventures and misfortunes. Finally after twenty years he reaches his homeland, Ithaca, a small kingdom in the Aegean Sea. Upon arriving he slaughters a horde of young men who had taken advantage of his absence to persecute his wife and eat up his fortune. In the end he regains kingdom and wife, and lives happily ever after. This is not a founding myth, or a cautionary tale. It does not explore the nature of death or courage.

Attempts to moralize the *Odyssey* fall short. Odysseus is no less a brutal pirate at the end of the poem than at the beginning. When he surveys his wealth, depleted by years of the suitors' gluttony, he consoles himself easily enough: "Take care of what is left me in our house," he tells Penelope,

> *as to the flocks that pack of wolves laid waste*
> *they'll be replenished: scores I'll get on raids*
> *and other scores our island friends will give me*
> *till all the folds are full again.*[3]

The brutality of his character does not prevent him from being loved. Telemachus, Menelaus, Circe, Calypso, Penelope, Eumaeus, Euryclea, Anticlea, Nausicaa: all adore him, and weep for him. Wherever he goes Odysseus provokes anger, fear or love, but not judgment, because moral categories have no place in Homer's poem.

Odysseus is nothing more, but nothing less, than an adventurer, a man "skilled in all ways of contending," outstandingly cunning, generous, egotistical, lovable, polite, rude, as the occasion demands. The brilliant foreground of the poem resists interpretation, which is why the *Odyssey* has caused such trouble for modern critics who deplore its pointless energy: "the mere endless up and down, the constant aimless alternations of glory and misery, which make up the terrible phenomenon called a Heroic Age." [4]

The adventures of the *Odyssey* cannot be explained or explained away, because adventure itself is the elementary subject matter of the story. In Homer's world, adventure is what is worth talking about, as Odysseus well knows, for he is a great story-teller. The swineherd Eumaeus tells Penelope:

> *the man could tell you tales to charm your heart.*
> *Three days and nights I kept him in my hut;*
> *he came straight off the ship, you know, to me.*
> *There was no end to what he made me hear*
> *of his hard roving; and I listened, eyes*
> *upon him, as a man drinks in a tale*
> *a minstrel sings—a minstrel taught by heaven*
> *to touch the hearts of men. At such a song*
> *the listener becomes rapt and still.* [5]

The adventurer brings back news of the gods. The lands of myth, Hades, even death and Elysium have been within his reach. His story recreates this distant world, enlarging the boundary of what men know.

Even time is reorganized by the adventurer's tale. Time becomes a neutral dimension in which the story takes place, not a medium of essential change, as in the novel. For how many years did the suitors besiege Penelope? Has she really remained splendidly beautiful all this time? We need not know the answers to such questions. Nor are we disturbed when Odysseus is described alternately as old enough to resemble a withered beggar, and young enough to be in the budding maturity of his strength.

In the *Odyssey* time is elastic and transparent, a modulation of space. The darkest mysteries and the most vibrant meanings do not lie out of reach in the past, to be recaptured by philosophers and historians; they lie beyond the horizon, where the earth shades over into myth. Like the gods, the past has not vanished; it is far off, in the blessed isles, mythically but geographically located. A great traveller could get there, if he were gifted for such voyages. In Homer, omens and prophecies are not miracles; they are signs from afar, hints to man from the overview which the gods possess, from their perspective on Olympus, of the spatial and temporal landscape.

Between the adventurer and his goal, there is only a distance to be traveled. Time is not important, because nothing has ever been left behind. The loftiness of the gods, the prodigious magic of unknown races, the fields of the blessed isles and the shadow beings of Hades, the aura of beginnings and the desolation of endings: all are enmeshed in the vast contemporaneity of the cosmos.

In this sense, the adventurer's most serious obstacle is himself. The world extends before him like a fabulous text. Only his ability to "read" it is in doubt. His quest is also an excercise in "self-overcoming," to use a Nietzschean expression. Every successful action hardens the adventurer's identity, every failure erodes it. The theme of the journey as test and ordeal is universal in romance and mythology. Homer evokes it ironically in the *Odyssey*, when Odysseus identifies himself to the Cyclops as "No Man." Only through risk and trouble will the adventurer finally gain his identity. But after he has proved himself, by surviving the mythic assaults of the monster, his name bursts from him irresistibly, through arrogance perhaps, but also through a sort of natural overflow.

George E. Dimock's important essay, "The Name of Odysseus," [6] makes this point in another way. In Homeric Greek the name "Odysseus" is also a verb denoting a "general sort of hostility," something between being angry at, and making trouble for. When Odysseus' grandfather Autolycus is asked to name his grandchild, he says: "I have odysseused many in my time, up and down the wide world, men and women both; therefore let his name be Odysseus." [7] Dimock comments: "All we know from the Odyssey about Autolycus' career is that he was the foremost liar and thief of his day. Most naturally, by 'odysseusing many' he means that he has been the bane of many people's existence." [8] Dimock suggests therefore that we translate Odysseus as "Trouble": making it for others, suffering it at the hands of others. Odysseus certainly does enough of both. He makes a name for himself, by living up to his name. Thus, he is not merely concealing his identity from the Cyclops when he calls himself "No Man." At this point in the adventure, his name has yet to be earned. But here is where the *Odyssey* differs from other "quest" stories. For Odysseus will never reach his goal. His ordeal is unendable. Or rather, each end becomes a defeat, each repose an obliteration of his name. Odysseus will be himself only in the midst of trouble. Trouble will be its own end and will breed more trouble. Odysseus will not advance triumphantly to the fullness of his identity as king of Ithaca; he will struggle from trouble to trouble, adventure to adventure, for that is the only defense he knows against the oblivion of No Name. His arrival on Ithaca repeats the drama of the Cyclops' cave: he starts again as No Man, an anonymous beggar; only gradually, as the trouble unfolds, does he become Odysseus. The name Odysseus has made is, of course, the song by which he is remembered. The song is his identity, and Homeric song, we remember, tells of acts, not idleness. To be Odysseus, he must court trouble; he must make, and suffer, hardship. Otherwise he will be forgotten, a fate suggested by another Homeric name: Calypso. Dimock writes:

Calypso is oblivion. Her name suggests cover and concealment, or engulfing; she lives "in the midst of the sea"—the middle of nowhere, as Hermes almost remarks—and the whole struggle of the fifth book, indeed of the entire poem, is not to be engulfed by the sea. When the third great wave of Book Five breaks over Odysseus' head, Homer's words are: ton de mega kyma kalypsen —"and the great wave engulfed him." [9]

Odysseus spends his life avoiding engulfment: by the sea, by the narcotic forgetfulness of lotus flowers, by the watery mouth of Charybdis, by the Cyclops' cave, and by its seductive equivalent, Calypso's grotto. Dimock concludes: "It is a choice between Scylla and Charybdis—to face deliberately certain trouble from the jaws of the six-headed goddess, or to be engulfed entirely by the maelstrom. One must odysseus and be odysseused, or else be kalypsoed." [10] To be kalypsoed is to fall outside the poem, as Odysseus does for seven idle years. To odysseus and be odysseused is to be at one with trouble, to be an adventurer. The "Apollonian" clarity which Nietzsche admired in Homer, is the clarity of remembered acts; it represents the emergence of the adventurer into his unshadowed identity as a man of actions. Odysseus does not need to meditate on his destiny, like T. E. Lawrence in *Seven Pillars of Wisdom* or like Marlowe in *Heart of Darkness*. The pattern of his story does not need to be "deepened" by a setting of moods lending bulk and authenticity to its mystery. The tale of the *Odyssey* exists already in its fullness; its every action makes a plenitude.

What, then, do we make of Odysseus' longing to return home? That, after all, is what the poem is about: the unhappy wanderings of a hero, whose homecoming is thwarted by an angry god. In the Land of the Lotus Eaters, in Circe's den, on Calypso's island, on Scheria, Odysseus struggles against danger and temptation, in an effort to regain his Penates. He wants only to be a

good husband again, a desire which would bring with it another sort of oblivion if it were fulfilled, for there would be nothing more to tell about him. The song, and the name it made—Odysseus—would vanish. Odysseus would have struggled against Calypso, only to be kalypsoed more subtly by his wife, who is in her own right a woman of witchlike powers. If Circe can turn men into swine, Penelope can turn the suitors into boisterous animals, unable to do her any real harm. When Odysseus comes, they will be slaughtered in their tracks, like helpless cattle. Where Calypso, Circe, and Nausicaa fail, Penelope succeeds. Even across the distances of myth, her magic does not weaken, for Odysseus is drawn ever nearer to her. Of all the women whose magic is evoked in the Odyssey, Penelope is without a doubt the most formidable. Odysseus' return home therefore is both a victory and a defeat for him. It is the culminating, and most elaborate, adventure of his odyssey, but it is also the end of his name making. Or almost the end. For Odysseus, in Hades, receives good advice from the prophet Tiresias, who tells him of the misfortunes that await him on his voyage home, concluding:

But after you have dealt out death—in open
combat or by stealth—to all the suitors,
go overland on foot, and take an oar,
until one day you come where men have lived
with meat unsalted, never known the sea,
nor seen seagoing ships, with crimson bows
and oars that fledge light hulls for dipping flight.
The spot will soon be plain to you, and I
can tell you how: some passerby will say,
"What winnowing fan is that upon your shoulder?"
Halt, and implant your smooth oar in the turf
and make fair sacrifice to Lord Poseidon:
a ram, a bull, a great buck boar; turn back,
and carry out pure hekatombs at home
to all wide heaven's lords, the undying gods,
to each in order. Then a seaborne death
soft as this hand of mist will come upon you
when you are wearied out with rich old age. . . .[11]

Arriving home, Odysseus will leave on a further voyage. Remaining true to his name as a bringer of trouble, he will carry an emblem of seagoing mystery on his shoulder, an oar sweep, and travel until he finds a place so landlocked and settled into the peace of domestic routines, that the people do not recognize the oar for what it is: an instrument of adventure, a traveling tool, echoing the name of its prophet, Tiresias, which Dimock translates: "the weariness of rowing." Only through the weariness of rowing will the adventurer escape engulfment at the hands of Calypso. After all, the *Odyssey* is about going home, not being at home. Going home sustains Odysseus when he is hemmed in by the mysteries of engulfment. Going home keeps him on the move, precipitates him from one adventure to the next. As he wanders through the perils of the magic countries, Odysseus preserve his human shape, his name, by homegoing. That is why he is never lost, never dissolved into forgetfulness by the allurement of lotus blossoms.

This aspect of the *Odyssey* presents an interesting analogy to the shamanistic dream-voyage. The shaman interprets his trance experience as a journey to the spirit world. His skill lies in his ability to enter the magic countries, and then return. Ordinary people are victimized by the perils of the invisible world—as Odysseus' crew is victimized. Only the shaman knows how to go, and then come home. The resemblance is striking too with R. D. Laing's record of a young girl's prepsychotic experience:

I was about twelve, and had to walk to my father's shop through a large park, which was a long dreary walk. I suppose too that I was rather scared. I didn't like it, especially when it was getting dark. I started to play a game to help pass the time. You know how as a child you count the stones or stand on the crosses on the pavement. Well, I hit on a way of passing the time. It struck me that if I stared long enough at the environment I would blend with it and disappear just as if the place was empty and I had disappeared. It is as if you get yourself to feel you don't know who you are. To blend into the scenery so to speak. Then, you are scared of it because it begins to come on without encouragement. I would just be walking along and felt that I had blended with the landscape. Then I would get frightened and repeat my name over and over again to bring me back to life, so to speak.[12]

By reasserting her name, the girl finds her way back from "unreality" into the familiar environs of home. Her "technique" resembles the shaman's skill at returning. Indeed, shamanism has often been interpreted as a sort of self-cure, an ecstatic technique for yielding to the changes of inward disorder so as to overcome them.

Of course, one must exercise the greatest caution when drawing parallels between psychic voyaging of the kind I have just mentioned, and the wholly objectified outward voyaging of Odysseus. If the *Odyssey's* preliterary roots are, in part, shamanistic, its precise poetic quality is quite a different matter. The literary theme of the fantastic voyage may well be connected to the family of trance tales told by shamans; adventure and action literature—including folktales, epic, and myth—may well be attempts to objectify the vertigo of inward disorder which is our most intimate knowledge of the unknown. It is possible that in man's early experience, the psychic unknown and the outward unknown seemed related, each supplying a means for expressing the other. Surely the proliferation of drug epics in modern literature, and the theme of the hallucinatory voyage, suggest a connection between the two sets of adventure. Yet the *Odyssey* itself is too well-lit, too serenely objective to allow the modern reader a free rein in such speculation. From a Nietzschean point of view, the *Odyssey* represents a brilliant triumph of the clearly lit outward shape, over the inward plunge which shamanistic societies cultivated, and which the Orphic religions would reassert in Greece during the centuries following Homer. Nonetheless, one sees how suggestive the homegoing theme becomes from this point of view, how closely connected it is to the central theme of adventure. In the *Odyssey*, going home and making trouble are one. Reasserting his name, Odysseus finds his way back into the human world, where he crowns his achievement in a paroxysm of name making, before leaving once again, on his unendable quest.

It is no surprise therefore that the return to Ithaca has taken so long. If Odysseus' longing for home expresses his connection to the human world of names, his provocation of Poseidon expresses his equal devotion to trouble. In their opposition, the two impulses are one, each perpetuating and strengthening the other. Odysseus is destined to travel forever between nobody and somebody, never wholly humanized into his name, yet never wholly lost to the engulfments of anonymity. Odysseus' mobility expresses a profound sympathy for the mysteries of the extrahuman world. The instability of his human definition represents a strange encroachment of unhuman definition.

The tradition of a homeless Odysseus survived the temporary loss of the *Odyssey* itself, during the Middle Ages. When Dante places Odysseus in the eighth circle of the *Inferno*, he is speaking at second hand, from a knowledge of classical tradition. He probably invents his account of the adventurer's death in mid-

Atlantic. But one recognizes the character who speaks these words:

> *not fondness for my son, nor reverence*
> *for my aged father, nor Penelope's claim*
> *to the joys of love, could drive out of my mind*
> *the lust to experience the far-flung world*
> *and the failings and felicities of mankind.*[13]

In Dante's view, homegoing was another form of the need for adventure. Odysseus' arrival on Ithaca was not a culmination, but simply a more elaborate episode, prelude to further episodes. When death overtakes Odysseus, it will be in mid-ocean, still probing the mysteries of the "far-flung world."

This reading of the *Odyssey* as an adventure story is reinforced by Erich Auerbach's famous analysis of Homeric style. Not only is the narrative of the poem "episodic" in the way I have argued, the style of the poem is episodic, or "paratactic," to use Auerbach's expression. Because the poem is made up wholly of foreground, there is no subordination of one scene to another; no "background" effect of motives or memories to flesh out and situate the action. Every scene is fully rendered in all of its details, with nothing merely suggested or left partly in shadow. This is the brightly lit, Apollonian quality that Nietzsche remarked. Scenes, regardless of their importance or their emotional impact, emerge at a leisurely pace, never hurried by an impending climax or weighted by a past: "Never is there a form left fragmentary or half-illuminated, never a lacuna, never a gap, never a glimpse of unplumbed depths. And this procession of phenomena takes place in the foreground—that is, in a local and temporal present which is absolute." [14] Auerbach points out that suspense counts for little in the *Odyssey*. Moments exist for themselves, not for their freight of future or past. As complex as the poem's syntax can be when it describes the relationships of characters in a scene, their actions and the place setting which surrounds them, it is extremely simple when it comes to connecting the different scenes one to another. The scenes simply follow like hypnotic stills, with no complicated sequential link, yet no hint of disconnection either. Homer's style presents the paradox of time itself: it passes in the medium of an unflagging present.

Auerbach's example is the story of Odysseus' scar, in Book XIX. The old nurse, Euryclea, is preparing to bathe Odysseus, whom she believes to be a wanderer. While she bathes him, Odysseus suddenly realizes that Euryclea will know him and give his disguise away, as soon as she touches an old scar on his thigh, which she cannot fail to recognize. Euryclea does in fact touch the scar, but before she does Homer interpolates a seventy-line digression describing the incident in Odysseus' youth when he received the scar. On the verge of an important climax, the larger story of the poem vanishes, its place taken by a leisurely reminiscence. The effect of the digression is not to deflate the climax, or to heighten the reader's impatience. It simply lays open its riches, and concludes, like all the other moments in the poem. In this sense, every scene of the Odyssey has a quality of beginning and ending. Perhaps that is why Homer can pay so little attention to questions of age and the passage of time. Such measures are peripheral in the medium of presentness which the poem creates.

The subject of the *Odyssey*, therefore, is not an epic event, or a moral fable. The subject is adventure. From the poem we learn that the adventurer is a man gifted for wandering, who has mastered the secret of travel between the worlds. Like the shaman, the adventurer crosses over into the mythic realm and returns with the story of his journey. By extruding his humanity beyond the frontier of human events, he embodies a victory over the invisible world. For this he is condemned to a life of endless mobility. Because he is at home everywhere, he will be at home nowhere. His existence will be humanly pointless. The gods are angry with him, for he is a thief; men distrust him, because he is not entirely one of them. That is the sort of man Odysseus is: a danger to himself and to everyone he knows, a bringer of trouble, yet a figure worthy of epic, for he brings the knowledge which men need. He is a great storyteller too, because stories are his bond to the human world. Only they are able to vanquish the distance which his character secretes around him. He enthralls his audience, while remaining separate from them, expressed but also hidden by the tale he tells.

The *Odyssey* dramatizes the adventurer's destiny of solitude. Before Odysseus can find his way home, his crew, his ship, even his clothing have been taken from him. Clearly he is not gifted for ordinary heroics. Menelaus too had no easy time returning from Troy, but when he did come home he was rich beyond measure with loot and merchandise. When Odysseus is washed ashore on Scheria, he is alone and naked, possessing only the news he brings of the magic countries. The wanderings which Tiresias predicts for him will be no different: he will carry word of the ocean's mysteries to landlocked farmers. The story will be Odysseus' essential wealth. Aeneas, Apuleius, and Dante will only follow in his footsteps. If we except Gilgamesh, whose story was unknown until the nineteenth century, Odysseus is the first hero in Western literature to have crossed even into death to bring back stories of the world beyond men.

CHAPTER

3

Heroes and Adventurers

HY do we say that Odysseus is a hero? As a leader of men he is a remarkable failure. He is neither virtuous nor loyal, and he is a compulsive liar. When we first meet him on Ogygia he is weeping for home, but that is only because, after seven years, he has become bored with Calypso's easygoing beauty. Anyway, by this time, largely through his fault, his ships have been destroyed and his men are dead.

The problem, I think, lies in our use of the word "hero," which has overlapping meanings. In literature it refers to the central character in a story: the hero is simply someone who is worth talking about, and that is certainly true of Odysseus. In our usual parlance, however, the word has a wider meaning with moral overtones. By hero, we tend to mean a heightened man who, more than other men, possesses qualities of courage, loyalty, resourcefulness, charisma, above all, selflessness. He is an example of right behavior; the sort of man who risks his life to protect a society's values, sacrificing his personal needs for those of the community. Virgil's Aeneas is a hero, in this sense of the word. He devotes his warrior skill, his pleasures, and finally his life to the historical destiny of founding Rome. Dante climbing to heaven in the *Divine Comedy* is a hero. Sergeant York risking his life to "end all wars" is a hero.

Clearly NASA had a heroic model in mind when it chose America's astronauts. The men are usually in their late thirties, at a balance point between youth and age, when a man's character has been formed, his face visibly etched with experience. Despite their fantastically mechanized exploits, the astronauts are not bland, but they possess character only in an impersonal way. They are veritable models of character. Clean, firm-faced, their speech clipped, obedient, but resourceful in a pinch, and a little unpredictable, as in Shepard's golf club exploit on the moon. They are perfect—all too perfect?—images of the brave, loyal, individualistic, law-abiding, personally powerful man America wants to admire. If someone made a robot portrait of the perfect citizen, it would resemble an astronaut. The astronaut is a vanishing point for our flawed selves; he is a hero. We tell our sons to be like him.

There is, of course, another sort of heightened man who bulks large in the popular imagination, as an antitype to Sergeant York and the astronauts. He is not "loyal," not a model of right behavior. Quite the contrary, he fascinates because he undermines the expected order. He possesses the qualities of the "hero": skill, resourcefulness, courage, intelligence. But he is the opposite of selfless. He is hungry; "heightened," not as an example, but as a presence, a phenomenon of sheer energy. One thinks of certain sports heroes, who boast and indulge their whims; who cannot be relied on, not because they are treacherous, but because the order of their needs is purely idiosyncratic. One thinks of criminals like Dillinger, or the old Hollywood stars, who thrilled us because they were such grandiosely bad examples in their private lives. These heightened men get too much pleasure out of their lives. We do not want our sons to be like them, yet they hold our attention. We perceive them as rebels and violators, encroaching on forbidden territory. Because they lack the other hero's aura of loyalty and selflessness, they seem to be more alone, more vulnerable. The more extraordinary their presence, the more desolate is the unsocialized space around them. They are not charged with the sympathies of a nation;

35

there is no warmth to shield them from the humiliations of failure. These heightened men, are self-derived, self-determined. Therefore they walk on delicate ground; an abyss opens at their feet. Why do they court dangers and isolation? For no reason. For themselves. To "live dangerously" is for them an act of self-indulgence, not of loyalty. The applause they receive will be charged with distrust, and with a secret longing to witness their downfall. From the viewpoint of the common good, these men are worthless. Apparently that is why we are thrilled by their acts. They stand outside the categories of duty and obligation. They give us the spectacle of the self-determined man who defends not us, but himself. His inner destiny is his law. He reclaims for man an area of the forbidden ground.

Obviously, Odysseus belongs to this second category of heroes who are not heroes at all. They share all the qualities of the "moral" hero, but one: they are not loyal, nor are they disloyal. The question simply does not arise for them. Their loyalty is directed toward the turns and chances of their own destinies. We call such a hero an *adventurer*.

These two sorts of characters are strangely intertwined in the early European epic of *Beowulf*, which mingles pagan and Christian values in a unique way. The character of Beowulf is very much heroic in our first sense of the word. "Master of manhood of all mankind,/Great-framed, greatheart," [1] he arrives in Denmark to serve as King Hrothgar's champion against Grendel, "mankind's enemy, the terrible solitary." [2] The poem's central episode describes Beowulf's victory over Grendel and his dragon mother, which restores Hrothgar's great hall to the joys of good companionship.

There is an atmosphere of exuberance and mystery in *Beowulf* which makes it unlike the Homeric epics. Grendel and his mother embody the horrors of the inhuman world. They are shaggy and evocative. Beowulf himself has a more fluid emotional life than Odysseus or Achilles. The poem is closer to the sort of individuality that will flourish in European literatures. But the world of *Beowulf* is no less a cosmos than is Homer's. The geography of the poem is shaped by a subtle mix of moral and physical characteristics. Hrothgar's hall is profusely human, dazzling with lights, friendships and nobilities. Grendel's country is dark and demonic; it resembles the Nordic wilderness, a place of

> *moors*
> *mist endless night . . .*
> *the gliding ground of demon and damned.*[3]
>
> *Unholy that place is:*
> *Up from it mounts the tumult of waters*
> *Black to the clouds, when the wind rouses*
> *Malice and tempest darkens the air*
> *Till weeping of the skies. . . .*[4]

All of life, in the poem, is lived near the frontiers of the human world, where the proud manhood of heroes struggles to maintain itself against the energies of the abyss.

A cloak of Christianity is drawn over this primal confrontation. The demonic geography is said to be derived from Cain and the fallen angels. The humanity of Beowulf and Hrothgar embodies the influence of God and His merciful son. More important, however, the moral-physical landscape of the poem creates a medium in which great actions can take place. As in the Homeric epics, the hero's deeds and appearance are suffused with a quality of transparency. Beowulf's identity is resplendent on his face, not buried in the secrecy of his character. To see him is to know him. When a sentinel meets Beowulf and his men disembarking on the Danish coast, he exclaims:

> *I never looked on*
> *A finer man living than one of you seems,*
> *He there in his armour: no mere retainer*
> *Tricked out with weapons, unless looks belie him,*
> *Looks without equal.*[5]

Just as Grendel is perfectly known by his hellish appearance, so is Beowulf by his magnificence. In this atmosphere of epic disclosure, Beowulf launches the conversation of his deeds. He reveals his nature and character in a history of acts which, because they already form a language of sorts, are linked essentially to the act of storytelling itself.

Foreshadowing the medieval Christian figure of Saint George, Beowulf is a dragon killer, an exemplary defender of the human form against the badlands of this world. As an old man, he becomes king of the Geats and dies selflessly in a final struggle against the creatures of evil. He is decidedly a hero, a model for all sons. Yet overtones of another sort complicate Beowulf's character as a hero; hints of a denser, more problematical nature, as in the brutal language he speaks:

> I am here
> For this fiend, for Grendel, to settle with these hands
> The demon's account. . . .
> Let me despise . . . yellow shield, sword,
> Broad-rimmed buckler, and let me rather
> Grapple with the fiend in mortal wrestlehold,
> Hated against hateful. . . .[6]

Beowulf longs for Grendel. He wants to strip away his armor, to grapple with the monster, flesh against flesh. Grendel's challenge stirs a raw berserker rage that wells up in Beowulf. In the fury of battle, he and Grendel will be twins: a single knot of energies rolling and hugging in the night.

When he arrives at Hrothgar's court, Beowulf is challenged by Unferth, a jealous warrior, who accuses him of impure motives and a reckless spirit:

> Are you that Beowulf who challenged Breca
> In a proof of swimming strength on the great sea
> When the two of you out of vainglory made trial of the waters
> And for a foolish vow ventured your lives
> On the skin of the abyss? The man was lacking,
> Either friend or enemy, who could turn you back
> From the hazardous undertaking as you swam from the shore.
> There with your arms you embraced the tide,
> Traced out the surging miles and with flailing

> *Palms thrust flashing through the waves; the swell*
> *Was bridling up with its wintery seethings.*
> *Seven nights' laboring on in the brinehold,*
> *And he outswam you, he had the mastery.*[7]

Unferth's accusation is strange, because it does not mainly impugn Beowulf's courage or his skill as a warrior. It impugns his claim to heroic stature, to the quality of exemplary form which the hero possesses. Unferth charges that Beowulf is fascinated by the demonic world; that he longs to plunge into it for nothing but the exaltation of adventure itself. If Beowulf longs to grapple with the evil, according to Unferth, it is because the evil belongs intimately to his nature. Amazingly, Beowulf does not deny Unferth's accusation. Brushing aside the claim that Breca outdid him in the undersea contest, he actually goes on to amplify Unferth's account, glorying in his pointless struggle against the creatures of the sea:

> *We had naked swords, iron to our hands,*
> *When we swam out to sea; we looked to defend ourselves*
> *Against whale and killer. . . .*
> *And so we two were on the sea together*
> *The space of five nights, when a current split us,*
> *A churning of the waters, in the chillest of weathers,*
> *Blackness louring and north wind bending*
> *Hostile against us; the waves were a chaos.*
> *The temper of the sea-fish was stirred and irritated;*
>   *. . . A raging attacker*
> *Dragged me to the bottom, savage, had me*
> *Fast in his grip; yet it was given me*
> *To reach and to pierce the monstrous thing*
> *With the point of my battle-sword; storm of conflict*
> *Took the strong beast of the sea by this hand*
>   *. . . Never have I heard of*
> *A harder fight under night and heaven*
> *Or in streaming ocean a more desperate man. . . .*[8]

There is exultation in Beowulf's description of the battle. He is proud to have struggled with the ocean for sheer pleasure. This ambivalence defines Beowulf's power as a character; in him the exemplary figure of the hero intertwines with the darker figure of the adventurer. Later when he plunges under the water to challenge Grendel's mother, his victory will result from his quite literally amphibious nature.

In the second half of the poem, Beowulf becomes a venerated king. Hardened by adventure, aged, made wise, Beowulf finally takes his place as ruler of the Geats, replacing Hrothgar in the poem as an epitome of human strength and values. In this sense, *Beowulf* describes the taming of the demonic warrior into a hero; the process of learning whereby the adventurer's strength is capped and siphoned into civilizing acts. As a warrior, he discovered within him a mirror of the demonic world; more than he knew, he belonged to the realm of dark furies against which his bravery strove.

When he leaves Denmark and Hrothgar's hall, Beowulf will not be the same man. Having grappled with the demonic darkness and discovered the resonance it awakened within him, Beowulf makes a choice. Previously he had been a man of adventures, a warrior; now he chooses loyalty, and the clear light of the human world. To his kinsman Hygelac, he brings gifts and friendship:

> . . . *as a kinsman should,*
> *Shunning secret and crafty web-weaving*
> *Of spite for another, the setting of death-traps*
> *For a comrade in arms. To the hardened fighter,*
> *To Hygelac his nephew was strongly loyal,*
> *And each of them strove to give joy to the other.*
>
> *The son of Ecgtheow showed thus his valor,*
> *A man famed in battle and good deeds,*
> *His acts sought glory; wine-flushed hearth-comrades*
> *Took no death from him; nothing barbarous in his heart*
> *But he guarded, war-bold, with the greatest wisdom*
> *Of the race of man, that liberal favour*
> *Which God had given him.*[9]

Epic tells the story of the demonic character who learns slowly, perhaps tragically, that his final allegiance must not be to his

own crazy needs, but to the shared vision of the culture which reveres him, and fears him. Epic describes the essential cultural act: the capturing and taming of forbidden energies. Just as Beowulf kills Grendel and his dragon mother, he must tame the Grendel in himself which is both the source of his valor and the limit of his humanity.

Beowulf is often thought to be an inferior example of epic because it lacks formal unity. The poem's central episodes—young Beowulf's fight against Grendel, old Beowulf's struggle against the fire-dragon and his resulting death—do not appear to be linked in any important way, as if they were fragments from separate poems set side by side, with little or no thematic reworking. *Beowulf* may well be made of separate fragments, but the ideas expressed in this chapter suggest a dramatic unity which has, I think, been overlooked. Having killed Grendel, and tamed the Grendel in himself, Beowulf becomes a loyal king, a defender of man against the dark world of ocean and earth. For a generation, he reigns prosperously, growing old in peace. When the fire-dragon appears, Beowulf knows that he must destroy the monster, but the demonic rage within him has calmed, his inward connection to the demon world has become blurred. He has become a heightened man, a hero, but only at the cost of sacrificing the furor within. As a result, his strength will fail him in the new struggle. With help from Wiglaf, he destroys the fire-dragon, but he is already dying of his wounds. To establish himself as king, Beowulf had to vanquish his warrior nature; because of this he became vulnerable, and was condemned to die. The two parts of *Beowulf* are bound together tragically. In the style of archaic Greece, they signify that the triumph of the human is also a defeat.

A similar theme emerges in other great works of heroic literature: *Gilgamesh*, the *Iliad*, the *Aeneid*. In each of them, the culminating mood is one of tragically earned reconciliation with the needs of the human. Gilgamesh is inwardly mutilated by the death of his demonic twin, Enkidu; he is worn and wearied by his own fruitless quest for everlasting life. The final words of the poem describe him carving on a stone tablet the wisdom he has brought back from the demonic countries. The result of his adventures has been to extend the knowledge and resilience of his culture. He has been defeated into humanness where he remains enthroned in a splendor which is tragically trimmed, but humanly honored.

The figure of the hero as we initially defined it may well be a late moralizing development in a tradition whose original traits are somber and problematical. Among traces which have survived of the lost Indo-European literatures, we find, in place of the exemplary hero, another equivocal sort of hero: a defender whose inclination to violence and adventure makes him dangerous to his friends and to his enemies alike. At the climax of risk and fury, this hero rises up in terrifying splendor, as a man of no society: drunkenly solitary, an embodiment of all risk, all transgression; as if the violence of his character had traced a boundary on all sides of him, which severed him from the world of social values, hierarchy and family—that very world which had empowered him to act on its behalf, to be its champion.

One finds these equivocal hero figures in the mythology of Vedic India (the warrior god Indra); in the early Roman history myths (Tullus, the Third Horace); in the mythology of the north (Starcatherus); in Irish legend (Cuchulainn).

The story of Cuchulainn's battle with the sons of Nichta contains an example of the warrior's demonic wildness. When he is still a child, Cuchulainn journeys to the distant border of Ulster where he defeats three brothers who are traditional enemies of his people, the Ulates. After the victory he returns home to Emain Macha, where his coming has been foreseen by the witch Leborchann: "A warrior arrives by chariot, terrifying to behold. If we are not careful tonight, he will destroy the warriors of Ulster." And the king repeats: "We know this traveller who arrives by chariot, it is the small boy, my sister's son. He has travelled to the border of the neighboring country, and his hands are red with blood. He has not had his fill of combat, and if we are not careful, he will destroy the warriors of Emain." [10]

Although he is still a child, Cuchulainn has experienced the deadly furor of warfare. He has become a creature of pure anger, irresistible in battle; a tower of demonic intensity, who cannot distinguish between friend and enemy. In this condition he returns home, victorious but deadly. The energy which fed his triumph has blinded him to moral distinctions and family allegiance. He has become the intense berserker radiance of his acts. To avoid the disaster which he sees approaching, Conchobar, the king, makes a decision. He sends a troop of naked women out of the city to meet Cuchulainn:

The troops of young women went out, they showed him their nakedness and their modesty. But he had his face against the side of his chariot so as not to see the women's nakedness and modesty. Then he was taken from his chariot. To calm his fury, three barrels of cold water were brought. They plunged him into the first barrel, and the water became so hot that it burst the staves and hoops of the barrel like a nutshell. In the second barrel, the water boiled up with bubbles as big as a fist. In the third barrel, the heat was of the kind that some men can bear, others not. Then the fury of the little boy passed, and they put his clothes on.[11]

Only when Cuchulainn has literally been cooled off, can he safely be admitted to the city. Indeed, the problem so quaintly solved by King Conchobar is an essential one. How can the order of the city be preserved from its own defender? How can the invincible furor of the warrior be sufficiently tamed so that he will not endanger those he apparently must serve, and yet not so tamed that his efficiency in battle will be impaired? With his curious dosing of female magic and cold water, Conchobar manages to cap the torrent of Cuchulainn's anger. In the future, Cuchulainn will reserve his solitary furor for battles and adventure, without peril to his fellow men.

In Cuchulainn's mystical rage one recognizes a resemblance to Achilles' anger in the *Iliad*, and Gilgamesh's restlessness in the Babylonian *Epic of Gilgamesh*. These heroes are not at home in the human world. Their somber energy—the very energy which defines their greatness—creates for them a kind of exile, a solitude vanishing only in the fullness of action. Their adjustment to human aims is necessary, yet difficult to achieve. At their moments of splendor, they belong only to themselves.

The lives of these equivocal heroes are articulated by a series of dramatic faults. Starcatherus, in the *Gestum Danorum*, is a dangerous betrayer. The Third Horace, after his exciting victory over the champions of Alba, kills his own sister in a fit of uncontrollable anger. Indra's career involves a number of forfeits committed in the line of duty, but nonetheless reprehensible. Behind these widely different heroic figures, one glimpses the

44

profile of an archaic Indo-European adventurer god, a profoundly ambivalent character whose gift for violence and extreme action creates a problem for those who need to make use of him. The unruly wanderer, which his mystical vitality has made of him, must be harnessed and tamed. He must be caught in the snare of civilization (Conchobar's procession of naked women, the harlot seducing Enkidu in the *Epic of Gilgamesh*) before he can be calmed into a hero. Even then the hero form will alter and slip; the archaic energies will assert themselves.

This brutal solitude is remarkably represented by the Vedic texts describing the adventures of the warrior god Indra. Unlike the other major Vedic gods (Mitra and Varuna, gods of order and sacred hierarchy; the two Asvins, gods of plenty, of fertility), Indra is never a partner in any stable couple or group. He is alone, or else he is described as a partner in innumerable fleeting couples, none of which alter his essential aloneness. He is the only functional god whose social attachments are forever problematical, forever called into question.

Another trace of the original difference which defines these archaic adventurer gods is found in Saxo Grammaticus. Saxo, with the precautions of a converted Christian historian, relates the pagan tradition of Starcatherus' origin.

This is an incredible folk tradition, completely contradicting all the rules of common sense. Some people claim that he was born into the race of giants, and that he betrayed this monstrous origin by the unusual number of his arms. They also claim that it was Thor who crushed his muscle-joints and tore off four of the arms which had been created by the mistake of an over-fertile nature. Thor also cut off his extra fingers, leaving him a normal body. As a result he had only two hands, and his body, which before was grotesque and lopsided from the over-abundance of members, was trimmed down to a better, more correct measure, and reduced to a human pattern.[12]

This marvelous passage describes the dilemma created by the character of torrential energies and irresistible strength. Made for a life of struggle with the obscure spirits surrounding the human sphere, devoted to the pursuit of an enemy who prowls beyond the border of life itself, these solitary warriors are themselves not fully human. Their fate of savagery and warfare calls forth in them qualities which belong to the enemies they combat. They are themselves inwardly grotesque, according to the socialized standards they ostensibly must defend. Just as Cuchulainn must be doused and seduced, Starcatherus must be mutilated, before he can be brought sufficiently close to the "human pattern" to serve it. Even then, he serves it with a bewildering combination of bravery and duplicity.

In *L'Heur et Malheur du Guerrier*, Georges Dumezil summarizes the problem of the Indo-European warrior god with remarkable clarity. In order to defend the social and cosmic order against overwhelming demonic hostility,

> *they must themselves possess and cultivate qualities which resemble very closely the faults of their adversaries. In the midst of battle, in order to guard against certain defeat, they must answer boldness, surprise, feints, betrayals, with operations of the same nature, only more powerful. Drunk or exalted, they must put themselves into a nervous, muscular and mental condition which increases their strength, which transfigures but also defigures them, making them strangers in the group they are protecting. Above all, devoted to Force, they are the triumphant victims of the internal logic of Force, which proves itself only by transgressing limits, even its own limits, even those which define its reason for being. . . .*[13]

Compared to the archaic warrior, our own image of the good hero, defender and founder of the social order, is strangely flat. Neither Diomedes nor Hector, nor much later Aeneas, possess the power of fascination, the sheer splendor of Achilles. In the *Odyssey*, it is evident that Telemachus, the exemplary son, will never equal his cruel, restless father. Nor will the astronauts, for all their lonely voyaging, stir us as deeply as Dillinger.

Our image of the adventurer appears to be rooted in the half-vanished traditions of Indo-European mythology. The adventurer is older, more essential than the hero. Only when the half-human warrior had been trimmed and tamed to the "human pattern" did the possibility of the exemplary hero emerge. And only a people—the Romans—whose passion for mythology, whose awareness of the problematical vitalities of risk and confrontation had taken the form of patriotism and militarism, could recognize itself in a gray loyal hero like Aeneas.

Although the Greek sculptors Phidias and Praxiteles had created an aesthetic of exemplary humanity in the ideal forms of their statuary, it was the Romans who raised the hero to the place he has since occupied for us as the defender and highest embodiment of human values.

CHAPTER

4

The Tragic Guest

THE hero and the adventurer are opposite figures. One stares at us from army recruitment posters all over the world. The other flits across the screen in forgettable pirate movies. As perfect types, they are curiously unsatisfying. We know that life is more complicated than that. Surely a shadow of privacy darkens the hero's jutted jaw. Surely a tremor of loyalty flaws the adventurer's perfect freedom. When Aeneas painfully makes himself into a "hero," he is simplified and fades. The wholesome face on the recruitment poster looms behind him. Conversely, the perfect adventurer is perfectly insubstantial. He is Loki, the Nordic prankster, or the Winnebago Indians' Trickster hero. His mobility becomes frivolous and dreamlike, because he is not freighted with human cares and needs. Popular literature seizes hold of him, and paints him with gross features as the pirate, the mobster, or the picaresque figure of fun.

In *Heart of Darkness*, Joseph Conrad introduces a strangely airy character who emerges from the jungle like a will-o'-the-wisp. "He looked like a harlequin. His clothes had been made of some stuff that was brown holland probably, but it was covered with patches all over." [1] This Pierrot-like figure has passed untouched through the jungle's mysteries. Occasions have burst over him like bubbles, leaving no residue and no history.

The Tragic Guest

For months—for years—his life hadn't been worth a day's pur-
chase; and there he was gallantly, thoughtlessly alive, to all ap-
pearance indestructible solely by virtue of his few years and of
his unreflecting audacity. I was seduced into something like ad-
miration—like envy. Glamour urged him on, glamour kept him
unscathed. . . . If the absolutely pure, uncalculating, unpractical
spirit of adventure had ever ruled a human being, it ruled this
be-patched youth. I almost envied him the possession of this
modest and clear flame. It seemed to have consumed all thought
of self so completely, that even while he was talking to you, you
forgot that it was he—the man before your eyes—who had gone
through all these things.[2]

For Conrad, the pure spirit of adventure is feathery, almost
nameless. The "be-patched youth" is a breath of inconsequence
in the heavy darkness of the jungle. His nature is not mixed
enough for him to be drawn back into the human world of
names, like Kurtz or Marlow, who walk both sides of the line
between the demonic and the human worlds, between adventure
and loyalty.

It was Homer's extraordinary triumph to have created in
Odysseus perhaps the only fully-fleshed, believable, and happy
adventurer in all literature. As for the other heroes, caught between law and the dream of escape, they abide, restrained by
the freight of human limitations, while they struggle with their
longing to plunge into the demonic world. Here we find Gilgamesh, Sir Gawain, and Beowulf; here we find Melville's Ishmael
and T. E. Lawrence: characters for whom adventure has an over-
tone of suicide; who must fight through webs of involvement to
glimpse the mobility which Odysseus embodied with such ease.
Here is the mid-ground where adventure shades over into tragedy; where the dream of escape encounters limits, and fails.

The Greeks understood these distinctions better than any
people in the world. Their epic and dramatic literature is based
upon a vast fund of saga material which supplied adventure
stories and heroic types in abundance. Here too, Homer stands
out as the greatest artist of the warrior mentality. His characters
form a pantheon of heroic types. Diomedes, Odysseus, Hector,

Agamemnon, above all Achilles, act together, dispute and kill each other. Their relationships in the *Iliad* create a network of dramatic moments which is one of the central subject matters of the poem.

Hector and Diomedes are presented as moral heroes: obedient to the order of kings, brave, possessing the furor of battle, but never overstepping the limits which divide the mutable world of men from the carefree world of gods. Agamemnon is a political hero. His prestige arises from a feudal agreement of sorts, sanctified by Zeus who reigns on Olympus through a similar agreement. Agamemnon embodies the fact of social contract, along with its ambivalence. In his shadow, the Achaeans form an irresistible army; their separate powers complement each other, and achieve what the separate warriors could never achieve: a power so vast that it can change the order of relationships in heaven, since the gods too take sides in the struggle. Yet Agamemnon, the separate man, is foolishly proud, unwise, and probably not an outstanding warrior. As such, he weighs upon the Achaeans, reminding them of the rankling loss which they agreed to when they accepted society's contract: the loss of their unsocial, but glorious freedom as simple warriors. All of these issues are united in the character of Achilles, who is caught in the tragic mid-ground between loyalty and adventure, between social needs and demonic separateness. In Achilles, Homer explores the limits of the heroic enterprise. He underscores the irony of a society whose values depend upon a warrior ideal which, in its highest form, is brutally antisocial.

The *Iliad's* most telling irony occurs in the final books describing Achilles' reconciliation to the patriotic ideal, in the funeral games he has staged to honor his dead friend, Patroclus. Achilles knows that he will soon be killed. His mother, the sea nymph Thetis, has told him of an old prophecy: if he stays at Troy as a warrior, he will die young. Thus, when Achilles chose to avenge Patroclus, he accepted an early death. The funeral games announcing Achilles' reconciliation with Agamemnon, and with the social order he represents, also announce his own death. The triumph of the social is Achilles' defeat; society is his Achilles' heel, and this is right. Achilles dies because, unlike the gods, he is human, a social animal.

Yet Achilles will never be assimilated into a framework of human aims. We know that he is partly a god: his demonic strength and his clairvoyance—he knows his own destiny—result from his divine ascendance. On the other hand, he is not a god either. Belonging to neither world, he is a living portal between them; a true, if desperate, "amphibian," to misuse Sir Thomas Browne's famous image. Achilles' nervous rage expresses resentment at his isolation. His quarrel with Agamemnon, and his withdrawal from the war, dramatize the precariousness of his attachment to human aims. Achilles' anger burns away chivalry, virtue, compassion—the human qualities which Hector and Diomedes possess in abundance. He is not a moral hero; his uncontrollable rage is dangerous even for his friends. Patroclus dies of it, along with hordes of nameless Achaeans. When he finally returns to the battle, after Patroclus' death, it is on his own terms and for his own reasons, creating a mood of surrealistic violence in which he alone participates. The results of Achilles' return—defeat for the Trojans—fall from his rage like accidental fruits. His violence defines an envelope of intensity: in it he is alone. Later when his rage is spent, he will perform acts of conciliation. But this is because he is haunted by one link he cannot break with the human world. He knows that he will die. He shares mortality with men. Therefore, he also shares their obsession with honor: the quality of heroic stature which is the subject matter of song and guarantees for one who achieves it immortality in the memories of future generations.

Because he is mortal, Achilles will return from his solitary violence. He will reenter the world of conventions, aims, and virtues, in order to perpetrate a kind of fraud: he will encourage men to admire his acts of heroism which saved the Achaeans and won the war, as if those acts had been done for their sake. Born between two worlds, Achilles' mortality forces him to choose the world of men, no matter how uneasy he feels in this world, no matter how much its narrow limits confine him. In reality, the choice had been made long before, though imperfectly, when Achilles chose to become a warrior, winning honor in battle. But he could not always keep the bargain he had made. Under the stress of his unshared, ungovernable energies, he broke down. The *Iliad* tells the story of this breakdown.

Because Achilles moves uneasily between the two worlds, he violates the decorum of both. He is not to be trusted. But he is great, unspeakably great. There is, in Achilles, a quality which cannot be apprehended in human terms; a quality whose natural outlet lies in self-directed, self-perpetuating actions. The inward necessity of such actions may parallel that of the moral order, but only by accident, or by ruse. Achilles is the most completely conceived example I know of the archaic warrior whose affinities with the extrahuman create in him an aura of morally gratuitous splendor. As such, he clearly differs from Hector and Diomedes, who are patterns of human chivalry; from Agamemnon, whose power is politically, not demonically, derived. Closer to him is Odysseus, as he appears in the other great Homeric poem, the *Odyssey*.

Both of these characters overshadow their insertion in the human order. Both are unpredictable, even dangerous, because their allegiance takes them beyond the human world. This is expressed by the insatiable wanderlust and curiosity of Odysseus; in Achilles, by his capacity for blind rage. Nonetheless, the two characters are markedly different. Odysseus emanates a kind of Nietzschean gaiety. Even when he is desperate and facing the most exotic dangers, there is an exuberance in his character which comes from the sense of simple, unwithheld energies. That is why the *Odyssey*, despite the dangers it portrays, is a swift, happy poem. By comparison, Achilles is complex and gloomy. He broods more than he acts. His "godlike" energy accomplishes nothing. Achilles was made for the gaiety of wholly expressed actions. But instead he is paralyzed, turned morbidly inward until he breaks free in the final debacle, at the cost of his life.

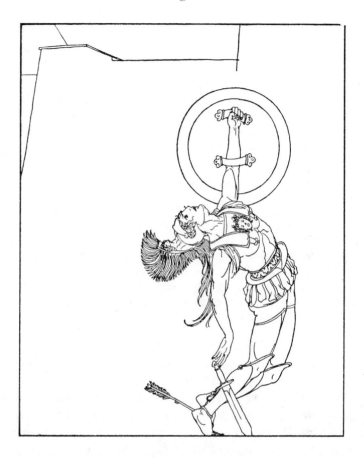

Achilles is the archaic warrior in chains. He will not be "cooled off," like Cuchulainn, or trimmed by a brutal god, like Starcatherus. His fate is more complex and more deadly, for he is caught in the webs of his own character. Whatever choice he makes will be wrong. To stay or to go; to fight or to be idle; to honor his "contract," or to retire. None of these alternatives will do. Achilles is trapped in a "double bind": he will die young, or he will be forgotten. He will die, or he will die. The choice, ultimately, is no choice, and Achilles sits in his tent, increasingly bitter, increasingly isolated.

Nietzsche was the first modern philosopher to express puzzlement at the beautiful sunlit faces of Greek statuary. These images of serenity and health were deceptive, he felt, because they represented only one voice in the conversation with death and mystery which haunted the Greeks. The "classical ideal," for Nietzsche, was not so much a belief as a precarious affirmation uttered against the weight of terrible evidence. Closer to the truth was an episode from Greek mythology, which Nietzsche retells in *The Birth of Tragedy*:

A legend has it that King Midas hunted a long time in the woods for the wise Silenus, companion of Dionysius, without being able to catch him. When he had finally caught him the king asked him what he considered man's greatest good. The daemon remained sullen and uncommunicative until finally, forced by the king, he broke into a shrill laugh and spoke: "Ephemeral wretch, begotten by accident and toil, why do you force me to tell you what it would be your greatest boon not to hear? What would be best for you is quite beyond your reach: not to have been born, not to be, to be nothing. The second best is to die soon." [3]

This terrifying denial of life is closely related to the conception of individual destiny which is described so powerfully in the *Iliad* and the *Odyssey*. The Homeric hero had to quarry out a space of achievements in the forest of divine prerogatives; he had to realign the boundaries of the human world in order to express the control he had established over his own destiny. Where gods had been, now man was, or tried to be. And often there was a price to pay: divine revenge against merely human greatness; a secret but widespread anxiety that greatness itself was a crime against the old order. Perhaps that is how we must understand the Greek belief in the vulnerability of heroic achievement. The folk myth of Silenus expresses a nightmarish tension between the glory of human accomplishment, and hubris, a crime against the gods.

The gloomy power of the *Iliad*, especially the destiny of Achilles, expresses the tragic wisdom of Silenus, as can be seen from a closer look at Homer's "epic machinery." Throughout the *Iliad*, the Trojan War is anxiously scrutinized by the gods on

Olympus. Zeus, Hera, Athena, Aphrodite, Ares, Poseidon engage in endless arguments about the fate of individual heroes, and of the war itself. Homer is not especially reverent to the gods. He shows them squabbling and playing pranks on each other, although the result of their frivolous behavior is often dreadful in the world below where men die in the gloom of battle. The *Iliad* has often been described as a secular poem, because the gods, though actively present, are not solemn and lofty, but reflect the divisions and inconsequences of the world of men. This may be so, but surely a bitter metaphysical irony is intended by the spectacle of airy gods whose actions result in the horrors of war and destruction. The gods may not be serious, but men are their victims. Homer's message is properly Jobian.

But the gods serve a more positive function in the poem. Entering the action at crucial moments, they provide an "explanation" for the sudden turns of fate; they create a language to express the power which molds human circumstances. At the height of his quarrel with Agamemnon, Achilles draws his sword in a fit of blind rage, intending to slaughter the Achaean leader on the spot. Suddenly Athena appears, and takes him by the hair. She whispers in his ear that no good will come of killing Agamemnon. Achilles listens to Athena's advice. He abuses Agamemnon verbally, then he withdraws from the war in protest over the bad treatment he has received. This is an important moment in the poem. The outcome of ten years of war, the life or death of Troy, the honor of the Achaean army depend on Achilles' decision. Even an Achilles does not often have the power to influence such matters. Few men ever have it. But sometimes circumstances combine mysteriously with character, and the power surges forth. By choosing to act or not to act, Achilles alters the equation of human energies. For this moment, he proposes and disposes like a god. Athena's intervention identifies the extraordinary privilege of the moment. It also suggests that such power has its origin, ultimately, beyond the human world. When Agamemnon is duped by Zeus's false dream; when Paris is coaxed by a god to break truce with the Achaeans; when

Diomedes and Hector sweep armies before them, these men have stepped outside the human world. They have focused in themselves, for better or for worse, an energy drained from the reaches of the cosmos, a godlike energy.

The intervention of the gods, in the *Iliad*, proposes nothing less than a theory of human power. It suggests that the source of power lies, ultimately, with the gods; that the excellent man, or the powerful man, or the politically dominant man is, as Homer so often writes, godlike.

But the godlike man is not always fortunate. When the power surges in him, he is in danger, for as he leaves behind the decorums and constraints of the human world, as he becomes open to the flux of divine power breathing through him, he steps beyond the limit of properly human worth; he trespasses among the gods who are the source of his excellence. Igniting himself to memorable achievements, he is caught in a strange bind: he is spurned by the gods, who turn against him for his trespass, but isolated from men, because the greatness which he has achieved is not properly human. Achilles, throughout the *Iliad*, is a permanent example of the tragedy of excellence. The poem's slow, murderous rhythm is rooted in this dilemma.

Three centuries later, this implicit drama emerges fully in the *Oresteia* trilogy by Aeschylus; especially in the *Agamemnon*, where the chorus envelops the action like a flock of terrified birds, warning that all human greatness contains the seed of disaster, and is a disaster; that the most vigorous aims of men are transgressions which must be punished. Greatness is the disease. To be a man to the fullest is to deserve, along with immortality in song, the bitterness of punishment. The space of the human is precarious and deadly. To fill it well is to deserve death. Therein lies the tragedy which envelops Orestes, which condemned Achilles to die young. For the choice in the *Iliad* had been clearly stated: if Achilles renounces his demonic origins and becomes a peaceful farmer, he will live prosperously; if he pursues his "godlike" destiny, he will be condemned to anguish, loneliness, fear of death, and finally death as a young man.

The Tragic Guest

The crisis in tragedy comes, it might be said, from a lack of space. Too many possibilities need to be worked out for the available rooms to bear. Oedipus discovers that there are not rooms enough in the house of the world to prevent him from inserting his key into the fatal lock; a lock which does not let him out, but rather in. At every turn, Oedipus advances further into the narrowness of his fate, no matter how aimlessly he wanders over the face of the earth, until, putting out his eyes, he locks himself into the inmost room of his blindness.

I will have more to say about the confining walls which force the tragic hero to his catastrophe.[4] But first, let me remark that the adventurer too suffers from this essential housing shortage. Gilgamesh, in the Babylonian epic, is stifled by the city which he himself has fortified. He cannot accommodate his restless needs to the decorums which, as king, he ought to uphold:

The men of Uruk muttered in their houses, "Gilgamesh sounds the tocsin for his amusement, his arrogance has no bounds by day or night. No son is left with his father, for Gilgamesh takes them all; yet the king should be a shepherd to his people. His lust leaves no virgin to her lover, neither the warrior's daughter nor the wife of the noble; yet this is the shepherd of the city."[5]

Like Achilles, like Odysseus on Calypso's island, like Don Quixote, or rather Don Quixada in his forlorn manor house in La Mancha, Gilgamesh finds that life has become small in the confined rooms of society. His energies are bent inward and he is haunted by morbid fears:

Here in the city man dies oppressed at heart, man perishes with despair in his heart. I have looked over the wall and I see the bodies floating on the river, and that will be my lot also. Indeed I know it is so, for whoever is tallest among men cannot reach the heavens. . . .[6]

At this point, which is the nexus of tragedy, Gilgamesh makes the discovery of his life. He discovers that he is not irrevocably bound to the house he has built. The walls of the city, and the walls of his nature as a socialized, moral hero, are not binding forever. With the coming of Enkidu, his wild nature twin, Gilgamesh learns to articulate his needs. Having someone to whom he can talk, he now can bare his obscure energies in language, no longer victimizing them and being victimized by them. He learns what Achilles and Oedipus cannot learn: that the power to build walls can also undo them. With Enkidu as his companion, Gilgamesh lets himself out precisely at the point where the tragically bound hero can only let himself further in. He undertakes his expedition against the forest spirit, Humbaba, a prelude to his further quest for the secret of everlasting life.

It is the same with Odysseus. When the house becomes too small, whether it be Calypso's island, Scheria, or Ithaca, he escapes toward the wide regions of the world. His episodic career demonstrates an impunity for which the tragic hero can only long; for which the spectator, whose bound destinies are expressed all too clearly by the tragic nexus, can only long. The adventurer can trespass into great achievements without paying the price. He can display the wiles, the courage, the warrior skills, the berserker rage; he can play with the fire of the gods, and not be burned.

The archaic Greeks expressed a belief that they were guests in the world who knew they must humor their host, the god, by walking softly and speaking in a quiet voice. Because they were guests, they had to go timidly from room to room, their knees bent, their eyes demurely lowered. It was better not to take up too much place. It was better to observe the rules of the house, careful not to provoke the god who was the source of all they lived by, even their values, which, by the way, secretly despised guests. So that the guest found himself caught between an outward life of discretion and an inward life of self-hatred.

In this sense, the moralized hero was an exemplary guest, a kind of glorified majordomo. Brave, but only within reasonable limits; admiring the host and imitating his manners but only so the host would feel flattered, as when a child plays at being an adult. The tragic hero, on the other hand, represented the nightmare guests are haunted by: the dread that they may violate the decorum of the house. Every day the guest wonders what will happen if he wrongly understands the host's desire. The tragic hero, therefore, was the bad guest. Not because he refused to do what was expected of him—he was not essentially rebellious —but because somehow, despite his good intentions, he made a mistake. That is why he inspired terror as much as he did pity. For these were mistakes anyone could make. Could they even be considered mistakes? When Philoctetes stepped into the sacred grove and called down on himself the curse of the Furies, he did not know what he had done. Such boundaries are invisible, and the world is full of similar boundaries. Who can be sure he will not make a false step? There is another more frightening thought, too. At the moment a man triumphs humanly, he may be violating the etiquette of the gods, without knowing it. For the Greeks, this possibility was a probability. By doing his duty, Orestes is also committing a crime. Oedipus' "fault" is simply another aspect of his triumph over the Sphinx. To be humanly right, is to be divinely wrong. The tragic hero bears a desperate message: it is the message that there is no hope for the guest.

The adventurer refuses to consider the problem in these terms. He cannot, and will not, be a guest. The invisible boundaries, the decorum, the obsession with right behavior, do not extend very deeply into his psyche. When the stifling routines of guesthood press in upon him, he challenges them. He takes the god-power and turns it back against its source. The adventures thrown his way by chance are *peripeteia* in a lifelong warfare which he leads through the badlands of the extrahuman world, beyond the limit which the guest morality has traced around its cities, its farmed lands, and its familiar coastal waters. Like the tragic hero, he is not good at being a guest. Unlike the tragic hero, he knows what he is good at.

It is easy at this point to generalize the preceding argument. After all, the image of the guest is a familiar one. Men are always guests at someone's table: parents, teachers, government, god, or priest. How often do we act as if quiet deference and a smile were the safest way to deal with a policeman, an employer, or a famous man? There are so many rules and so many "faults" to be avoided. In such a labyrinth of dangers, it is a good idea to be polite and clean and proper, all the time, just in case.

The furthest development of the guest morality occurs, of course, in Christianity, where the world itself becomes a sitting room in a mansion whose owner is "merciful," but who nonetheless knows what is going on everywhere, even in the depths of the human heart. To be a good guest, it is not enough to act properly—"meekly"—one must be proper to the limit of one's being. In this view, all of life is an incipient tragedy—for who can be inwardly meek all the time?—which is staved off only by the host's forgiving nature. It is a case in which the host's—God's —mercy is as binding to the guest as is his anger; in fact, more so. Job at least could argue with Jehovah. What can the Christian saint do, but lacerate himself and perform "good works"?

It is no surprise that the adventurer has continued to fascinate the ages of Europe, in the form of the medieval knight, the Spanish picaro, the explorer heroes of endless volumes of travel literature from the sixteenth to the nineteenth centuries, the rogue, the pirate, more lately the mobster. These men refuse the pieties of guesthood. They are escape artists. We are stirred by the key we imagine they have found in their courage and their reckless needs, to the all-too-close-fitting lid of the human condition. The adventurer pokes holes in the walled city, and we breathe more freely for having seen that it is possible to do so, for someone, though not for us.

CHAPTER

5

The Flight from Women

THE unrelenting masculinity of adventure literature—from the *Iliad* to James Bond—has often been remarked. What has not been remarked is the enveloping influence of the feminine which haunts adventure tales in subtle but definite ways. The adventurer cannot be contained by situations. His life is a flight into danger, as if he were pursued by an enemy which he feared more than danger itself. And this appearance of flight is altogether apt, for the adventurer does have such an enemy. The adventurer is in flight from women. Because he cannot cope with the erotic and social hegemony of women, he flees them even into death.

The *Iliad* is not, strictly speaking, an adventure story; in many ways it is closer to the mood of tragedy; nonetheless, it provides a convenient first example of what I mean.

The *Iliad's* major characters single-mindedly create a vision in which men act and become great among, and for, other men: few works of literature are so fiercely dedicated to glorifying male exploits and male ideals. And yet, every decisive moment in the poem is governed by the power of women. It is Helen who creates the epic occasion, by running off with Paris. It is Hera who causes the major twists and turns of the war in her continual disagreements with Zeus. A dispute over women causes the quarrel between Achilles and Agamemnon. It is Achilles' mother who pleads with Zeus to let the war go against the Achaeans during Achilles' absence. Although no woman is present during the embassy scene in Book IX, it is notable that this sequence, in which Achilles' tragic isolation is dramatized, is one of the very few indoor scenes in the poem. It is appropriate that Achilles' tragic self-confinement should appear most strikingly within the walls of a tent, a domestic, "female" space. In short, men may act in the *Iliad*, but the space of the action, its cause, its major turning points, are occasioned by women. The archaic power of Achilles is contained, finally, not by men, but by a bind in his character which the poem attributes to his mother. It is, after all, she who has told him the secret of his fate which afterwards gnaws at him and isolates him from other men, exploding finally in his rage against Agamemnon.

The pattern, eventually the stereotype, of later adventure literature has made this a familiar theme. As in the *Iliad*, the adventures of medieval romance are occasioned by women, performed by men. In Grimm's fairy tales the most frequent motif has young, adventurous men performing dangerous tasks to win the hands of princesses. In the literature of popular romance, sublime "defenseless" women invariably require the bravery, daring, and loyalty of men capable of risking their lives.

But this popular simplification contains within it the outline of another reality which works against the moral symmetry of romance. According to this other reality, the woman not only inspires the adventure hero to his bravery; she is also, perhaps principally, the adversary he needs to master. The adventure performed for the woman is also performed against her. In many written or filmed Westerns, for example, the main character is a drifter who arrives in a town where he gets mixed up in a local dispute involving the safety or the well-being of a woman. Inevitably things take their course and the woman falls in love with him. From this point the story works in two directions. The drifter is inspired by the woman; she reveals in him a strength which he had been reluctant to recognize in himself, even more

reluctant to use. Because of the woman, he manages to win out, proving himself and guaranteeing her safety.

But his newly won strength of character is needed for another purpose now: to protect him from the woman, whose seduction he is able to resist by riding off into the hills, still lonely but still unmarried. The action of the story develops as if, at some level, it were a ceremony whose purpose was to ward off the binding power of the woman—and, by extension, of the community itself—by turning her own wish to be protected against her.

This counter-romantic theme is present throughout medieval

literature, in a number of forms. In *Sir Gawain and the Green Knight*, it is explicit in a negative way. Sir Gawain's final humiliation at the hands of the Green Knight results from Gawain's failure to resist the seduction of his host's wife. The woman's beauty performs a sorcery which binds Sir Gawain and weakens him; he becomes vulnerable and is defeated. The larger symbolisms of the story support this reading. The Green Knight is often interpreted as a pagan spirit of nature. Although the story presents him as a man, his concealed potency is derived from the earth, it is feminine; which is why Sir Gawain's defeat is accomplished in the seductive space of a bedroom, and concluded in a chapel which resembles a mound of earth.

In the poem's opening scene, the Green Knight rides into King Arthur's court, to challenge Gawain. He asks mockingly if any of the knights present will dare to behead him. Gawain answers the challenge, lopping off the head of the intruder with a single blow of his sword. But the mysterious Green Knight picks up his fallen head and rides off amid peals of frightening laughter. The dramatic symbolism of the episode is complex. The Green Knight is beheaded, and yet he doesn't die! The source of his life is not the head, but the womb; nature has no head. But Sir Gawain does. To sever it is to destroy him doubly: by cutting off his masculine intelligence; by symbolically severing that other projecting member which is the source of male potency. In the opening scene, the Green Knight performs a savagely ironic act. He demonstrates how effortlessly Nature survives the very wound which man must fear the most. This, too, is the humiliating lesson he will teach Gawain at the end of the poem, when the two meet a year later in the earth chapel, and Gawain waits in turn for his deathblow with a bared neck.

But on the whole, medieval romance follows an implicit pattern which enables the adventurer to triumph over his female adversary. Typically, the romance opens as the knight gratefully swears oaths of love and loyalty which bind him to the lady of his choice. Before the story even begins, he is "defeated," helplessly in love. All he desires, apparently, is to sit idly at the feet of his queen. What could be more painful than to leave the lady's presence? But that is precisely what he must do; because his lady requires proof—he encourages her to require proof—of his love. And so the knight is banished into the wandering, unattached life of adventure, proving his courage and improving his reputation, all for the greater glory of the lady, whom he may, in fact, never see again.

The pattern of romance expresses an unexpected cunning here. The adventurer knows the danger he is in. He meets it by lulling it to sleep, by giving in without a fight. Once a woman has safely bound him, he encourages her to test the quality of his love. And this is what she does. She traces a magic circle as vast as the world, one which contains all the mysteries of fate, all the challenges of adventure; one which contains, indeed, everything but the lady herself. Within the circle, whatever the knight does enhances the lady's glory, but it also confirms his own freedom. What is done for the lady, need not be done with her. Like the kings Frazer describes in *The Golden Bough* who are so loaded with cosmic potencies that they must live isolated from the community they rule, excluded more than any prisoner from the life of the world, the lady of the chivalric ideal is "elevated" until she is no longer dangerous; she is bound with her own ropes: the feminine goddess neutralized by resourceful male cunning, or at least by the wishful thinking of male ingenuity.

The examples of this counter-romantic theme in adventure literature are numerous. In Conan Doyle's novel *The Lost World*, the hero is a young newspaper reporter who aspires to lead a simple, unadventurous life and to marry a certain young woman whom he has courted very properly for some time. Finally his fiancée lays her cards on the table. She couldn't possibly love a man who had not proved how exciting and brave he was. The young man is stunned, but decides that he must indeed prove himself, for her sake perhaps, but also for his own. He joins an expedition into a lost region of the Amazon jungle, the journey making up the bulk of the novel. It is a marvelous tale of prehistoric monsters, and pre-Stone Age humanity. In the course of it, the young man becomes a true adventurer. Returning home, he finds that his beloved meanwhile has married a local store-keeper, who is quiet, bald, and extremely tame. The book ends as the hero, after a despairing moment, heaves a sigh of relief. He has escaped a fate worse than death. The woman was a trap which her own fantastic ideals have enabled him to escape.

A masterly use of the theme occurs in Conrad's *Heart of Darkness*. Marlowe, the narrator, describes his meeting with the Belgian adventurer Kurtz in the heart of the Congo jungle, where Kurtz has become a sort of living god to the tribes of the region. Kurtz's sojourn in the tropical wilderness has decomposed him morally and physically, until all that remains of his driving ambition and the talents which have made him a legend is his voice: cavernous, hypnotic, almost disembodied. As Marlowe's steamer lags down the river toward the coast, Kurtz dies, the two enigmatic, famous words on his lips: "The horror! The horror!" These words become a focus of the story. As the wisdom of the dying man, or his last delusion, they radiate their judgment into the depths of Kurtz's maniacal egotism. All of life, for Kurtz, is the horror: the rapacious colonial enterprise no less than the "enlightened" ideal of the white man's burden; the drive of personal ambition no less than the impersonal darkness of the archaic wilderness. All of these are the horror. But Marlowe does not end the story with Kurtz's death.

Returned to Europe, Marlowe is led to look up Kurtz's fiancée, his "Intended," a pale, wraithlike woman. As she questions Marlowe about the dead man, one begins to feel a strange ruthlessness in her idealism, a hunger for purity as steely and dangerous as Kurtz's hunger for the darkness of the Congo. Kurtz's Intended seems magical, almost predatory, the hunger of death itself. At last she turns to Marlowe with unbearable, whispered intensity, and asks him the one thing she needs most to know: What were his last words? Marlowe, horrified by his position, horrified also, perhaps, by what he is beginning to understand, answers: "The last word he pronounced was—your name," at which the Intended cries out exultantly. Marlowe is troubled

by the lie he has told—or is he troubled rather by the possibility
that it was not a lie? That this ghostlike queen of the dead was,
indeed, the horror, or one of the horrors?

The irony of this revelation becomes even more gripping if
one recalls the scene of Kurtz's departure from his station in
the inner jungle. His "people" are gathered on the riverbank,
wailing with fear and grief at losing their god. As Kurtz looks
back at them from the deck of the steamer, suddenly a fierce,
baroquely jeweled woman steps toward him. She stares at Kurtz,
and raises her arms as if commanding him to stay. Her silence
is as compelling as the darkness of the jungle itself; she is the

predatory soul of the emptiness which haunts the great river. She, too, then, is the horror. She, too, is a queen of the dead, the hungry mother who, with her white shadow-counterpart in the "sepulchral city," has taught Kurtz the "horror" of her inescapability.

Women have the power to bind; they are witches whose secret ropes confine the adventurer's energies. From Conchobar's procession of naked women, sent out to dampen Cuchulainn's asocial frenzy in the Irish legend, to the paralyzing wiles of Circe, Calypso, and Penelope in the *Odyssey*, women possess the key to the adventurer's divine mobility. They offer him his freedom or confine him, according to their whim and his cunning. But what the woman can withhold—the adventurer's freedom—she can also give. She is the mistress of embraces, chains, and domestic magic, but she is also the mistress of the demonic mysteries which the adventurer confronts. It is through women that the archaic warrior is trimmed to fit "the human pattern," but at the darkest end of his episodic travels, the mysteries which he encounters, which are the source of the stories he brings back to tell, are more often than not profoundly feminine.

The lady herself is bound, on the one hand, by her own powers, but on the other she remains the presiding spirit of the knight's adventures, the gateway through which he must pass into the domain of the magical. One need only mention the frequency with which the adventurer's encounters in the magic countries involve monsters, dragons, caves, descents into darkness, temptations, which comparative mythologists easily identify as essentially feminine. Survivals of the great mother religions, they have been exiled by patristic morality to the distant badlands, where they live on, transformed into dangers which the male energy of the adventurer must overcome, as Saint George overcomes the dragon, as Beowulf overcomes Grendel and his dreadful mother, as Odysseus overcomes Calypso, Circe, Scylla, and Charybdis.

The constancy of the theme, at least in Western adventure literature—but probably elsewhere as well—is undeniable. The adventurer's essential triumph is masculine. His gift is to bind the binder, to outwit and defeat the mysterious identities of woman. The woman he defeats expresses the bewitching domesticity of the house, the space of the community—which is immobile, predictable, fenced off against the amoral potencies of the extra-human world. She presides over the safe breathing-space of human —that is, social—needs. Woman rules the home, and home is where the arts of man are nurtured. She creates the ambiance within which culture flourishes. The *Iliad* is a poem sung by men for men, at festivals from which women may well have been excluded. But the larger space of Mycenaean life, as all of communal life, is sociologically, but also symbolically, feminine. The male festival is inserted temporarily, like the male penis, into a feminine element.

The psychologically oriented mythologist finds obvious analogies between the womb, harbor and shelter of life, and the tent, house, or room: female enclosures which harbor and shelter life. The image of Penelope weaving and unweaving her tapestry comes to mind: making and unmaking the fabric of the household, mastering the unruly energies of the suitors; Penelope on whom the fate of Ithaca depends, because the bonds which hold together the community are the same as the bonds by which she holds Odysseus through marriage. If she dissolves them, the community is dissolved; if she remarries, it is reconstituted.

Undoubtedly, as Lewis Mumford has argued, the most ancient development of community required the presiding influence of women. Mumford writes:

In the early neolithic society, before the domestication of grain, woman had been supreme: sex itself was power. This was no mere expression of fantasy heightened by lust, for woman's interest in child nurture and plant care had changed the timorous, apprehensive existence of early man into one of competent foresight, with reasonable assurance of continuity—no longer entirely at the mercy of forces outside human control. Even in the form of physical energy, the agricultural revolution, through domestication, was the most fundamental step forward in harnessing the sun's energy: not rivalled again until the series of inno-

vations that began with the water mill and reached its climax in nuclear power. . . .

Certainly "home and mother" are written over every phase of neolithic agriculture, and not least over the new village centers, at last identifiable in the foundations of houses and in graves. It was woman who wielded the digging stick or the hoe: she who tended the garden crops and accomplished those masterpieces of selection and cross-fertilization which turned raw wild species into the prolific and richly nutritious domestic varieties: it was woman who made the first containers, weaving baskets and coiling the first clay pots.

Under woman's dominance, the neolithic period is pre-eminently one of containers: it is an age of stone and pottery utensils, of vases, jars, vats, cisterns, bins, barns, granaries, houses, not least great collective containers, like irrigation ditches and villages.

In form, the village, too, is her creation: for whatever else the village might be, it was a collective nest for the care and nurture of the young. Here she lengthened the period of child-care and playful irresponsibility, on which so much of man's higher development depends. . . . Woman's presence made itself felt in every part of the village: not least in its physical structures, with their protective enclosures, whose further symbolic meanings psychoanalysis has tardily brought to light. Security, receptivity, enclosure, nurture—these functions belong to woman; and they take structural expression . . . in the house and the oven, the byre and the bin . . . and from there they pass on to the city, in the wall and the moat, and all inner spaces, from the atrium to the cloister. House and village, eventually the town itself, are woman writ large. In Egyptian hieroglyphics "house" or "town" may stand as symbols for "mother," . . . In line with this, the more primitive structures—houses, rooms, tombs—are usually round ones: like the original bowl described in Greek myth, which was modelled on Aphrodite's breast.[1]

From these multiple swaddling clothes, the adventurer of fiction and legend sets about freeing himself.

Bruno Bettelheim has argued that puberty rites are, at least in part, symbolic rebirths: through such rites, the initiated adult undoes his original birth from woman, replacing it by a wholly masculine birth. But adventure, too, is an initiation. Through it, the adventurer becomes a child of his own deeds, his own bravery. He becomes not only his own father—that represents the "Oedipal" side of the initiation—but also his own mother. He creates the pattern of the wholly freed, wholly male fate. His career embodies the essential escape from the domains of women into the unconfined spaces where he can perpetually create and recreate his own beginnings.

It is an erratic career, requiring virtues which seem almost to be vices, triumphs which apparently lead nowhere, because they must be endlessly repeated in a series of encounters with no logic other than the compelling wildness of each. For the adventurer, the world is like the dragon whose heads sprout anew as quickly as he can sever them. If adventure is a form of initiation into the emperion of the masculine, then it is curiously imperfect, because it must be reaccomplished incessantly. Like Odysseus on Calypso's island, the idle adventurer is less than no man. The project of self-birth is keen and exciting, but unlike the original birth it cannot be done once and for all.

In a sense the adventurer's career violates all standards of responsible "male" behavior. It does not uphold morality; it lacks the productive logic of work. By yielding intuitively to the rhythms of chance, by courting the favors of Lady Luck, Dame Fortune, or the Fates, the adventurer becomes profoundly sympathetic to the wiles of the extrahuman. He learns how to abandon himself to adventure—*ad venio*, "whatever comes"—to be permanently available, his mind emptied of sequence like a Zen master's, at one with the heartbeat of the world, profoundly passive. Don Quixote, who embodies so wonderfully the profile of chivalric adventure, is sublimely nondirective; the world solicits him and he follows its occasions, as water follows the slope of a hill. The adventurer's unsequential, passive temperament is, in fact, strangely feminine. It is as if, to escape the social bonds of woman, the adventurer had internalized the shape of her sensibility in a new, androgynous harmony. Where he least thought to find his enemy, then, he finds her again: in the very temperament which makes him so responsive to the mysteries of the world.

71

Here is where the adventurer discovers the elusiveness of woman. She is the house from which he frees himself in order to give birth to himself as a pure male. But she is also the means within him by which he escapes. And she is still more: her various incarnations appear before him as occasions for adventure, mysteries beckoning to him out of the obscure fertilities of chance. The forests of Grimm's fairy tales are full of witches, bad fairies, and stepmothers whom young wanderers must overcome or die. Think of the Sleeping Beauty story in this light. A witch charms a princess, causing her to fall asleep, while a deadly barrier of thorns grows over her castle, killing those men who attempt to penetrate it. The innocent maiden asleep in the castle, and the thorns which tear men's flesh to shreds, as the Maenades tore the flesh of Dionysus, are part of the same meaning. They are the adventurer's danger, and yet, by creating the episodes he craves, they are the very sense of his life. As for Kurtz in *Heart of Darkness,* and Gawain in the medieval epic, the adversary in the bedroom and the adversary in the forest are one.

The most complete expression of these themes occurs in the oldest of the traditional adventure stories, the Babylonian *Epic of Gilgamesh.* The ancestor of Eve, Circe, Dido, Guinevere, is undoubtedly the sacred prostitute whose seduction of Gilgamesh's companion Enkidu sets the story in motion.

Enkidu is the "natural man" created by the goddess Aruru to be a companion for Gilgamesh, "as like him as his own reflection":

There was virtue in him of the god of war, of Ninurta himself. His body was rough, he had long hair like a woman's; it waved like the hair of Nisaba, the goddess of corn. His body was covered with matted hair like Samuqan's, the god of cattle. He was innocent of mankind; he knew nothing of the cultivated land.[2]

The male energies of war and the womanly energies of earth combine in Enkidu to produce a savage harmony. His androgynous existence is a form of original freedom. He will be to

Gilgamesh a living image of Gilgamesh's "other," buried self which longs for an unfettered existence.

The story tells how one day a trapper meets Enkidu in the wilderness and is struck with awe. Returning home, the trapper tells his father that he has seen "a man, unlike any other, who . . . is the strongest in the world, . . . like an immortal from heaven. . . . He ranges over the hills with wild beasts and eats grass. . . . He fills in the pits which I dig and tears up my traps set for the game; he helps the beasts to escape. . . ." [3] The trapper then goes to consult with Gilgamesh and receives from him good advice on how to go about capturing Enkidu—for Gilgamesh understands the vulnerability of the natural man: "Trapper, go back, take with you a harlot, a child of pleasure. At the drinking-hole he will embrace her and the game of the wilderness will surely reject him." That is what happens. In a marvelously suggestive scene, Enkidu comes to the waterhole and meets the harlot:

She was not ashamed to take him, she made herself naked and welcomed his eagerness, she incited the savage to love and taught him the woman's art. For six days and seven nights they lay together, for Enkidu had forgotten his home in the hills; but when he was satisfied he went back to the wild beasts. Then, when the gazelle saw him, they bolted away; when the wild creatures saw him they fled. Enkidu would have followed, but his body was bound as though with a cord, his knees gave way when he started to run, his swiftness was gone. . . .

Unable to resist the "woman's art," Enkidu loses his freedom. His body is "bound" by the harlot's erotic sorcery. Whereas before his life had been an androgynous harmony, a mingling of the warrior and the corn spirit, now he has fallen into erotic sexuality and is divided against himself, the man and the woman within him are at war. This, the epic tells us, is no ordinary fall: it is the essential failure out of which civilization arises. Enkidu, bound and bodily weak, discovers nonetheless that "wisdom [is] in him, and the thoughts of a man [are] in his heart." [4]

Like Cuchulainn subdued by the procession of naked girls, Enkidu is tamed to "the human pattern" by the divisive, thought-inducing sorcery of woman.

For the space of human achievements is presided over by women, created by women. The binding power of sexuality, a domestic, feminine magic, creates the bonds which make up the community. To learn the human arts, Enkidu must sit at the woman's feet and listen to what she says. He must do this before he can be a companion for Gilgamesh.

Even friendship, the socializing bond which creates the need of one man for another, results, we are told, from the original fall into sexuality. Before meeting the harlot, Enkidu has not been self-reflective; his desires and his fulfillments have been one. He has lived in a thoughtless present, like the animals. Autonomous, blessedly unsocial, he has needed no one, like Rousseau's natural man. But now that he has fallen partway into civilization, now that he is bound by womanly sexuality as Gilgamesh is bound by the walls of Uruk—for they are the same walls— Enkidu needs someone to "understand his heart." Before he can help Gilgamesh to understand the demonic longings which impel him toward the life of adventure, Enkidu must be flawed; he must be tamed into the ongoing "failure," civilization, over which women preside, a "failure" to which the dream of male companionship is a partial remedy.

The complexity of themes in *Gilgamesh* is fascinating. The coming of Enkidu frees Gilgamesh by clarifying his desire for adventure. Gilgamesh's freedom, however, is the same freedom which his friend loses: freedom from lust, which has haunted Gilgamesh, as the opening lines of the poem have told us: "His lust leaves no virgin to her lover, neither the warrior's daughter nor the wife of the noble. . . ."[5] And yet it is by means of a woman, the harlot, that Enkidu is brought to Gilgamesh. Both the bonds which the adventurer unties and the power to untie them derive from women.

Nor do hints lack in the poem that the friendship between

Gilgamesh and Enkidu is partly sexual, as if the adventure heroes, in binding their passions to each other, become less vulnerable to the erotic call of a woman. When Enkidu arrives in Uruk, for example, he learns that Gilgamesh is about to snatch another woman from her family. "At these words Enkidu turned white in the face." He challenges Gilgamesh, and the two men fight until Enkidu is finally thrown. It is then that he and Gilgamesh swear friendship to each other. The bride has apparently been forgotten; Enkidu has, so to speak, taken her place.

This motif recurs in the literature of adventure: uprooting himself from women, the adventurer forms a masculine friendship so intimate, so passionate, that it reasserts, in male terms, the emotional bond which formerly anchored him within the world of the city. One thinks of Achilles and Patroclus in the *Iliad*, or, closer to the modern period, of Don Quixote and Sancho Panza. The adventurer, in his desire to reinvent himself as a man, reinvents his emotions, so that they may be served wholly by male pleasures: the rooted society of women superseded by the mobile society of men.

I do not mean to argue, on the basis of such slender evidence, that Gilgamesh and Enkidu—or Achilles and Patroclus, for that matter—are homosexual lovers, though that is the way fifth-century Athenians understood the latter friendship. Homosexuality, latent or expressed, may or may not belong to the equation of adventure. What does belong to it is the reassertion of a strangely deflected, one might say sublimated, femininity in the adventurer's character.

Later in the poem, when Gilgamesh and Enkidu return from their first adventurous quest, having killed Humbaba, the spirit of the cedar forest, Gilgamesh is faced with a new, deadlier incarnation of the feminine: the goddess Ishtar. Woman is no longer the domestic binder or the liberating harlot; she is frankly, horribly, the adversary the adventurer must cope with. Ishtar, the spirit of creation, the queen of life, invites Gilgamesh to be her lover. She has the power to offer and to withhold growth

75

from the earth, and it is she, we learn later in the epic, who brought down the flood to devastate humanity. Men fertilize her, but they die in the act, like Adonis, Dionysus, and all the other dying gods. Ishtar remains. This is the fate which Gilgamesh sees —and refuses. In the course of his refusal, however, he loses Enkidu, who dies as a result of Ishtar's spite. The dying Enkidu curses the day he gained access to civilization, and reveals to Gilgamesh a terrifying vision of the world of death in which the city of death strangely resembles the confined city of life. Both are unbearable to Gilgamesh, who sets off alone, mourning the loss of his friend and in search of the secret of eternal life.

A question remains: does Gilgamesh triumph over Ishtar or not? In their initial confrontation, he holds fast, but the poem ends on an ambiguous note. Years later, after Gilgamesh has traveled to the ends of the earth and has overcome formidable obstacles—very much, in this poem, like the heroes of later romance—he reaches the land of Faraway, where lives Utnapishtim, the only man to whom the gods have confided the secret of eternal life. Utnapishtim is not a warrior, not an adventurer. Like Kierkegaard's Knight of Faith, the signs of his divine gift are in no way visible. He is a peaceful, ordinary man who lives in domestic happiness with his wife. The contrast is startling when Gilgamesh introduces himself:

"I have wandered over the world, I have crossed many difficult ranges, I have crossed the seas, I have wearied myself with traveling; my joints are aching, and I have lost acquaintance with sleep which is sweet. My clothes were worn out before I came to the house of Siduri. I have killed the bear and hyena, the lion and panther, the tiger, the stag and the ibex, all sorts of wild game and the small creatures of the pastures. I ate their flesh and I wore their skins; and that was how I came to the gate of the young woman, the maker of wine, who barred her gate of pitch and bitumen against me. But from her I had news of the journey; so then I came to Urshanabi the ferryman, and with him I crossed over the waters of death. Oh, father Utnapishtim, you who have entered the assembly of the gods, I wish to question you concerning the living and the dead, how shall I find the life for which I am searching?" [6]

The Flight from Women

Gilgamesh has delivered himself up to the hazards of fate. The goal of his haunted quest has been to wrest the secret of life from the hands of the gods, especially from Ishtar, queen of life and death. Yet at the end of his quest he finds, as a model for the life he seeks, a quiet, apparently domesticated man, reconciled to the confinements of woman.

Upon leaving, Gilgamesh is told of a certain underwater plant whose virtue restores lost youth. He gathers the plant, but on his journey back to his own kingdom, a snake creeps out of a well, while Gilgamesh sleeps, and steals the plant. Gilgamesh's quest is finally an empty one. His errant sexuality, represented by the snake, snatches away from him the secret of eternal youth. Now he too, like Enkidu, is condemned to have his body bound as by a cord, the cord of old age. That is Ishtar's revenge. Gilgamesh's misused sexuality will bind him. He is condemned to the common fate of man.

In the *Epic of Gilgamesh*, the male strategy of adventure is glorious, but it is desperate; and it fails. At the beginning, in the middle, at the end of his quest, the adventurer discovers the many faces of his single adversary—woman, the goddess of sexuality and of life itself, the spirit of the confinements which men erect, the walls of the city.

Various interpretations can be offered of this motif in adventure literature. Reconstructing a hypothetical history of mythologies, it is possible to argue that the archaic adventurer participates in the struggle which opposed the new patristic religions to the more ancient mother religions. Some evidence exists to support this idea. The Greeks, for example, interpreted their own myths along these lines, as in the *Oresteia* trilogy, where Zeus, Apollo, and Athena represent the new male order, while the Furies represent the older blood power of the Mother Goddess. Odysseus gaily triumphing over the perils of the feminine exemplifies the rise of a new male character able to neutralize the old sorcery. It is well-known that the Greeks were haunted by the dangers of woman. The best solution that Plato could devise, in the *Republic*, was to educate women to act and look so much like men that the city would forever be purified of the traps of femininity.

The theme has been no less lively in the European literatures. Here too, the comparative mythologist detects a long-standing struggle between the patristic morality of Christianity, and the older mother religions which, according to Tacitus, prevailed throughout Germanic Europe during the Roman conquest:

Reudignes, Aviones, Angles, Varins, Eudoses, Suardones and Nuithons live in the shelter of their rivers and streams. . . . These tribes . . . share in common the cult of Nrthus, the Earth Mother who, according to their belief, intervenes in human affairs and periodically travels among the nations. On an island in the ocean grows a holy forest with a veiled chariot in it. Only the priest can touch the chariot, and feel the presence of the goddess in her secret sanctuary. The chariot is hauled by cows, and is accompanied with enormous veneration. There are days of rejoicing, festivals wherever the goddess deigns to visit and sojourn. Truces are observed; weapons are set aside and kept well locked up. Peace and tranquility reign until this same priest has brought the goddess back to her temple, weary of her contact with humanity.[5]

Chased by stern Christian authority from the altars of the city, the Mothers took refuge in the forest, as witches and evil stepmothers. They took refuge in the human heart, in the cult of love which developed in Provence and spread throughout Europe during the twelfth and thirteenth centuries. They even reconquered their former churches in the guise of the Virgin Mary, whose festivals gave, and still give, rise to the same festive wildness which Tacitus describes. The adventurer continues to win and lose against his ancient enemy: Saint George against the dragon; fairy-tale heroes against the witches of the woods; Sir Gawain against the earth magic of the Green Knight.

Another explanation for the woman motif in adventure literature is psychobiological. Psychoanalytic theory has made us aware of the vastly complex role played by the mother in the development of the adult psyche. According to Freud, man is haunted throughout his life by a stifled "Oedipal" longing for his mother. During the Oedipal crisis, when he is forced to repress his mother craving and internalize the moral interdictions represented by his father, the male child becomes bound to the ideals of his society. But the suppressed mother is never forgotten. She reappears in numerous "sublimated" forms, as the phantasmic aim of all his sexual longings. She influences his taste for other women, who are no more than failed replacements for the mother. Wife, home, community, even mother country and mother tongue, substitute lamely for the repressed object of his longing. But if language, home, and country are shadows of a hidden mother need, then culture itself can be interpreted as an intricate attempt to sooth man's failure. The harsh male ideology which governs official culture today is, from this point of view, an attempt to reshape language and culture, freeing it from the nightmare of failure which presides over its source in the psyche. The savage distrust of women expressed in Mohammedan and Christian morality, acknowledges how desperate the issue is, because they tell us that salvation from "sin"—from the woman-haunting which destroys men's natures—lies only beyond society, beyond the flesh, and beyond the world itself. Whatever is alive is marked by the original need which man, as long as he lives, can never satisfy.

In a psychoanalytic perspective, the adventurer represents a poignant male fantasy: moved by his desire to vanquish the many faces of woman, he reinvents the shape of manhood itself so as to free it from its multiple attachments to the feminine. As we have seen in the case of Gilgamesh, it is a desperate fantasy. Of all the great adventure stories, only the *Odyssey* brings this purely male longing to a triumphant conclusion. Elsewhere the adventurer must pay for his escape, like Kurtz, forced to recognize "the horror"; like Gawain; like another erotic adventurer, Giacomo Casanova, of whom I will speak in Chapter Nine.

These interpretations of the adventure myth help to organize what I take to be facts of cultural history, but they both contain serious drawbacks. The hypothesis which claims that an ensemble of archaic mother religions has gradually been displaced by the patristic vision, which now predominates throughout most of the world, is far from proved, although it has been extravagantly documented by Robert Briffault in his study, *The Mothers*. The psychoanalytic emphasis on the role of the "dreadful mother," in and before the Oedipal crisis, can be criticized as simply one more way in which patristic morality is haunted by women. Its explicative value, therefore, can be doubted. What cannot be doubted is the endless struggle which the adventurers of myth and literature undergo against the triple presence of woman: as domestic binder, as demonic adversary, and as shaper of the adventurous character itself.

CHAPTER

6

The Adventure of Storytelling

ODERN fiction has abandoned the effort to tell stories. Since James Joyce, a convention has been established which defines "experiment" in literature as the attempt to say how words will behave when there is no tale to tell. Samuel Beckett's increasingly brief fragments of prose and drama—probably the last perfect examples of the genre—pare away actor and action alike, until a disembodied voice remains as witness to the bewildering fact that man speaks on, groping toward his nonexistent story as an amputee gropes for the arm he no longer possesses. This contributes to one's sense of unreality upon reading the great modernist classics, for it has become increasingly clear that a literature purified of storytelling is also distant from life. It also helps to explain why the subject matter of adventure has declined so much in repute. Adventure and storytelling have always gone hand in hand. The great adventurers have not only been great doers, they have been great talkers, like Odysseus returning from the magic countries with his essential tale, or Gilgamesh engraving his adventures on a stone tablet. Even the archaic warriors of the *Iliad* experienced their exploits as raw material for a "song" without which their lives would not have been well-lived.

There is a paradox here, for the experience of adventure seems, at first glance, to be quite the opposite of literature. Adventure fulfills itself in the excitement of risk and personal danger, not in words. If the mystic sheds language in ecstasy, the adventurer sheds language in action.

But actions pass, and the adventurer, like the mystic, is left stranded in the slower world of time. Then words are needed to clothe his idleness. In the trough of the wave, the adventurer tells his story; his words give a permanence to the illuminating moments of action he has lived. They help to preserve his identity through the *little death* which follows the climax.

There is another explanation too. Because the adventurer is fully alive only when he acts, he is a man without a past. Each episode is for him a fresh identity, a beginning of sorts, as for the actor who becomes another self with each role he plays. The adventurer's, "biography," therefore, is the sum of his separate stories. By recalling, and telling, his adventures, he defeats time, inserting his past lives into the present. In this sense, the adventurer's only effective memory is the one he performs in his tale.

That is why the adventurer-storyteller appears so often in literature from Homer, to the Knights of the Round Table, to the ritual boasting of the American frontiersman. The story he tells is not a luxury, but a shape required by adventure itself. One thinks of Admiral Scott, during his fatal return from the South Pole, recording each daily tragedy in his journal, even when he knew that he had only hours to live in his frail tent engulfed by the polar blizzards. His adventure needed the words, like messages in a bottle sent floating out of solitude.

This link between adventure and storytelling motivates one of the few conventions which the modern tradition of adventure literature has adopted. Ishmael, surviving the wreck of the *Pequod* in *Moby Dick*, returns home like the servant in the *Book of Job*, exclaiming: "I only have escaped alone to tell thee." The book is his tale of disaster, and we are Job, learning as we read the extent of the catastrophe which is our lives. Both *Heart of Darkness* and *Lord Jim* are yarns spun by Marlow, to whom they happened. A similar connection between adventure and storytelling is created by writers like T. E. Lawrence and Jean Genet, in whose hands the adventure story becomes an odd permutation of autobiography. As for André Malraux, his novels, though presented more conventionally as fictions, are studiously connected to the episodes of his life. They form a sort of personal odyssey, as Malraux hinted by naming the sections of *Antimemoirs* after his novels.

Like Job's servant, the adventurer returns, crying: "I only have escaped alone to tell thee." And he does tell us, as if the act of adventure and the act of literature were one. Isn't this what Cervantes humorously implies in the episode of *Don Quixote* in which the Don has tried in vain to provoke a lion into battle. The lion yawns and goes back to sleep. But Quixote turns to its keeper, saying:

Come then and shut the cage door, my honest friend, and give me a certificate under thy hand, in the amplest form thou cans't devise, of what thou hast seen me perform; how thou dids't open the cage for the lion; how I expected his coming, and he did not come; how upon his not coming, I staid his own time, and instead of meeting me, he turned tail and lay down. I am obliged to do no more. So, enchantments avaunt! and heaven prosper truth, justice and knight-errantry. Shut the door as I bid thee.[1]

Quixote's story is more substantial, finally, than the adventure itself. In a curious sense, it precedes the adventure and provokes it. Quixote acts in order to legitimate the words he wants to tell. But when the adventure doesn't work out, he decides comically to negotiate anyway for "rights" to the story of what might have happened.

Stories may be "invented" or they may imitate the "real" world —one has no trouble recognizing the difference between a fairy tale and a newsreel. But all stories have this in common: they beckon us out of the visible, providing alternative lives, modes of possibility. Merely listening to a story—"losing oneself" in it —creates a vision of other spaces and times. A man reading *Robinson Crusoe* is penetrated by the loneliness of desert islands, for he has been to one. He understands the sweep of the years, for he has experienced their inexorable passage. The story resembles a wind filtering through cracks in a wall: it gives evidence of the vastness. It provides a mobility through time and space, like the magical mobility supplied in some old tales by flying carpets and seven-league boots.

The Arabian Nights describes a succession of fabulous characters and events, but the central magic which the tales demonstrate is the magic of storytelling. Endless numbers of characters save their lives in the nick of time by coming up with a good story to tell. The entire cycle of the tales becomes a talisman which saves the life of Scheherazade who, day after day, displays more wizardry than Circe or Penelope ever had to: the wizardry of the storyteller who can halt the progress of destiny by exploding any mere minute in time into a bundle of alternative ways. According to the Arabian fabulist, stories were not simply fun; they saved lives.

The peculiar power of storytelling was dramatized for me, one day, on a visit to the marketplace of Djama el Fna, in Marrakesh. Toward the end of the afternoon, the small booths of the market began to close down. The multicolored awnings were rolled up. Swarms of merchants who had squatted all day beside blankets covered with odd objects for sale folded up their wares and disappeared. Within a few minutes, the clash and vibrancy of the market had been replaced by another, even more fantastic scene. Acrobats, desert dancers, and snake charmers appeared all about the cleared space, surrounded by rings of onlookers. Here and there in the noise and turmoil, I noticed several especially dense circles of spectators, and at the center of each one sat a storyteller. The men listening had come down from the Atlas Mountains early that morning to buy and sell wares in the market. But now they sat like pools of quietness in the pushing and shoving of early evening.

The contrast between the quiet of the listeners and the wild activity on the square was startling. The men seemed to have turned their backs on the world, creating a circle of vacancy with their slumped bodies and their expressionless faces.

When I thought about it later, it seemed as if that ring of absorbed faces had made the deepest shape of the story visible. They formed a barrier of unreality, like the one Nietzsche describes in *The Birth of Tragedy*, erected by the chorus around the surges of grief and action in Greek tragic drama. Imagine a visitor pushing his way through the crowd, almost stumbling over these men squatting quietly in the middle of the square. He is startled by their passiveness, which is haunting, as if the men were not wholly there. And that is, in fact, the truth. They are inside the story, having been transported inward on a journey so elusive and sudden that a man could search for that road everywhere over the earth and still not find it.

Transport of this kind is probably what distinguishes storytelling from other uses of language. A story does not primarily require thoughtfulness or critical judgment from its audience; it requires self-abandonment, an act of depersonalization. To enter a story, one must give up being oneself for a while. Self-abandonment to a story is probably one of the crucial forms of human experience, since few cultures have been discovered which did not value it; as if man could be defined by his willingness to appreciate, and tell, that peculiar sort of lie known as a story.

The word "transport" itself evokes the mystery of depersonalization. Primarily, it means traveling or being taken from one place to another. But it can also mean quite the opposite, as when we say that a person is transported with joy or grief, or by music, or by a story. "Transport" in this sense, becomes a way of going nowhere, of being nowhere. The connection which our language has preserved between the geography of the world and the displacements of the psyche suggests that we continue, at some level, to ask questions which the shaman or the archaic adventurer might have understood.

When someone is "ravished" by a strong emotion, or is absorbed in a story, or daydreams "absentmindedly," it seems as if that person were no longer here. A hole has gaped open in the continuum of the visible reality. When he returns, our idiomatic speech asks the right question: Where have you been? The shaman answers this question when he wakes up from his ecstatic trance, by telling the story of his visit to the spirit world. To be "absent" is to be in some other place: *dans la lune*, perhaps, as the French say, or in some aimless nook of time, as when we say "the mind wanders." Apparently the two meanings of "transport" are not as contradictory as they seemed. Both refer to modes of traveling, both describe ways of getting elsewhere.

But where is elsewhere in the case of storytelling? Is it the same as the elsewhere of daydreams, or trance? Do transports of emotion take one to the same place? Is "tripping" with drugs a way of getting there, too? Another more difficult question suggests itself: Does the adventurer, by extravagantly different means, travel to the same elsewhere?

Before attempting to answer these questions, I must point out that the idiomatic expressions I have used contain, in fossilized form, an interpretation of "transport" which has had wide course in various parts of the world. This sort of interpretation is generally described as "soul-loss" or "soul-journey" by anthropologists, and its claim is this: someone who is "absent" has become unstuck from his body in the real world. In different cultures, different reasons are given to explain why this happens. It can, for example, be a punishment for some wrongdoing; that would be a moral version of soul-loss. Or it can result from malice on the part of the spirits. The "absence" can also be intentional, as in the case of the shamanistic priest, who controls his trance movements between the world of men and the spirit world. Intentional "absence" can serve to accompany a dead man's soul to its resting place in the underworld, or to guide back the soul of a sick man (someone whose interior being has been kidnapped by spirits). It can also be part of a spiritual learning process, as in the system of peyote-induced episodes described by Carlos Castaneda, in *The Teachings of Don Juan*. It can even be for "joy alone," as among Eskimo shamans, according to Rasmussen.

To interpret "absence" as soul-loss or a soul-journey is logical enough. If a man is not *here*, he must surely be somewhere. And since, according to the traditional view, the visible and invisible worlds are joined together along unknowable seams, like a coat and its lining, it is possible that holes will gape open at any point in the visible reality. Through these holes the kidnapped or the adventurous man sweeps without warning. The soul lives with the incessant possibility of voyages, welcome or unwelcome. The most dramatic shifts in personal destiny can be interpreted in this way: illness, hysterical seizures, sudden changes of fortune, fainting, dreams, even death. All of these, in different cultures, have been thought to result from intrusions from or into the spirit world.

This view of "transport" was held widely among North American Indians during the nineteenth century. An example occurs in John G. Neihardt's *Black Elk Speaks*, in which an Oglala Sioux holy man tells of receiving his first call from the spirit world. One day when still a young boy, he found that he had trouble walking. He fell quite ill and had to be carried home. For days afterward he lay paralyzed with fever in his tepee. During this time, he experienced a complex revelation which took the form of a journey to the peaks of the spirit world. There he learned his spiritual destiny in a series of visionary encounters with the "Fathers of the World." Upon "returning" to his body, he found his family solemnly gathered around him as if he had been ill. He understood that the illness was an exterior form assumed by his revelation, but the situation frightened him, and he waited several years before he finally told of his visit with the "Fathers of the World," thereby assuming responsibility for the journey, and the knowledge he obtained in the course of it.[2]

Another example of a soul-journey occurs in a lovely Hasidic tale, adapted into English by Meyer Levin. A handsome prince has no sooner been married, than he falls into a deathlike trance:

. . . The bride sat by his body, and held his hand, and waited. The hand became cold as stone. The face became white as snow. The brow shone in the pallor of death. From moment to moment, she leaned her head on his heart, and she heard how the heart beat ever more faintly.[3]

Finally the prince wakes up and tells his bride the meaning of what has happened to him:

Know . . . that this night I pierced to the highest of heavens and stood before the Unnameable Presence. And I asked what would become of me.[4]

For the Hasidic storyteller, the trance is a portal through which the prince journeys beyond the world, outside the reaches of ordinary geography.

In short, the soul-journey resembles very much the sort of adventure one encounters in folklore and myth. According to the archaic view, all men apparently had the chance to become a sort of Odysseus, whether they liked it or not.

Two remarks are called for at this point. Soul-loss or the soul-journey unites in a remarkable way the experience of physical adventure and that of psychic adventure. It establishes between them a relationship in which the adventure story is called upon to describe the experience of a "soul" unstuck from its attachments to conventional reality. For modern readers this is a familiar connection. Since the early nineteenth century, we have learned to respond to the ramifications of "inward" adventure. Romantic and modern literature have supplied a variety of idioms to describe the spirit plunging into its own depths: reviving the older conventions of dream narrative, as in Gerard de Nerval's *Aurelia*; ransacking the language of insanity for literary effect; adapting themes from mythology, as in Joyce's *Ulysses*. The Romantic view of the artist as hero reflects our sense of the encounters sustained by the artist in the secrecy of his mind, to bring "home" the forms of artistic truth.

The Adventure of Storytelling

Such inward traveling was perfectly understood by archaic cultures, with this difference: the reality of the trip, and the realism of the tale it gave rise to, were unquestioned. The soul-journey, and the central importance of the stories told about it, expressed a belief that the principal reality was to be found in the meanders of the invisible world. The mysterious ground of life itself could be known only by the traveler.

A resemblance exists between the adventurer exploring the countries of the marvelous and the "absent" one: each finds his way to the "other" world and returns to tell the story. For each, the story is what he brings back; it is all he brings back, sug-gesting an essential connection between adventure and story-telling: a connection which becomes all the more complex, if we recognize the "transport" of the listener, the self-abandonment which it is the story's business to create, as a form of soul-journey. By entering the story, the listener not only allows him-self to be transported into a particular narrative, he crosses the elusive barrier which divides the worlds. He makes a controlled excursion into the "elsewhere" of life itself.

Remember the men squatting around a storyteller in the marketplace? Their relaxed faces have excluded the welter of ordinary affairs, until only the story remains, like a timeless en-velope within which other places and lives emerge. The listener has detached himself from needs and responsibilities. He has accepted the story, gripped by the images emerging serenely, confidently. The world of the story is controlled and purposeful. Even chance, even the unpredictable strokes of fate, seem "necessary." The aesthetic unity of the story provides an essen-tial luxury: unlike the "real" world, the story reveals all the ele-ments of its form. It reveals what men hope for and believe in, but cannot otherwise see: the complex geography of fate, the longitudes and latitudes which locate men absolutely among the contours of the world. Notice that I have said nothing about the subject matter of the story. I am describing the form of attention the story creates, the "transport" it provides into the neighboring space of realities, resembling in this the shaman's ecstatic trance, the absence of illness or seizure, the trip accomplished by dreams, the kidnapping of death itself.

An important distinction must be made here—and this will be my second remark—between the wildcat transports of illness or death, and the controlled transport of the shaman or the listener. In the first case, the absent one is a victim. He has been defeated by malign spirits. The obscurity of life has ravished his humanness. And his defeat signals a more terrible danger threatening the community: the danger that their minimal island of humanity, their precarious enclosure of customs and needs, will be overrun by the demonic element which surrounds it and temporarily tolerates its existence. Men are guests in the world, their dependence is absolute. Soul-loss therefore becomes a form of punishment, not for some personal fault, but for life itself.

Voluntary "transport" is something else again. It offers an escape from the timorous rituals of guesthood, a confirmation of human prerogatives. The shaman differs from other sorts of priest because his contact with the spirit world is ecstatic. He, more than most men, is susceptible to seizures of "absence." His vocation as priest and healer is usually decided because of this "illness," which descends upon him disruptively, warning that he must learn to master it, or succumb. Before anything else, the shaman discovers his vulnerability to the demonic element. His ties to conventional reality have been loosened, and this provides him with a terrifying personal knowledge of the world beyond men. I. M. Lewis writes in his study on *Ecstatic Religion*:

The shaman is not the slave, but the master of anomaly and chaos. . . . Out of the agony of affliction and the dark night of the soul comes literally the ecstasy of spiritual victory. In rising to the challenge of the powers which rule his life and by valiantly overcoming them . . . man reasserts his mastery of the universe and affirms his control of destiny and fate.[5]

The shaman's vocation as an ecstatic traveler resembles that of the archaic adventurer. Both forge an immunity to the perils of

the demonic world by mastering them. Both return from their journey bearing stories which sustain the humanity of those who are destined to exist within the circle of domestic realities. The story itself is a way of naming the unnameable, extending the net of language into the obscure seas which defy human foresight. Telling his tale of struggles and triumphs in the demon countries, the shaman pushes back the essential ignorance in which men live, by exposing a further reach of darkness to the clarity of words.

Like the adventurer, the shaman learns to possess the possessor. He learns to neutralize the demons by demonizing in his own name, thereby turning the malignity of "absence" into a revelation. He steals fire from the gods, a controlled, sustaining fire, which creates comfort in the place of fear: the fire of culture.

The resemblance between the shaman's inward journey and the adventures attributed to the heroes of epic and folklore has often been remarked. Mircea Eliade suggests that, at least in some known cases, stories which originated in shamanic séances as narratives of the trance journey, came to be preserved as part of oral literary tradition.[6] Eliade reproduces an Eskimo shaman's tale about his visit to Takanakapsaluk, Mother of the Seal, in order to obtain the release of a sick soul:

When he reaches the bottom of the ocean, the shaman finds three huge stones before him, in continual movement, blocking his way: he must go between them at the risk of being crushed. Having passed this obstacle, the shaman follows a path and arrives at a sort of bay; on a hill stands the house of Takanakapsaluk, made of stone, with a narrow entryway. He hears the sea-animals breathing and panting, but doesn't see them. A snarling dog defends the door to the house: he is dangerous to anyone who is afraid of him, but the shaman flies over him and the dog knows that he is dealing with a very powerful magician. . . .

If the goddess is angry with humanity, a thick wall stands before her house, and the shaman must break it down with his shoulders. . . . All kinds of sea-animals are gathered around a pond to the right of the fireplace, and you can hear their cries and their breathing. The face of the goddess is covered with hair; she is dirty and neglected: the sins of man have almost made her sick. The shaman must come close to her, take her by the shoulder and comb her hair (for the goddess doesn't have fingers to comb herself). Before he can do this, there is another obstacle to overcome: Takanakapsaluk's father mistakes the shaman for a dead man heading toward the Land of Shadows, he wants to grab him, but the shaman cries out: "I am made of flesh and blood," and manages to get by.[7]

Such stories, which resemble folktales or the episodes in traditional mythology (for example the clashing rocks in the story of Jason and the Argonauts or Menelaus' encounter with the old man of the sea in the *Odyssey*), are at the heart of the shaman's vocation. Even his role as healer can be supplanted, on occasion, by that of storyteller. At his patient's bedside, as the shaman chants the adventures he has undergone, "one has the impression that the quest for the sick man's soul—the initial motive for the ecstatic journey—has become secondary, and may even be forgotten, as the subject matter of the song becomes the shaman's own ecstatic experience." [8]

Civilization is an affair of storytelling. In oral cultures, the wisdom, moral standards, and skills handed from one generation to the next are kept alive in the repository of tales. For Homer, the memorable life was modeled on a story, and had as its goal to become a story. This, perhaps, is the shaman's most profound function: to extend the clarity of words—of human power and knowledge—ever further into the realms of the unnameable.

The story provides a "safe" analogy for the eruptions of the ungovernable world. The storyteller's art creates a circle in the marketplace. When men enter it, they leave their lives behind them, as if they had crossed beyond the furthest limit of the culture itself, into wilderness, trance, or death. Yielding to the story, the listener plunges, analogically, into the other space which encloses the human world. In this sense, the story's function is homeopathic, and this may be the truest meaning of the shaman's role as healer: by manipulating the "soul's" inward mobility, teaching it to be "lost," and then found again, his story fortifies men against the dangers of the extrahuman.

Armed with the safe-conduct which the story provides, the listener ventures across the border of the visible world, experiencing a fate analogous to that of the character whose adventure he "sees." In the *Poetics*, Aristotle identifies reversal and recognition, preferably both together, as the indispensable elements of tragedy, a judgment which can be extended to include all stories. The happy man becomes desperate; the poor man, rich; the virtuous man, corrupt; the lonely man, loved; the lovers, separated. Men, it would seem, are worth talking about only when the pattern of their lives is broken. The unforeseeable erupts; fate suddenly becomes palpable, making and breaking what, until then, had been merely human. It is Philoctetes accidentally stepping into the grove of the Furies. It is Jacob assaulted in darkness by an angel. It is the poor soldier in Grimm's story, "The Twelve Dancing Princesses," who finds himself caught in an underground kingdom. Each of these characters experiences a form of "transport," a fateful slide into the domain of the invisible. When they return, they will no longer be the same men. Oedipus recognizes that Jocasta is his mother, that Laius had been his father. Suddenly his power, his wisdom, his angry superiority, his very kingship, crumble. Before this moment, he had been a colossus, now he is nothing. Recognition, for Oedipus, *is* reversal; both represent the raw power of the world beyond men, which sweeps chillingly in to overwhelm him.

The "transport," which characterizes the subject matter of the story, also characterizes the experience of the listener. The change of fortune expressed in the plot is mastered by a controlled change of fortune to which the listener submits when he yields to the story. Perhaps this is another way of taking up the old argument for the identity of form and content. Stories tell about changes of fortune, while providing, for the listener, a controlled "absence," which is also a change of fortune, albeit reversible and safe.

At the same time, the story is an act of obeisance. It acknowledges what men must not lose sight of: that their middle ground of customs and security, their existence as men, depends upon forces spinning beyond the human world. What man provides for at the center, in the cleared space of what he knows, originates far from the center, among the gods. At the beginnings of narrative, the tale, whether sung or spoken, was part of other cultural forms: shamanistic séances, sacrifices, initiations, whose purpose was to maintain the trickle of communication between men and the gods or spirits. Often, as in origin myths, the story describes how some implement or custom, or the culture itself, descends from "the time before time began," that is, before the dense barriers which separate the worlds were firmly fixed in place.

Virtually all cultures "remember" a time when gods and men mingled freely. Is it an accident that storytelling grows in importance and autonomy as the divisions are thought to be more impenetrable, the distance more terrifying? Which is to say, as new forms of "transport" become necessary to prevent men from stifling in the human, or being victimized by what they have no name for?

It is not difficult to see why storytellers have often been honored as wise men, as Walter Benjamin points out in his essay on the Russian storyteller Leskov. There is wisdom in the store of tales he tells, but also in the frame of spirit his story creates, the "transport" it induces.

Storytelling is a form devised by men to control the journey away from the visible world which the adventurer first accomplished at the risk of his life. What prayer, ritual, and sacrifice have done in one register, the adventure story does in another: it creates a possibility for "transport" beyond the familiar world, a controlled encounter with the raw power surging over and around that world.

In the preceding chapters an idea of adventure has emerged, expressed in the language, and within the framework, of traditional cultures. The adventurer has been presented as an ontological voyager, a traveler between the worlds. His unstable character has made of him an "amphibian," afloat between the human and the inhuman worlds, between the security of domestic routines and a sea of demonic troubles.

The ur-myth of the adventurer represents a victory over the instability of human nature. If the boundaries of the human world are precariously and imperfectly defined, if all men must live with the peril of involuntary odysseys, then the adventurer figures the triumph of the voyager, for he brings the original good news that man is capable of hewing out a place in the forest of divine prerogatives. Responding to the demonic call in his nature, the adventurer flees the walled city, but in the end he returns with a story to tell. His escape from society is a profoundly socializing act.

It is difficult today for us to respond to these traditional categories. The supernatural is not a shared reality for us. Distance has become a geographical, not an ontological, fact. Gods, demons, and monsters have become figures of speech which do not describe the world, but the way we experience it. Our witches and warlocks lurk not in the forests but in the psyche. This is what Georg Simmel meant when he defined adventure as a "form of experiencing." To render the quality of adventure, we must no longer present the simple contour of acts, but the subtleties of feeling which flesh out "mere" acts. Eventually the truest adventure was found to lie in emotions alone. The language of the quest became involute and rich, rendering the dimensions of inward space.

Nonetheless, the traditional adventure myth has provided us with a clear, almost geographical definition of the adventurer's mobility, which it will be useful to keep in mind. For our subject now will be the fall of adventure in the modern world, the blurring of the mythic geography through which the adventurer once traveled in his quest for the demonic adversary. Having restored the primitive map of adventure, it will now be possible to trace the transformations of that map which our psychologically and sociologically oriented civilization has brought about.

PART TWO

CHAPTER

7

The Interior Monk

THE birth of the modern age was a grim event. During the sixteenth century, England and Germanic Europe were assaulted by a relentless new vision. Within decades the boisterous spirit of Falstaff was dead, replaced by a new morality, and a new method of piety. Max Weber has given us the most sweeping description of the change:

Christian asceticism, at first fleeing from the world into solitude, had already ruled the world which it had renounced from the monasteries and through the Church. But it had, on the whole, left the naturally spontaneous character of daily life in the world untouched. Now it strode into the marketplace of life, slammed the door of the monastery behind it, and undertook to penetrate just that daily routine of life with its methodicalness, to fashion it into a life in the world, but neither of nor for this world.[1]

Christian distrust of the world had been expressed by the massive walls of monasteries dominating the medieval landscape. Around the monastic islands spread a continent of forests inhabited by witches and stubborn gods who would not die out. As late as the seventeenth century, with its monstrous sabbats and its witch trials, Europe was still a surprisingly pagan continent. The monastery walls resembled breakwaters holding back the pagan spirit of the world.

But, during the sixteenth century, the walls had begun to fall; not only the monastery walls, but the secular walls of the castle, and the battlements of the medieval city. There were many reasons for the change: a weakening of feudal prerogative, as the dynasties of France, Spain, and England consolidated their royal power; dramatic shifts in population, as cities like Paris and London grew beyond their established limits; the Protestant revolt, with its doctrine of spiritual self-reliance, weakening the institutional life of the Church. The bulky stone walls which had stood for so many centuries suddenly became vulnerable. When Montaigne, from his tower, surveyed the world he had come to know, he saw movement without boundaries, change without limits or principles:

The world is but a perennial movement. All things in it are in constant motion—the earth, the rocks of the Caucasus, the pyramids of Egypt—both with the common motion and with their own. Stability itself is nothing but a more languid motion. I cannot keep my subject still. It goes along, befuddled and staggering, with a natural drunkenness.[2]

Yet Weber's passage describes a remarkable victory, not a defeat. Instead of letting the worldly enemy in, the monastery's broken walls loosed a spirit of asceticism which gripped the countries of northern Europe. Previously the monks had lived their methodical lives in seclusion, but now the monastic spirit influenced whole cities and countries. The walls had fallen, but the world itself, for Puritans and Jansenists, had become a vast, inhospitable monastery, and all of its inhabitants incipient monks.

Two centuries later, William Blake would speak of "mind-forged manacles." Hegel, Marx, and Nietzsche would formulate the modern worry about "alienation." Freud and the early Wilhelm Reich would develop their view of character as a form of interior wall-building, or "repression." But in the heroic days of the modern age, the interior monk was not thought of as an oppressor. He stood for a spirit of self-reliance; he democratized the capacity for epic solitude by teaching each man to be an island in the sea of the world. At least that was Daniel Defoe's opinion in the early eighteenth century. The portable walls of the soul were dearer to God and truer to man, he felt, than the barbaric monastery walls. Solitude was the element of thoughtful lives: "Everything revolves in our minds by innumerable circular motions, all centering in ourselves. . . . Hence man may be properly said to be alone in the midst of crowds and the hurry of men and business. All the reflections which he makes are to himself; all that is pleasant he embraces for himself; all that is irksome or grievous is tasted but by his own palate." [3] Instead of complaining about lonely crowds, Defoe glories in the discovery of a new resource for man: his aloneness. Some years later Adam Smith would rework the very conception of social enterprise, founding it not on community but on solitude, what he called "self-interest." This newly discovered aloneness in the world was far superior, in Defoe's opinion, to the mere geographic aloneness which monasteries and hermit cells had once enforced in "primitive times," when men

separated themselves into deserts and unfrequented places, or confined themselves to cells, monasteries, and the like, retired, as they call it, from the world. . . . A man under a vow of perpetual silence, if but rigorously observed, would be, even on the Exchange of London, as perfectly retired from the world as a hermit in his cell, or a solitaire in the deserts of Arabia. . . . For the soul of a man, under a due and regular conduct, is as capable of reserving itself, or separating itself from the rest of human society, in the midst of a throng, as it is when banished into a desolate island. [4]

At the heart of this new monasticism was the rule of "due and regular conduct." What in "primitive times" had been enforced by opaque battlements and explicit codes was now to be enforced implicitly, by a commitment to moral limits whose advantage was their ubiquity: no voyage, however extravagant, could extract a man from the jurisdiction of interior walls. Conversely, wherever he might be, the interior monk was at home. On the London Exchange or an island in the Caribbean, "due and regular conduct" would monasticize his portion of reality.

The medieval monastery had been a center of spiritual discipline; but it had also fostered a busily productive life style among the monks. Along with Christianity, the first fruits of Western technology had taken refuge in the monasteries. Weber called this inclination to regular, productive behavior, "the spirit of capitalism." And now it was loose in the world, producing visible works and private solitude, public wealth and productive aloneness.

The inadequacies of Weber's view have been argued by many critics. The "spirit of capitalism" never won the clear-cut victories Weber described. Neither Restoration England nor Regency France were "monastic" by any definition of the word. Where the rationalization of behavior ("due and regular conduct") which Weber described did occur, it resulted from more complex causes than he acknowledged: not only the secularization of Calvinist ideals, but the prior pressures of economic development during the late Middle Ages. Another perhaps more important factor was the emergence, during the seventeenth and eighteenth centuries, of the modern city, which disrupted traditional obligations, forcing men to regulate their lives in a more lonely, less explicit fashion. Weber's interior monk is essentially an urban character, as Defoe well knew. The ideal of freedom —"solitude"—which Defoe claimed for him was possible only in the city, where each man, sociologically, was indeed something of an island. This development occured not only in Protestant London, but in Catholic Paris.[5] It was described not only by Dissenting moralists, but by Enlightenment *philosophes* like Montesquieu, whose *Persian Letters* constitutes one of the great stories of the eighteenth-century city. About the same time, Defoe was the first in England to express the drama of urban insecurity in *Moll Flanders, Roxana,* and *Journal of the Plague Year.* In his *Serious Reflections During the Life and Surprising Adventures of Robinson Crusoe,* Defoe draws repeated parallels between "the silent life" of his famous island hero and the portable solitude of man in the modern city. He even hints that in

Robinson Crusoe he had used the cover of a fictional adventure to tell his own real-life story. It is striking to read the preface to *Serious Reflections*, while keeping in mind what we know of Defoe's actual life:

The "Adventures of Robinson Crusoe" are one whole scheme of a real life of eight and twenty years, spent in the most wandering, desolate and afflicting circumstances that ever man went through, and in which I have lived so long in a life of wonders, in continued storms, fought with the worst kind of savages and man-eaters; by unaccountable surprising incidents, fed by miracles; suffered all manner of violences and oppressions, injurious reproaches, contempt of men, attacks of devils, corrections from Heaven, and oppositions on earth; have had innumerable ups and downs in matters of fortune, been in slavery worse than Turkish, escaped by exquisite management. . . . raised again and depressed again, and that oftener perhaps in one man's life than ever was known before; shipwrecked often, though more by land than by sea. In a word, there is not a circumstance in the imaginary story but has its just allusion to a real story.[6]

Defoe himself experienced vicissitudes very much like these: bankruptcies, rash political involvements, imprisonments, humiliations, numerous economic shipwrecks "by land," isolation, betrayal by members of his family, the gnawing servitude of his work as a secret agent for political masters who used and abused him with cunning. Defoe apparently never knew a moment's security during his long life. The city of London was his ocean; embattled self-reliance was his island; every uncontrollable turn of politics or the market was his shipwreck. Sutherland's biography of Defoe describes him convincingly as a sort of urban adventurer, for whom risk had become a way of life. "Though he tried to make money as long as he lived, and once or twice made a good deal of it, the impulse that drove him along through a quite extraordinary career was not so much the desire for riches as an incurable love of excitement."[7]

Defoe was probably the first writer to grasp the exotic possibilities of city life with its unpredictable energies tempting the urban adventurer into ever new situations. Defoe literally domesticated adventure, by discovering a new home for it: the streets of London, the vast patchwork geography of the city. Defoe's urban novels prepared the way for a literature which would not fully emerge for another century: the literature of popular crime romance, founded on the experience of the city as a place for exotic encounters. For Defoe, the quintessential urban character was mobile, unsentimental, cunning; he was self-reliant, good at taking risks, because his life was composed of risks. He might not be a criminal, but the difference between his sharp dealings as a businessman or entrepreneur, and those of the criminal were subtle. In Defoe's London, success replaced morality as a source of legitimacy; failure lapsed normally into crime. As he wrote in *The Review:* "How many honest gentlemen have we in England, of good Estates and noble circumstances, that would be Highway Men, and come to the Gallows, if they were poor?" [8] For Defoe, crime, like business, was an act of survival. His two most interesting criminals, Moll Flanders and Roxana, were simply engaged in the city's most demanding enterprise: staying alive and well.

We have come some distance from the interior monk to the criminal. Indeed, what connection is possible between these opposite models for the self-reliant citizen? Is the criminal simply the monk gone bad, the godly busyness of the one degenerating into the egotistical busyness of the other? Defoe doesn't bother with such distinctions. His criteria are simpler and more vigorous: it is better to be busy than not, rich than poor, cunning than foolish, enterprising than timid. The moral shadings of cunning, busyness, and enterprise are not entirely forgotten; but they carry less weight than the realistic urban need to survive. Defoe has an activist's view of human nature. Among the talents of man, there is one to which all the others are subordinate: the ability to keep alive. And since, in Defoe's opinion, "Man is the worst of all God's creatures to shift for himself," [9] he cannot be choosy about the means: "I tell you all, Gentlemen, in your Poverty the best of you will rob your Neighbor; nay go farther,

. . . you will not only rob your Neighbor, but if in distress, you will EAT your Neighbor, ay, and say Grace to your Meat too— Distress removes from the Soul, all Relation, Affection, Sense of Justice, and all the Obligations, either Moral or Religious, that secure one Man against another." [10] For Defoe's urban character, crime represents a sort of vanishing point, an organizing limit for his ambitions.

The criminal, therefore, was the quintessential individual. The successful shopkeeper, the entrepreneur, even the landed gentleman, were shielded by money from the actual nature of their acts. A shove of misfortune, and the superfluities would be swept away. The criminal would emerge from his concealment, continuing his career in the open now. A century before Proudhon, Defoe launched the potentially anarchistic opinion that "property is theft," along with this unanarchistic corollary: theft is a form of business. Moll, Roxana, and Singleton resemble entrepreneurs as much as criminals. They calculate profits and losses, and prove, untiringly, that crime does indeed pay. In their own way, their episodic careers are governed by "due and regular conduct." They work hard, rate their adventures, opportunities, and human relationships in terms of money, and know, with wise exactness, the monetary value of most human occasions. The result of their prudent management is inevitable: they become rich; they flesh out their criminality with comfort, social position, and, ultimately, with legitimacy. In Defoe's novels, the wayward individual works hard at his crimes, improves his lot quantitatively by "earning" a lot of money and spending only a little. At last the quantitative improvements result in a qualitative leap: the criminal is converted into a citizen, his wealth solidifies into cleanly possessions. I wrote earlier that Defoe had "domesticated" adventure by creating the mode of popular crime romance and the literature of urban adventure. It is now clear that he domesticated adventure in another sense as well: he converted it into good business. He recuperated it for society, by redefining it as the central activity of the citizen. If we are all adventurers (that is, enterprising urban individuals), then adventure is not too strange, not too wild. It takes place amid a thicket of interior limits, among men whose lives, devoted to "due and regular conduct," have managed to regularize the excitement of adventure. If we are all adventurers in Defoe's sense, then none of us are adventurers in the old sense. There is nothing demonic about Moll, Roxana, Captain Jack, Singleton, or any of Defoe's criminals. Their situations are all similar. Impoverished by birth or bad luck, they are forced to roll up their sleeves and get down to the unambiguous labor of staying alive, which means accumulating "substance." When at last they are "converted," the reader is only mildly surprised. Whatever vagaries of crime they have undertaken, they have worked at it calculatingly and regularly. The financial accountings which are so much a part of Defoe's fiction are signs that the "lost" hero or heroine has retained his sense of direction, that he has been safely headed all along toward the haven of "conversion." There is no satanic protest in Defoe's criminals. Vautrin, Melmoth, and the Monk would not recognize them as ancestors. The small difference between Defoe's criminal and Weber's interior monk is underscored in the novels: Roxana is fascinated by pious costumes; the pirate Singleton's best friend is William the Quaker. Even amidst an ocean of murder and shady dealings, the walls remain intact, the portable limits assert their influence.

With Defoe, the experience of adventure has been democratized; it has been tamed into a socialized and socializing activity. The adventurer-hero is no longer an extravagant, half-human character; he is no stranger among men. On the contrary, he has become the well-known, familiar citizen engaged in enlarging his interests. Moll does what we all do, in the mode of crime. Robinson Crusoe does what we all do, in the mode of solitude. With a journalist's acumen, Defoe understood the as yet unspoken needs of his audience, the class of newly literate shopkeepers and small businessmen, most of them Dissenters or at least Dissenting sympathizers. In the unstable world of the city, these men held on tightly to the one regularity which they could depend on: their interior monkhood, which enabled them to be at home in a crowd, harnessing for their "profit" (that is, their survival) the financial cannibalism and the stormy changes of mercantile London.

Defoe has a place of choice in the history of adventure. He is also Europe's first novelist, after Cervantes, and the two facts are not unrelated. In Defoe's fiction, for the first time, we encounter a new attitude toward adventure, amounting in fact to a new subject matter: the fall of the adventurer. Defoe himself saw a connection between *Robinson Crusoe* and *Don Quixote*, the greatest novel ever written about the adventurer's heart-rending fall from grace. When a critic accused his island hero of "quixotism," Defoe answered by acknowledging the similarity. "Perhaps [the critic] will be a little startled when I shall tell him that what he meant for a satire was the greatest of panegyrics." [11]

The parallelism between the two books is interesting. In Cervantes' novel the adventurer is a madman who has read too many books and can no longer see the world for what it is. In Defoe's novel, the adventurer is equally deluded; he is a sinner, who will remain stranded in the "silent life" of his island until he has learned the advantages of "due and regular (that is, realistic) conduct," whereupon he will be "saved" from the sin of adventure, and from the island. Cervantes' novel describes the discovery of "reality" as a squalid place with no room for wonder and heroism. Defoe's novel describes an equally grim world in which survival does not depend on heroism and action, but on obedience, on deference and methodical virtues. Cervantes' novel exposes the divorce which "natural philosophy" had begun to pronounce between science and imagination, facts and values, knowledge and opinion, ultimately between the world of "reality" and its wayward, exiled inhabitant, man. Defoe's novel explores a similar divorce between the individual and "reality"; it is the divorce between the sinner's episodic nature and the structure of God's will as the world reveals it. *Don Quixote* would eventually become a text of sorts for the Enlightenment's preoccupation with "nature" (scientific reality) and theories of knowledge (psychology). *Robinson Crusoe* embodies the grim cosmology of English Puritanism. But in both books, the episodic life is a delusion, the adventurer a fool. That is the lesson which the novels impart; that is, in fact, their subject matter. Don Quixote is a noble fool who dies mad, because he prefers his foolishness to all the "common sense" in the world. Robinson Crusoe is a lost fool who "finds" himself when he is most lost and thereby learns how to make himself as much at home at the ends of the earth as the monk was in his monastery. These parallels between *Don Quixote* and *Robinson Crusoe* suggest a relationship between the secular realism which triumphed in Europe during the Enlightenment and the intensely Christian vision of English Puritanism which influenced Defoe. Neither the *philosophe* nor the Dissenting moralist had any use for the adventurer. For both the episodic life was unrealistic—unrepentant—and therefore to be scorned. The adventurer was a man who skirted the serious business of life, who ran away, like Robinson Crusoe, or who stumbled helplessly over his crazy misinterpretations, like Don Quixote.

Until recently, *Robinson Crusoe* was considered by critics to be something of a fluke. It had been one of nature's jokes that Daniel Defoe, an overworked, slightly principled journalist, should have stumbled on the formula for the most famous book of the eighteenth century. Defoe was credited with luck and a gift for mimetism: he could "lie like the truth," as it was called, and he could recognize an engaging fact when he saw one. But he had no "imagination," and he couldn't give any convincing shape to his half-connected stories. It has since been demonstrated that Defoe was a more complex writer than anyone gave him credit for; that his sources for *Robinson Crusoe* were not only travel books and newspaper stories—in particular the story of Alexander Selkirk, a sailor stranded for several years on an island off the coast of Chile—but the vast tradition of Christian "Providence" literature, and spiritual autobiography, which formed the reading matter for England's literate Puritans. From this tradition of exhortatory writing, Defoe borrowed his structure of biblical allusions and the form of his narrative: the straying sinner who is punished by God's will and is taught to understand the error of his ways. From it he also borrowed his judgment of the adventurer as a disobedient son, who cannot read the stern messages of God the Father as they are revealed by the phenomena of nature and the events of his personal destiny.

J. Paul Hunter and George Starr were the first to see the connection between this popular tradition in the late seventeenth and early eighteenth centuries and the novels of Defoe.[12] The "Providence" books were usually compilations of "case histories," each one telling how God's miraculous intervention saved the day when disaster of one sort or another seemed certain. A favorite source of examples was the life of the sea, especially shipwrecks, spectacular storms, and such, where some unexpected turn of events caused a shipful of lost souls to be saved. The storms, shipwrecks, and rescues were presented as evidence that God's will was omnipresent in nature; that the world displayed a mysterious continuity between the moral and the physical. The aim of these books was to convince the reader that his life was in God's hands at all times, but especially in moments of crisis. The world of nature revealed a mysteriously interconnected grammar of divine intentions. Every event contained a "signature," every disaster and good fortune bore a sign revealing its place in the pattern of God's will. The lexicon of these signs was overwhelmingly simple: all things in nature were to be "read" as a reward for good behavior, or else, more frequently, as a retaliation for sin. As the Anglican John Tillotson wrote:

The hand of God doth sometimes as it were by a finger point at the sin, which it designes to punish: as . . . when a sin is punish'd in its own kind, with a judgement so plainly suited to it, and so pat, that the punishment carries the very mark and signature of the sin upon it.[13]

The "Providence" books describe a world governed by relentless moral laws. In them, nature itself became an agent of morality. The world, in its unexplored corners and its familiar neighborhoods, among cannibals and Christians, expressed the inescapable consequence of each man's obedience or disobedience.

The influence of this moral tradition on the literature of adventure cannot be underestimated. The judgment it pronounced on the adventurer's wayward career was unambiguous. Evoking the parable of the Prodigal Son, John Goodman, in *The Penitent Pardonned* (1694), writes that the Prodigal is typical of sinful man; he "grows mal-content with his condition; and finding himself restrained, the proud waves of his passion rage and swell against all that bounds and checks them. . . . He finds his condition not to his mind, and . . . he is tempted to run upon adventures. . . ." [14]

The monastery of the world was guarded by invisible walls from which there could be no escape. Adventure was a form of "mutiny"; what is more, it was foolish. In a world governed by God's law, only a "lawful" life made any sense. "Due and regular conduct" was not merely recommended; it was a necessary tactic for survival. Only the unrepentant "natural man," could be so deluded as to follow his hunches to their conclusion. As Obadiah Sedgewick affirms:

Every sinful man is a wandering Meteor, a very Planet on earth; he is gone from the fold, as a silly sheep; he is gone from his Father's house, as a silly Child; he is gone out of the right path, like a silly Travellor in the Wilderness. Sin puts us into a Maze, into a Labyrinth; we go from one sin to another sin, out of one by-path into another by-path; and the further we go in sinful paths, the more still we go out of the way. [15]

Still another spiritual autobiographer writes:

Man naturally loves changes of states and conditions, as feaverish palates do change of beer, and it may be none will please. . . . It may in some sort be said of every natural man's heart, as of Nebuchadnezzar's, a beast's heart was given unto him (Dan. 4:16).

Man would have change of pasture, as some beasts will not stay where they are put, but break and leap Hedges to get into new grounds.[16]

The adventurer is the "natural man"; he is the criminal, and his impulsive life reveals the devil in his soul. The unregenerate sinner—everyman—cannot control his appetites. His life is strewn with storms and shipwrecks, treacheries and temptations. Unable to read the "signatures" of Heaven, he fails to make his soul into a replica of the larger order of the world. "The lost man, he is out of the common and known Road; he is in the Woods, in the Ditches, in the Deserts, in the Fields, and he goes from one strange place to another strange place." [17]

Defoe's democratization of adventure is clearly anticipated in the popular literature of the Dissenters: all men are born into adventure; it is the "natural" tendency of their souls. Only a proper experience of God's wisdom will save the individual from the delusions of his erratic temperament. To be "saved" is to shed the adventurer in one's soul. It is to recompose one's inmost being in the shape of "due and regular conduct." The spiritual autobiographer typically looks back on the shipwreck of his life from the safe ground of his rescue: that is, his conversion. He is an Odysseus who went home to stay; a Gilgamesh who saw the error of his ways; a Don Quixote who shed his "madness" and became a good husband to a real woman.

The influence of "Providence" literature and spiritual autobiography on *Robinson Crusoe* is undeniable. Not only the moral framework of the book, but its subject matter, its familiar symbols, and its narrative stance are derived, at least in part, from these popular traditions. Defoe's audience was at home with his book because they found in it a familiar language turned to new, but not eccentric, use.

8

Robinson Crusoe,
The Unadventurous Hero

OTWITHSTANDING its alluring title, "The Life and Surprising Adventures of Robinson Crusoe of York, Mariner," *Robinson Crusoe* is not an adventure novel. Adventurous episodes abound: piracy, miraculous escapes, attacks by wild beasts, a shipwreck, savage storms, an earthquake, several armed assaults. The brute task of survival in a hostile world has never been described more tellingly. Yet *Robinson Crusoe* undermines the ethos of adventure. It does not glory in the episodic life. Its hero is exasperatingly cautious, paralyzed with terror at the dangers he encounters, forever regretting the "mistakes" of his past life.

Robinson Crusoe is paradoxical evidence for Georg Simmel's modern definition of adventure as "a form of experiencing,"[1] for it is an adventure novel without an adventurer. Its engrossing catalogue of disasters and rescues presents the singular anomaly that no one experiences them. Episodes burst into the story with an aura of risk and lonely affirmation, but they are deflated by Crusoe's lack of imagination, or they are drowned in his hysterical fears. The outward structure of adventure prevails, but the adventurer's energy is lacking. In this sense, *Robinson Crusoe* forms a negative prelude to the new adventure literature of the nineteenth century, for it clearly identifies the adventurer himself as the key to the revelations of "action." For modern writers like Conrad, T. E. Lawrence, and Malraux, adventure will no longer be a form of travel literature, but of autobiography. The mysteries into which the adventurer advances at the risk of his life will no longer take the form of a shamanistic bestiary in an objectively magical world; they will flow out of his inward madness, they will explode his personal psychology into a new perception transforming geography into revelation, like T. E. Lawrence in the Arabian Desert, political warfare into mystical confrontation, like Malraux in *Man's Fate*. *Robinson Crusoe* prepares the way for this transformation by demonstrating beyond question the dependence of the adventure story on its hero's "form of experiencing." It prepares for a new psychology of adventure by presenting a story in which the exotic episodes are flattened relentlessly into the ordinary by the ordinary character of its protagonist. The reader in search of adventure encounters what he is looking for, and yet, because of the hero's peculiar perspective, he is thwarted at every turn. The adventures of *Robinson Crusoe* are never what they seem. Or rather they are, far too thoroughly, what they must be for a character like Crusoe. Virginia Woolf has described as well as anyone the deflated perspective of Defoe's novel:

It is, we know, the story of a man who is thrown, after many perils and adventures, alone upon a desert island. The mere suggestion—peril and solitude and a desert island—is enough to arouse in us the expectation of some far land on the limits of the world; of the sun rising and the sun setting; of man, isolated from his kind, brooding alone upon the nature of society and the strange ways of men. Before we open the book we have perhaps vaguely sketched out the kind of pleasure we expect it to give us. We read; and we are rudely contradicted on every page. There are no sunsets and no sunrises; there is no solitude and no soul. There is, on the contrary, staring us full in the face, nothing but a large earthenware pot.[2]

This is the peculiar originality of *Robinson Crusoe*. Its hero is not an Odysseus, "skilled in all ways of contending"; he is not a Beowulf, dragon-slaughterer, or a Hercules, or a Gawain. Its hero is an old earthenware pot; its hero is Robinson Crusoe, whose character resembles a homely piece of hardware. But here is the rub. In the world of *Robinson Crusoe,* old earthenware pots survive, and adventurers do not. Old earthenware pots have an unimaginative way of conquering the wildness of the world where adventurers are apt to get lost while losing all their money. The impulsive character of the adventurer may get him cast away on a desert island, but he will be saved only if he can change himself into a lump of the obedient clay from which God made man as a "vessel" of His intentions on earth. This is the book's triumphant irony: domestic virtues and gross labor are precisely what are needed to keep Crusoe sane and civilized in the heart of the darkness. He survives because he dislikes risks. He survives because he lacks traditional courage. When he is cast up on the shore of his island to be, he is revealed for what he is: a nerve without a shell. "I ran about the shore wringing my hands and beating my head and face, exclaiming at my misery and crying out I was undone, undone, till, tired and faint, I was forced to lie down on the ground to repose, but durst not sleep, for fear of being devoured." [3]

Crusoe lives with fear; it is his native element. At every turning point in the book, it erupts hysterically, almost childishly. Like Jim's paralyzing cowardice in *Lord Jim,* fear is Crusoe's signature. Upon running away from home the first time he goes to sea, a storm, typically, frightens him to death: "I thought the ship had broke or some dreadful thing happened. In a word I was so surprised that I fell down in a swoon." [4] Later, on his island, he devotes a year of hard labor to building a boat. But one bad experience while circumnavigating the island terrifies him so thoroughly that he abandons the boat and never uses it again. When Defoe finally provides Crusoe with cannibals to worry about, one is relieved. The cannibals keep Crusoe sane.

They keep him from dissolving into something like paranoia, by providing real enemies to combat. There is a fine moment of psychological realism in the novel, when Crusoe sees the naked footstep in the sand. The more he thinks about it afterward, the less sure he is that the footstep is not his own, and that he is not simply terrified of his own shadow. It is fitting that Crusoe should brush up against the truth of his character at the very moment when an actual human situation looms before him.

Robinson Crusoe may be a nerve without a shell; he may be afraid of his own shadow, but he has the instincts of his vulnerability. Like a mollusk, he knows how to secrete around him a thick wall-like skin. Robinson Crusoe never stops building walls. For twenty-eight years of the "silent life," he ramifies, reinforces, camouflages, and naturalizes the walls of his enclosure. Upon first rescuing goods from the wrecked ship, he builds a wall with them: "as well as I could, I barricaded myself round with the chests and boards that I had brought on shore. . . ."[5] At this point Crusoe is all but naked in the wilderness; it is only common sense to build a barricade. But as the story progresses, Crusoe's wall-building takes on momentum. His walls become inventive and passionate, displaying an almost magical capacity to grow on their own. This is as close as Defoe's studiedly prosaic imagination comes to the conceptions of romance. When Crusoe decides that he must protect his home base so that he can live with peace of mind, he plants a thicket of tall, pointed stakes in the ground in the form of a wide semicircle, spending months at the task. "The piles or stakes, which were as heavy as I could well lift, were a long time in cutting and preparing in the woods, and more by far in bringing home, so that I spent sometimes two days in bringing home one of those posts, and a third day in driving it into the ground. . . ."[6] Here is Robinson Crusoe doing what he does best: laboring day in, day out, repeating his clumsy, persistent craftsmanship until it is almost ritualized, a psychic wall against the loneliness. Wherever he goes on the island, he builds walls like this one. They are his mark; they establish his identity in the limitless greenery of nature. The key to Robinson Crusoe's wall-building, as to his entire career of "silence," is "infinite labor." Creation, in *Robinson Crusoe*, is no mystery. It is the result of hard work, which defines Robinson Crusoe, just as compulsive wall-building defines his turf of home and confinement. In the end the labor bears fruit, quite literally. The walls sprout leaves and branches. They naturalize themselves into a green, womblike dome, nature domesticated into a wall; the bare nerve secreting its protective skin. Having discovered that walls can change themselves into nature, Crusoe completes his book-long compulsion to tame the powers of creation into a home:

I stuck all the ground without my wall, for a great way every way, as full with stakes or sticks, or the osier-like wood, which I found so apt to grow, as they could well stand; insomuch, that I believe I might set in near twenty thousand of them, leaving a pretty large space between them and my wall, that I might have room to see an enemy, and they might have no shelter from the young trees, if they attempted to approach my outer wall.

Thus, in two years time I had a thick grove, and in five or six years time I had a wood before my dwelling growing so monstrous thick and strong that it was indeed perfectly impassable; and no men of what kind soever would ever imagine that there was anything beyond it, much less a habitation.[7]

Crusoe has made a wondrous wood as dense as any in medieval romance. This birth of nature out of artifice has the flavor of a fairy tale, expressing the creative mystery of "infinite labor" and compulsive domestication.

Homer Brown proposes a connection between Robinson Crusoe's methodical wall-building, and Defoe's lifelong fascination with pseudonyms. None of Defoe's characters are presented to us under their "real" names. Singleton and Colonel Jack never knew theirs. Moll Flanders' name, on the other hand, is too well known in the registers at Newgate Prison, and therefore must be withheld for the sake of discretion. The title page of *Roxana* presents a catalogue of the heroine's aliases: "a History of the Life and Vast Variety of Fortunes of Mlle de Beleau, afterwards called the Countess de Wintselsheim in Germany Being the Person known by the Name of the Lady Roxana in the time of Charles II." Robinson Crusoe is the only character who seems to speak in his own name. And even he is hinted to be pseudonymous in the preface to *Serious Reflections*. But Defoe's pseudonymous heroes are removed even further from the privacy of their voices, for the "literary" pseudonyms are concealments for the unpronounced name of their author, Daniel Defoe. Privacy within privacy within privacy; natural-seeming faces turned outward toward the world, so that "no men of what kind soever would ever imagine that there was anything beyond" them.

Crusoe solves his terror of exposure by learning how to "lie like the truth." He creates walls which sprout leaves, coaxing nature into camouflaging his sedentary flesh, until the very wilderness is made into a lie. Crusoe's privacy is masked by a false reality which is, nonetheless, authentic, made of thick branches and real leaves. Similarly, Defoe's other novelistic characters reveal themselves by means of fences ("pseudonyms") which pretend to be natural contours ("names"); they expose themselves through a science of concealment.[8]

Defoe himself had a passion for concealment. During fourteen years he worked as a secret agent for successive Tory and Whig governments, signing his dispatches with the pseudonym Alexander Goldsmith, or with an anonymous symbol. The names under which he wrote his tracts, pamphlets, and novels were so various that it has taken over a century to fix with any accuracy the canon of Defoe's writing. At one time or another, almost every piece of unsigned popular writing published in England during the early eighteenth century has been attributed to Defoe. Time and again, Defoe went into hiding to avoid creditors or the police. He was protean in concealment; prolifically public in his writing, but private and cunning with his person. At the age of seventy, after a lifetime of concealments, he died on the run, hiding from pursuit by a stubborn creditor. Even Defoe's "real" name was a form of concealment. He was born Daniel Foe, but added the ennobling particle to dignify his identity.

Robinson Crusoe, The Unadventurous Hero

We have seen how "Providence" literature judged the "natural" human impulse toward adventure. This methodical morality is active in *Robinson Crusoe* too, but with startling results. Crusoe repents of his career as a Prodigal Son. He learns to distrust the wanderlust and the "devilish" curiosity which sent him to sea against his father's will. His stay on the island is not simply another venture into danger; it is radical cure for adventure. On the island he learns the curative power of labor; he also discovers the soothing familiarity of home. After one of his remarkably few attempts to explore the island—a task he never really achieves—he sighs with relief upon reaching his old turf again:

I cannot express what a satisfaction it was to me to come into my old hutch and lie down in my hammock-bed. This little wandering journey, without settled place of abode, had been so unpleasant to me that my own house, as I called it to myself, was a perfect settlement to me compared to that; and it rendered everything about me so comfortable that I resolved I would never go a great way from it again while it should be my lot to stay on the island.[9]

In the course of the book, Crusoe comes to interpret his misfortunes as punishment for having disobeyed his father. But Crusoe's fall turns out to be fortunate, and the suffering he undergoes useful, because it teaches him to value the security which his father's wisdom had preached. Robinson Crusoe, on his island at the ends of the earth, becomes his father's son at last, fulfilling the vision of contentment which he had scorned at the outset. By the power of the orderly temperament which he has newly won, he destroys the distance between his island and the other home he had fled as a child. His victory over the powers of geography characterizes the book. Indeed, it is fitting that in the *Further Adventures of Robinson Crusoe*, Defoe shows Crusoe founding a settlement of European colonists. For the ethos of colonialism was never more tellingly dramatized. One knows the myth of the lone English gentleman in the jungles of Africa who dressed for dinner every evening in shirt and tails, thereby defying the exotic darkness of the tropics to be anything but what he knew it was: a piece of the "home" he lived in wherever his English temperament operated. Although Crusoe wore the pelts of wild beasts, and probably looked like a Cyclops, the domesticating magic of the English—Puritan—temperament has never been described more convincingly. The result is unique and ironic. In *Robinson Crusoe*, Defoe has written the first great novel of the urban temperament. His story of survival in solitude is one of the eighteenth century's staunchest defenses of man's social nature.

The walls Robinson Crusoe builds are not the bulky public walls of medieval Europe. They are private walls. They objectify the containments which the "interior monk" has raised, brick by brick, in the solitude of his character. Like Defoe's pseudonyms, Robinson Crusoe's walls protect him, but they express him too. They are the solid shape he has given to his fear of exposure In *Serious Reflections,* Defoe confesses to an allegorical intent in his island novel, and perhaps we should take him at his word. With cunning irony, Robinson Crusoe represents the strengths and solitudes of the Englishman his father counselled him to be, the man whose place was "the upper station of low life, which he had found by long experience was the best state in the world, the most suited to human happiness. . . ." [10] When he sets out his barricades, Robinson Crusoe performs the ultimate civilizing act. He makes nature into the image of his character. Mastering the "natural man" in his temperament, he masters, simultaneously, the "nature" of his island. The two works are one and are accomplished by means of each other. Shaping himself into a proper stance of obedience to God and father, he shapes his island into an ordered, well-husbanded estate, complete with town house and country house.

E. M. Tillyard is perfectly right to place *Robinson Crusoe* squarely in the tradition of the English epic. In an earlier chapter, I defined the impulse of epic as an attempt to humanize forbidden energies, as Thor tamed Starcatherus to the "human pattern," and as Aeneas tamed his self-seeking warrior temperament into the good gray father of Roman history. Robinson Crusoe banishes the devil of adventure; he exiles from his temperament the unredeemed savagery which links him to cannibals and other witcheries of nature. He tames himself to the "human pattern," an act expressed in the book by his campaign of hard work and wall-building which tames his island to the human pattern. As he does so, he demonstrates the resilience of the new urban character. This new man—Weber's interior monk—no longer defines himself as a part in a whole; he no longer performs a specialized function in the pattern of relationships composing the traditional community. Instead, he carries the whole of society in the pattern of his character. The solitary citizen, making his choices and doing his labors, becomes a microcosm of the larger society—much as Plato theorized in *The Republic*, the first masterpiece of the urban temperament.

Robinson Crusoe is the hero of rational individualism. From inward and outward necessity, he spins the full repertory of human artifacts; he creates the pattern of essential limits which define man's presence in the world. By the reassuring method of hard work, all the resources of culture and society are extracted from the inward nature of man, in the person of Robinson Crusoe. The book is a declaration of human independence. Before the Enlightenment's theoretical formulations, it declares the primacy of the individual over society, because the individual, even wrecked on an island, even naked and alone, contains all of society within him. Therein lies the epic stature of Defoe's novel, its unexpected connection with the creation myths and the legends of civilizing gods like Prometheus.

Defoe is untiring in his praise of the domestic virtues of labor and regularity. But he is enough of a realist to know how dull domestic routines can be. As an old man in London, Crusoe discovers that "laboring for bread" is a drudge. He longs for his keen, active days on the island, where labor was happy because the needs it fulfilled were clear and undeniable. Perhaps that is the glory of Defoe's epic of the common man. Unlike the earlier epic or the later adventure literature of the nineteenth and twentieth centuries, Defoe does not provide an escape into the dangers of the heroic world. He provides instead a vision which nineteenth-century utopian writers would value: a vision of happy labor, unmutilating work.

Man, in the person of Robinson Crusoe, may be frail; his inward nature may waver between obedience and mutiny, between heavenly domesticity and satanic venturesomeness, but labor comes to his rescue. When Adam was expelled from Eden, he was told that his sin had cursed the earth. Henceforth he and his descendants would have to work for their subsistence. Milton puts it this way in *Paradise Lost*:

> *Cursed is the ground for thy sake: thou in sorrow*
> *Shalt eat thereof all of the days of thy life;*
> *Thorns also and thistles it shall bring thee forth*
> *Unbid; and thou shalt eat the herb of the field:*
> *In the sweat of thy face thou shalt eat bread,*
> *Till thou return unto the ground. . . .*[11]

Labor expresses God's curse on human nature. But in the Puritan epic, labor also enacts the redemption of that nature; labor tames man's inward mutiny while it softens the outward harshness of "thorns and thistles" through agriculture. *Robinson Crusoe* can be read as an exegesis on Milton's verses. By the sweat of his face, Crusoe does indeed eat his bread and fence out the wilderness. Just as Milton's rebels "clad their nakedness with the skin of beasts," [12] So Crusoe too covered his nakedness with the skins of beasts. But Milton was interested primarily in the first half of the Puritan epic, the fall. Defoe relates the second half of the story, the redemption. In this, he reflects a shift in the gloomy vision of English Protestantism. Perhaps the "pagan" optimism of the Augustan Age had begun to have its effect. In any case, Defoe's characteristically Puritan view of the world as a sea of punishments and temptations comes to a happy conclusion. Crusoe is redeemed and the island is redeemed by means of God's curse, which turns out to be God's blessing: hard work, redemptive labor. *Robinson Crusoe* is filled with a modern version of the original "good news." Men will be redeemed not by God's grace, and not by "good works" in the Catholic sense of charity; men will be redeemed by the activity, as much as by the results, of labor. This change in attitude represents an extraordinary reversal of values. Previously it was the adventurer whose experience of danger enlarged the human space, bringing "news" from nature's darkness. The activities of work were accomplished anonymously; they were humble and defensive. But in Defoe's "epic," labor becomes the essential warfare. Labor hardens the hero, readying him for his assault against fallen nature. Labor is also the assault. The reversal is complete, and the dream of redemptive labor will become one of the most potent of modern times.

Robinson Crusoe pioneered the eighteenth century's dream of sanity. When Crusoe peered into the abyss of nature and isolation, he did not discover an essential darkness, as Conrad did 180 years later. He did not discover the absurdity of human desire, as Swift did in Defoe's own time. Wherever Crusoe looked, he discovered lessons for man, tailored by God and nature for his personal, if painful, instruction; he discovered models of obedience and punishments for mutiny. Wherever Robinson Crusoe looked, whatever the cost he paid in suffering, exhaustion, and fear, he discovered a profoundly domestic, ultimately familiar world.

In this sense, Robinson Crusoe does not represent only the spiritual behaviorism of the Calvinist tradition. He also represents the radical vision of the Enlightenment: its faith in reason, its belief in the sanity, if not the sanctity, of nature. The book's very popularity demonstrates how much the high culture of the Enlightenment, and the popular religious culture of the eighteenth century, were inhabited by parallel ideals, however different the languages in which those ideals were couched. In *Robinson Crusoe*, Calvinist tradition and Enlightenment rationality conspired to create the model for a new heroism: the heroism of militant domesticity. Not many years later, Voltaire expressed the *philosophe*'s characteristic distaste for the extravagance of old-style heroics. "I do not like heroes; they make too much noise in the world. I hate those conquerors, proud enemies of themselves, who have placed supreme happiness in the horrors of combat, seeking death everywhere and causing a hundred thousand men of their own kind to suffer it. The more radiant their glory, the more odious they are." [13] Voltaire wrote these lines in a letter to Frederick the Great, and Robinson Crusoe would have understood the sentiments they express. His greatest care was to make as little noise as possible in the world. For Crusoe, the way to accomplish one's destiny was not self-affirmation, but obedience; not personal heroics, but conformity to the larger forms which govern life in the world. Crusoe's morality of obedience resembles Voltaire's distrust of heroic action. Both are based on a belief in the implicit reasonableness of life, which outweighs any merely individual exploit, however splendid. The hero is "odious," because the pain he causes has no point, his glory is merely decorative, not essential to the nobility of human actions. Montesquieu framed the eighteenth century's confidence in the larger patterns of experience in the following terms:

It is not fortune which rules the world. . . . There are general, intellectual as well as physical causes active in every monarchy which bring about its rise, preservation, or fall. All accidents are subject to these causes, and whenever an accidental battle, that is, a particular cause, has destroyed a state, a general cause also existed which led to the fall of this state as a result of a single battle. In short, it is the general pace of things which draws all particular events along with it. [14]

Like the natural world, the human world is governed by laws. Individual heroics may occupy the front of the stage; daring men may tempt fortune and seem to tip the scale of events. But they are merely counters in the sweep of cause and effect which shapes the life of nations. In keeping with the eighteenth century's belief in the social nature of man, Montesquieu, Voltaire, and others shifted their attention from the mysteries of heroic will to the patterns which secretly govern human affairs. It was more important to understand the spirit of a nation's laws—and the nature of law itself—than its great men.

The social and natural philosophies of the Enlightenment were profoundly legalistic. "Laws in their broadest sense are the necessary relations which are derived from the nature of things," writes Cassirer of Montesquieu's philosophy.[15] For Montesquieu, man was not the jurist, nature was. Long before society had created rules of conduct, the world was lawfully governed. "Before there were any enacted laws, just relations were possible. To say there is nothing just or unjust excepting that which positive laws command or forbid is like saying that before one has drawn a circle all of its radii were not equal."[16] Thus no historical event, no custom or exotic practice could escape from the network of patterns which rule "human nature." Similarly, no natural phenomenon, no beast however curious or place however exotic, was irreducibly strange. If it appeared so, that was because the laws of its nature had not yet been discovered by man's imperfect science. This legalistic view did not represent a spirit of system, in the manner of earlier philosophers like Descartes and Spinoza. It implied no effort to erect exhaustive explanatory formulae. It was rather a belief that the phenomena of nature and society, if methodically examined, would little by little yield up hints of their conformity to predictable patterns. As Ernst Cassirer writes: "The mind must abandon itself to the abundance of phenomena and gauge itself constantly by them. For it may be sure that it will not get lost, but that instead it will find here its own real truth and standard."[17] Because the world's reasonableness matches the reasoning capacities of the mind, the further one advances into the phenomenal world, the more familiar it becomes. "The power of reason does not consist in enabling us to transcend the empirical world but rather in teaching us to feel at home in it."[18] Reason, for the *philosophes*, was a form of wise passiveness. It supposed that the unknown world was not essentially different from the world it knew. The mood of the Enlightenment was serene, because it believed that the light cast by reason would reveal only what was reasonable.

The very use of the word "nature" by the *philosophes,* reflected their belief that the world was a cozy place: " 'Natural' [in the eighteenth century] has lost all reference to what is original or primitive, and has come to mean what is congenial to those in whom human nature is most fully developed, that is, to the educated in the most polite nations of the civilized world." [19] This congenial spirit is what the scientist, the philosopher, the historian, the artist discovered in the world. Science, indeed all reasonable human activity, was as much a celebration of the world's trustworthiness, as it was an act of discovery. In such a cozy world, the adventurer was a misfit. The soul-journey, the struggles of an Odysseus or a Beowulf, were misguided and superstitious. More could be learned by simply being reasonable. The heroics of the adventurer produced hardship, disorder, and death, but no essential knowledge. Only the scientist, or the *philosophe,* by obediently tuning his mind to nature's patterns, could obtain knowledge. Now, when he returned from his journey, the adventurer had only self-indulgent "tall tales" to tell, while the geographer brought back maps, the explorer information, the merchant riches. Adventure had become the figment of a fairy tale, but during the eighteenth century, according to Basil Willey, "the dry light of reason [penetrated] the furthest corners of the universe, scattering the yellow-skirted fays and all the last enchantments of the Middle Ages." [20]

Robinson Crusoe is merely the best-disguised version of a new sort of travel literature in which the scheme of adventure has been reshaped by the "dry light of reason." The resources of romance, fairy tale, the heroic journey, the magical vision of mysteries to be challenged and secrets to be revealed through action: all of this was harnessed, in the eighteenth century, by a new form, of which *Gulliver's Travels, Rasselas, Candide,* and *Jacques le Fataliste,* are examples. In these modern tales, the wanderer does not venture beyond "reality" into the demonic world. He does not lose himself in the extrahuman geographies of myth. The eighteenth century's adventurer is an ordinary man, loyal, unimaginative; he is not made for the illuminating risks of romance. The actions he undertakes do not enlarge his mastery over the hauntings of ghosts, spirits, and gods. The ordinary man, in the person of Robinson Crusoe, Gulliver, Candide, or Jacques's "Master," is stubbornly unventuresome, remarkably blind to the exotic geographies into which he is thrust. Wherever Gulliver is, he is in England. Whatever he sees belongs to the framework of old concepts and customs. He is simply not equipped to see anything else, even if it existed, which it doesn't. For Gulliver, Lilliput is England writ biting and small. Brobdingnag is England, and humanity itself, writ large and fleshy. Laputa, for all its bizarre science fiction, is England writ technologically. Even Houyhnhmn land, as strange a country as any Odysseus or Gilgamesh visited, impresses Gulliver as an idealized, somewhat chilling image of English common sense at work. Gulliver's stolid, plodding nature is remarkably at home in the world Swift created for him. The more fantastic his adventures, the more completely they turn out to express familiar customs and habits of mind. As Gulliver journeys through the world, he learns more and more about England (that is, about what he already knows) and nothing about anything else. That, of course, is the point of the book. Swift's realism in *Gulliver* is a ruse. The form of the adventure story is harnessed satirically to a moral intention. The reader is meant to enjoy the shock of recognizing, in each fantastic shape, the caricature of a familiar activity or a well-known type. The further Gulliver goes from home, the more he encounters the familiar forms of the civilized, and especially the English, mentality.

The conception of the satirical adventure story is instructive. It presents the world as a place to learn the lessons of the familiar. The hero's exotic travels are short-circuited by the utter sameness of the underlying realities. It is a world in which there is nowhere to go, nothing to do. What Gulliver learns about the world, and human nature, he might have learned by staying at home, had he been more "philosophically" inclined.

The irony generated by *Gulliver's Travels* comes from the recognition that there are no magic countries. The bizarre lands Gulliver visits are not mysterious at all. Their bizarreness is a joke played by reason on itself. Swift's narrative is, of course, far more sophisticated and intellectually controlled than Defoe's in *Robinson Crusoe*. His conception owes a debt to classical satire, rather than to popular religious literature. But Crusoe and Gulliver are brothers, and the worlds into which they are cast away have this in common: at the ends of the earth, the right lessons to teach, and to learn, are the lessons of home. Crusoe on his island and Gulliver in his fantastic lands are closer to the realities of England than they had ever been before. Crusoe learns that to survive in the solitudes of urban society, one must be an obedient son. Gulliver learns to pronounce a moral judgment on the corruptions of civilized life. Neither learns about the otherness of distant places. In *Gulliver* and *Robinson Crusoe*, distance is merely a geographical, not an ontological, fact. This is equally true in other works of the Enlightenment. Montesquieu, in the *Persian Letters*, instructs his French reader about the facts of life in France. Diderot's Polynesia, in *Supplement au Voyage de Bougainville*, creates a new perspective on the nature of European behavior. Harnessed to a satirical intention, we have here a version of the same colonial mentality which we encountered in *Robinson Crusoe*. The world, for the eighteenth century, is full of uses for man, in particular, for the domestically talented European man. Nature itself, as the Enlightenment understood it, was governed by a cosmic version of common sense. In this world, to be reasonable, unimaginative, and obedient was merely to be realistic.

Even this encouraging view of nature could not ignore the evils which befell men through no fault of their own. But *philosophes* and Calvinists alike were remarkably adroit at explaining away sufferings and misfortunes. For sufferings and misfortunes too had their place in the scheme of the world. Defoe believed that pain was a language spoken by God to instruct man in the error of his ways and punish him for his

recalcitrance. Pain, therefore, was reasonable. It resulted from man's depraved inclination toward adventure, from his original disharmony with the laws of the world. The *philosophes* were divided on the question of suffering. The optimistic view was that suffering seen from the limited perspective of man might appear to be evil; but if a larger view were taken, it would be seen as a note in the universal harmony. As Leibnitz had famously decreed, "All is for the best in the best of all possible worlds." The plenitude of nature's laws was a more important fact about the world than the partially understood "evils," of which men are victims. The panegyrics of Augustan deism culminate in this passage from Soame Jenyns' *Free Inquiry into the Nature and Origin of Evil:*

Man is one link of that vast chain, descending by insensible degrees, from infinite perfection to absolute nothing. As there are many thousands below him, so there must be many more above him. If we look downward, we see innumerable species of inferior beings, whose happiness and lives are dependant on his will; we see him cloathed by their spoils, and fed by their misery and destruction, inslaving some, tormenting others, and murdering millions for his luxury and diversion; is it not therefore analogous and highly probable, that the happiness and life of man should be equally dependant on the wills of his superiors? . . . The fundamental error in all our reasonings on this subject, is that of placing ourselves wrong in that presumptuous climax of beast, man, and God; from whence, as we suppose falsely that there is nothing above us except the Supreme Being, we foolishly conclude that all the evils we labor under must be derived immediately from his omnipotent hand: whereas there may be numberless intermediate beings who have power to deceive, torment, or destroy us, for the ends only of their pleasure or utility, who may be vested with the same privilege over their inferiors, and as much benefited by the use of them, as ourselves.[21]

Basil Willey calls this remarkable view of human misfortune "cosmic Toryism." That is as good a way as any to describe the Enlightenment's impulse to devalue suffering, while praising the immutable laws of nature. Whether the praise took the deistic, partly mythologized form of Jenyns' treatise, the scientific form of "natural philosophy," or the old-fashioned form of Defoe's Calvinism, the emphasis was the same: by scrutinizing the world, one discovered its laws; by scrutinizing oneself, one discovered the advantage of obeying those laws. In the larger scheme, misfortune was inconsequential, or it was the result of stupidity. Pain contained few important lessons. As man's experience of the world was leveled into "facts" and the ordering of facts, the adventurer faded as a figure of necessary striving. He became an entertaining occasion for moralizing, as in *Gulliver's Travels*; or he was chastised into obedience, as in Robinson Crusoe. What traditional literature had taken with utmost seriousness—the illuminations of risk and confrontation —became frivolous in the eighteenth century. The best adventure stories of the period are comedies, like *Roderick Random* or *Tom Jones*, deriving not from medieval romance, folktale, or epic, but from the grotesque unseriousness of the Spanish picaresque novel.

Voltaire's *Candide* may well be the Enlightenment's manifesto on adventure. Like *Robinson Crusoe, Candide* is cast in the form of an episodic tale. It was intended by Voltaire as an answer to the absurd optimism of certain *philosophes* who parroted Leibnitz's opinion about "the best of all possible worlds." Candide stumbles from disaster to disaster. He is slandered and accused of illicit sex; the woman he loves is raped and made into a whore; he is cheated and beaten; forced to witness an incredible sequence of cruelties, depravities, and natural disasters, and becomes himself an excellent killer. All the while, though with increasing bewilderment, he repeats to anyone who listens his incredible opinion, learned as a child from the absurd Doctor Pangloss, that this is the best of all possible worlds. Evil is not what it seems to be; things may look bad, but in the larger view they are really all right. Chapter by chapter, Voltaire's vision of horror corrodes Candide's optimism.

But Candide barely exists as a character. Throughout his odyssey of troubles, he is such a weightless presence that we hardly know he is there, except as a conventional figure with only the sketchiest feelings. The disasters which befall him also have an anonymous quality. Somehow, they are all alike. Rape, murder, theft, earthquake, auto-da-fé, and treachery merge into an indistinct rumble. After a while, despite its headlong pace, the book verges on boredom. The more extravagant the episodes become, the more boring the rumble of disaster. This, paradoxically, is the peculiar triumph of *Candide*. It succeeds in making adventure seem utterly pointless. Voltaire tells us that the world, far from being the best of all possible ones, is a vale of tears. Disasters exist everywhere, monotonous, undeserved, unprovoked. If the truth were known about any man, it would be an unhappy truth. The point is apparently to ridicule the Leibnitzian optimism. But another point is also made. Any adventure is likely to end in disaster. Any energetic striving will probably fall on its face. For Voltaire, pain has no redemptive quality, as it does in Christian morality. Its intensities reveal nothing. Candide is not sharpened or individualized by his odyssey of disasters. When finally the moral of the story is pronounced in the last chapter, we heave a sigh of relief. What indeed is there to do in such a sea of misfortunes, but to settle down behind thick walls and cultivate one's garden? Voltaire's picture of the world as a place in which something ventured is something lost is so relentless that we are finally convinced when a simple Turkish farmer gives Candide the best advice he has received: "Hard work solves man's three evils: boredom, vice, and need." The book leaves Candide enthusiastically cultivating his garden, grateful for the walls which protect him from a sea of troubles. Like *Robinson Crusoe*, *Candide* begins as an adventure story and ends with praise of the domestic life.

During the course of the eighteenth century it became clear that cultivating one's garden was not a simple affair. The garden served excellently to fence out the world and to maintain the integrity of "the upper station of low life." But the quiet of domestic routines made it progressively easier to hear mutterings of another sort: psychological torments, signals emerging from the previously unnoticed labyrinth of human character. A strangely complex world was discovered within the garden walls; a world as various and as treacherous as the excluded geographies of the adventurer. A new form of narrative, the novel, was created to describe a new order of adventure, extending not outward toward the horizon, but inward to the "human heart." The novel formalized the judgment which the eighteenth century had pronounced on the adventurer, by placing a new subject matter at the center of its cultural values: not action, but sentiment; not heroics, but psychology; not the voyage out, but the voyage in. The man who makes little noise in the world is all the more capable of listening to the interior noises which, properly heard, will tell another sort of truth about human nature. When Pope declared that "the proper study of mankind is man," he did not know how well he would be heeded, and by whom.

CHAPTER

9

Giacomo Casanova,

The Frivolous Adventurer

THE French Revolution has cast such a broad shadow across the history of modern Europe that it is difficult to look beyond it with any objectivity at the final decades of the *ancien régime.* Libraries have been written about the Revolution itself. Historians have described the failure of the French monarchy, the deepening split between the wealthy classes and the deprived classes, the scandal of conspicuous spending in a world of poverty. We have learned how the eighteenth century orchestrated its doom, coming closer each year to the brink of political suicide, and deserving it. But the century itself escapes us, with its peculiarly overwrought decors, its wholehearted frivolity which did not know or care that it was a dead end of history, a lull before the greatest political storm in centuries. For Hegel, writing only a decade later, the two great qualitative leaps in the history of the Western world were the birth of Christ and the French Revolution. Overnight, the Europe of Louis XVI and Marie Antoinette had become incredibly distant, like the world before the flood.

It is easy to condemn the declining years of the *ancien régime* for their political ineptitude, their blindness to the failures of the aristocratic life. It was a world curiously sheltered from history, unruffled by the "Protestant ethic," and the eighteenth century's ideal of domestic heroism. Yet, paradoxical as it may seem, the very frivolity of the age offered a stage for magnificent actions of the sort described in Laclos' *Liaisons Dangereuses,* which offers, in miniature, a sort of moral history of the time. In the course of Laclos' story, a grown man and woman devote all of their considerable talents to the work of seducing an innocent girl and a virtuous wife. And this activity is no simple game to wile away leisure hours. The "heroes," Valmont and Mme. de Merteuil, exist only for such bagatelles. The drawing rooms, bedrooms, and closed carriages of their world constitute a battlefield for brilliant actions which mock from afar the heroic actions of epic and chivalry. Demanding proof that Valmont has seduced the virtuous Presidente, Mme. de Merteuil offers herself as recompense for the great deed: "As soon as you have had your fair devotee, and can furnish me with a proof, come, and I am yours. . . . Come . . . bring me the proof of your triumph—like our noble knights of old who laid at their lady's feet the brilliant fruits of their victory."[1] Earlier in the century Pope had playfully dramatized the heroism of the bedroom and the ballroom in his mock-epic poem "The Rape of the Lock." But Laclos saw far more deeply into the world of the bagatelle. He saw it as a field not for comedy, but for terrifying actions fully as deadly as the actions of the old heroes. Valmont barely exaggerates his skill as a warrior in a letter to Mme. de Merteuil:

Hitherto, my fair friend, I think you will find I adopted a purity of method which will please you; and you will see that I departed in no respect from the true principles of this war, which we have so often remarked is so like the other. Judge me then as you would Frederic or Turenne. I forced the enemy to fight when she wished only to refuse battle; by clever manoeuvres I obtained the choice of battlefield and of dispositions; I inspired the enemy with confidence, to overtake her more easily in her retreat; I was able to make terror succeed confidence before joining battle; I left nothing to chance except from consideration of a great advantage in case of success and from the certainty of other resources in case of defeat; finally, I only joined action when I had an assured retreat by which I could recover and retain all I had conquered before.[2]

She in turn expresses, in terms which grow increasingly somber as the book proceeds, a longing for the untouchable splendor of a goddess devoted to harm and mutilation:

you have seen me directing events and opinions and making these formidable men the toy of my caprices or my fantasies; depriving some of will, others of the power of harming me; if in accordance with my changing tastes I have turn by turn attached to my train or cast far from me

> *Those unthroned tyrants now become my slaves;*

if through these frequent revolutions I have kept my reputation intact; ought you not to have concluded that, since I was born to avenge my sex and to dominate yours, I must have created methods unknown to anybody but myself?[3]

If this is a game, it is a serious one. Pope's mock world has become a true world in which artifice and the lie of appearances are matters of life and death. For Valmont, life was a theater, but the actions of the play were deathblows. Those who did not play well did not survive.

When the Revolution came, Laclos' world collapsed like a house of cards. The economic and social energies of the century had barely affected it, but secretly it had been emptied of substance. Voltaire and Rousseau bulk large for history; Mme. de Pompadour and the Count of Saint Germain are gilded skeletons. Yet that precisely is the magic of the age: because it had become "unreal," it preserved intact the morality of an older time, transposed into a mode of pure frivolity. According to the new domestic spirit of Defoe, adventure was a bagatelle. But the reverse had also become true in the courts and bedrooms of eighteenth-century Europe, where the bagatelle was a veritable adventure.

•   •   •

Giacomo Casanova, The Frivolous Adventurer

It is characteristic of the age that our best knowledge of its customs and pleasures should have survived through an accident. In the aftermath of the Revolution, a bitter old man, librarian at the Chateau of Dux in Bohemia, decided to ward off the loneliness of his declining years by writing the story of his life. He never quite finished, probably because the pages dealing with his old age would have been too full of humiliations to be remembered with pleasure. When he died, the unfinished manuscript was inherited by a distant cousin who sold it for a pittance to the German bookseller Brokhaus. Brokhaus published selections from the manuscript in German translation, probably counting on the erotic passages to attract some attention. The book caught on beyond anyone's expectation. By the 1820s, a doctored version of the text had been published or pirated throughout most of Europe. A new figure had appeared in the folklore of the *ancien régime:* Giacomo Casanova, adventurer, Venetian exile, spy, alchemist, lover, financier, and jailbird. But Casanova's great achievement was ironic. After a lifetime of perpetual movement, he managed, before he died, to become a fine writer.

The *History of My Life* is one of the great works of the eighteenth century. Besides his other talents, Giacomo Casanova was a remarkable storyteller, on the page as well as in person. Ebullient, ferociously entertaining, a student of laughter and dazzling effects, he was a sort of Rameau's nephew, though with far more pride and sophistication, who talked his way from Paris to Saint Petersburg and back again, through every high-living court and city on the Continent. The English woman writer Justinienne Wynne described in a letter the troubling effect the man produced:

In a loge near me [at the Comédie Italienne] was Casanova whom you know, making a magnificent appearance. He came to greet us and is now with us every day, although his company does not please me and he thinks this does not matter to us. He has a carriage, lackeys, and is attired resplendantly. He has two beautiful diamond rings, two different snuff boxes of excel-

*lent taste, set in gold, and he is bedecked with lace. He has
gained admittance, I do not know how, to the best Parisian
society. He says he is interested in a lottery in Paris and brags
that this gives him a large revenue, although I am told that he
is supported by a very rich old lady. He is quite full of himself
and is foolishly proud; in brief, he is insupportable except when
he speaks of his escape [from the Leads] which he recounts
admirably. I talk with him about you very often. . . .*[4]

Justinienne may not have been as annoyed as she says she was.
After all, the letter was addressed to her lover, André Memmo,
who knew all too well Casanova's reputation with women.

For years Casanova's entry into high society was the story
Justinienne mentions about his escape from the Leads, a well-
known Venetian prison. During his lifetime, Casanova was
famous throughout Europe for being the only man ever to accomplish this feat. The story in the memoirs is remarkable indeed.
Before Casanova is done, he has persuaded his cellmate that an
angel will descend through the ceiling—it does. He has duped the
warden into carrying a steel spike to an accomplice, concealed
under a plate of steaming spaghetti. He has dangled by his
hands from a roof ledge over the Piazza San Marco. He has
found time in mid-escape to refresh himself by falling asleep.
Most improbable of all, he has taken refuge in the house of a
local police chief, disguised as a hunter. It took Casanova two
hours to tell the story, and he was too canny a performer to
start unless he was given the full two hours.

Casanova's style is occasionally clumsy, and it is marred by
Italianisms. But he used his material like a sensitive novelist. It
is no surprise that the *History of My Life* became a literary
source book during the nineteenth century. Casanova's adventure
with Henriette, his escape from the Leads, his humiliation by
the London prostitute La Charpillon were fair game for novelists who retold them as fiction, though never with the sparse
clarity of the original. Had the *History of My Life* been offered
as a novel, its position in literature would have been assured:
admired as a precursor to the best Stendhal, a bizarre classic

matched only by Laclos' *Liaisons Dangereuses* or Diderot's *Jacques le Fataliste*. As autobiography, however, the memoirs present a problem, for the author and his subject matter make a troubling claim upon the reader: unlike a novel, they ask to be believed and that, for skeptical readers, has been hard to accept. For a century Casanova was accused of telling tall tales, because his story was simply too good to be true. As fiction it was all right; as truth, it had to be a lie, because no life could be so interesting. Besides, only a great novelist could tell such a good tale. Critics even accused Stendhal of writing the *History of My Life* in his spare time; a sort of fictional supplement to the *Souvenirs d'Egotisme*.

But Casanova scholars have gathered evidence for more than half a century, and their faith has been amply rewarded. Archives all over Europe have begun to yield their secrets. Most of the people mentioned in the memoirs have been identified;

events Casanova describes have been verified from other sources; the places he claims to visit have yielded evidence of his sojourns. On most occasions it seems that he told the truth. As for the other, more private occasions, we are left to assume what we like.

But the *History of My Life* does not only describe people and places. Casanova himself dominates every page as I suspect he dominated most of the situations he found himself in. His temperament is unmistakable: cunning, vain, and a great talker —maybe the greatest in a century when good talk was valued more than money, rank, and a good deal more than honesty, which was generally considered to be a boring virtue.

Casanova was a man of action. Not on battlefields, perhaps, but on Laclos's mock-epic field of honor. And not only there. Casanova was most alive when he was on display. Situations involved him in a sort of polite warfare, the weapons for which were good talk, good drama, and good clothing. Because he was always preparing for the next encounter, he came to know himself well. Not like Rousseau, or the later writers of *journaux intimes,* who explored the inward sources of their acts, but like a warrior who learns what he can expect of himself. Casanova had survival knowledge. He was an activist, with an activist's self-confidence. As he writes: "I have always had the pleasure of being my own student, with an obligation to love my mentor." ⁵

Casanova had no gift for introspection. He could not be said to "know" himself, as Montaigne did. He probably never made the attempt. The life he tells was bright and articulate, made of intricate decor and social scheming, actions and counteractions. Its sharply-lit foreground is positively Homeric: a patchwork of stories strung together like a picaresque tale. These qualities define Casanova's originality as a memorialist: he describes a world of surfaces, a public world, unshadowed by the newly discovered depths of the personality. But his autobiography is not frivolous for all that. No less than the great memorialists of the past, Casanova gave his life the form of a magnificent possibility. Great autobiography has always demanded greatness of conception. Like Whitman's "Song of Myself," autobiography must tell more than a limited life, however interesting; it must "contain multitudes." It must bear out Montaigne's profound insight that "each man bears the entire form of man's estate." Saint Augustine and Rousseau are important writers, not because they told the "truth" about themselves (Rousseau is no more factually truthful than Casanova), but because they conceived their lives in retrospect on a grand scale. Augustine's life became the Christian odyssey of sin and redemption: Rousseau's, the tragedy of man's "natural" self in a world of artifice and deceit. For both men, autobiography was programmatic, an act of exemplary philosophy. Another example of programmatic autobiography is Freud's *On the Interpretation of Dreams*, which describes the modern struggle between the conscious self and the protean energies of the unconscious.

Unlike these other great memorialists, Casanova was not a philosopher. There is no conceptual framework for his story. Quite the contrary, he let the vagaries of his life speak for themselves, with only a minimal order, for the most part chronological. But Casanova's storytelling is not as innocent as it seems. His avoidance of a program is itself a sort of program. Indeed, the form of Casanova's experience is no less grand than Augustine's or Rousseau's, although by design it is less thoughtful. According to the memoirs, Casanova's life was a flirtation with luck. His best moments were gratuitous, uncalculated, his main talent being quickness to recognize a chance when he saw one. To plan and premeditate was only human; to be irradiated by impulse was godly. Casanova comes back often to this principle. "It seemed that I was only doing what God wished, when I carried out an unpremeditated idea." The result was a strong element of fatalism in his character. He was always prepared to be driven by the winds of impulse or circumstance. "All things are governed by fate, and we are the author of deeds in which we are not accomplices. Therefore whatever befalls us in the world is only what must befall us. We are only thinking atoms, blown where the wind pushes us."

Casanova was an adventurer. Adventure was the form into which he cast his life story. For almost twenty years he traveled erratically throughout Europe, sometimes rich, sometimes desperately poor. During most of this time he was probably a secret agent for the French government, perhaps also for the Order of Freemasons. Yet Casanova says nothing about these activities in the memoirs, preferring to attribute his varied fortunes to the pure fatality of his character. There may have been good reasons for his discretion, though he surely had nothing to hide by the 1790s, with the royal government in ruins. On the other hand, he may simply have preferred the gratuitous aura of his travels, felt that it was truer to his life as an adventurer, than his other career as a paid agent.

The eighteenth century was proud of its *aventuriers*. Mme. de Pompadour, Cagliostro, the Count of Saint Germain, Mme. du Barry, and above all Casanova, are the ones we know best. But the cities of Europe swarmed with elegant, fast-talking men and women, who performed the rituals of the aristocratic life with brio. They played the expensive card games which were the rage of the century, catering to the cult of pleasure and gay appearances which characterized fashionable society. Their names changed, their fortunes were fluid, their appearance was subject to all the metamorphoses which clothing, cosmetics, and cunning talk could perform. Often they vanished without warning when poverty or the law threatened to intrude upon their habits, only to emerge again as someone else, somewhere else, with no questions asked or answered. Usually these *aventuriers* were of obscure social origin, forced to earn their disturbing social mobility by shady means. The triumphs of the domestic life were not possible for them. Like Casanova after his escape from the Leads, they chose adventure and hoped for the best. It was a choice remarkably in harmony with the century. One hardly thinks of adventure as a career, but the peculiar social realities of eighteenth-century Europe made it a viable one. As much as the *philosophes*, the *aventuriers* were quintessential characters of pre-revolutionary Europe.

Giacomo Casanova, The Frivolous Adventurer

During the seventeenth century, Louis XIV had used the flamboyance of the aristocratic life for political ends. Under the *Roi Soleil*, sumptuous spending and the grandiose architecture of Versailles became spectacles of magnificence which amplified the royal will. As Jean Starobinski writes in *The Invention of Liberty*:

The outward show . . . was a spectacle whose spectators were not to remain distant and objective; their freedom was lost in the captivating magic of the scene; they were systematically bewitched into participation, into ritual submission, in a magnificent demonstration of the monarch's irresistible will. The ostentation was not simply the sign of sovereignty: it was the expression of power externalized, made perceptible to the senses. . . .[6]

During the succeeding reigns of Louis XV and XVI, the art of conspicuous spending was elevated to a height never equaled in the history of Europe. Gradually this public brilliance lost touch with the exercise of power. No longer representing the divine will of the king, it became a private spell cast by men who had no other way to display their talents. The aristocratic world abandoned the ritual "magic" of ostentation, for pretense and expensive sham. This was the "superficial" world which Rousseau and the Romantic generation turned their backs on. But the surfaces were splendid in their own right, as the paintings of Watteau and Fragonard remind us:

When ostentation aims at personal enjoyment rather than political influence it is evident that a person's immediate possessions (clothes, furniture, jewelry, curios, the decor of intimate rooms) take on added importance. At the same time fashions are bound to change very quickly, because tastes based primarily on the criterion of pleasure demand constant variety, surprises, originality. For the privileged, the artificial surface existence (which Rousseau calls "the arts" and we call "culture") becomes increasingly fine and complex, multifarious and evanescent, teeming with dainty knick-knacks, delighting in the slanting play of light in mirrors or polished surfaces.[7]

Because the glitter and ostentation aimed only at "personal enjoyment," because the "real" world of works and needs was concealed by the glitter, in a sense annihilated by it, the world
Starobinski describes had a purely existential quality: minute
by minute, it was entirely what it appeared to be. To question
its past or future, to examine its roots in social reality, was a
breach of decorum. For there were rules to the game. In a world
of pure show, everything is what it seems to be, and nothing
more, but also nothing less. Casanova writes: "It has reached
a point, in good society, where to be polite one must no longer
ask the name of a man's country. . . . You had also better not
ask a nobleman what his arms are, for if he doesn't know the
heraldic jargon, you will embarrass him. You must avoid com-
plimenting a man on his fine hair, for if it is a wig, he'll think
you're making fun of him, or praising a man or woman for their
lovely teeth, for they might be false."

There was no need for psychology in such a world, for a man
needed to know only enough about himself so that he could seem
to be the right sort of person at the right time. Rousseau's passion for self-interpretation seemed foolish, and Casanova, visit-
ing Rousseau one day, found him predictably ridiculous. In
Casanova's world, sham was the great equalizer. Success belonged to anyone who could master the art of appearances.
Money, nobility, proper connections gave one an advantage in
this game, but the advantage could be overcome by talent. Again
Starobinski comments:

*Fortune in the 18th century was if anything capricious; servants,
farmers, charlatans, all were favored. They knew how to get
their way, through honest crafts or underhand craftiness. The
absolute monarchy was tolerant, often even welcoming, to the
nouveaux riches who offered their services or bought lucrative
offices. The hierarchical structure and corporation restrictions of
the ancien régime were not so strict as to preclude absolutely the
social advancement of talented men—or of agile adventurers.*[8]

Adventurers like Casanova represent a peculiar, almost parodic
form of the Enlightenment's obsession with liberty. It is no acci-

dent that the adventurers were drawn to cities like Paris, Venice, Amsterdam, Saint Petersburg, and London, for they embodied an aberrant version of the new urban mentality. Like Robinson Crusoe they were devoted to self-creation, though in the mode of sham. Like Defoe, their identities were pseudonymous, as much to protect as to define themselves. No longer depending on social function or the family or the land for their "names," they invented them from the debris of used-out traditions, the way Crusoe invented himself from the debris of his shipwreck. More than any single influence, the city devoured the *ancien régime* and created a new one. The energetic, unstable regime of urban life and the *aventuriers* were creatures of this change: hybrid characters patched together out of old roles and old languages, but nonetheless free, in love with luck, which they honored as the "Blind Goddess," Fortune.

Defoe's Moll Flanders, too, was an adventurer of sorts. Like Casanova, she was forced to live by her wits, as confidence artist, thief, and prostitute. But Moll was not a renegade from public morality. On the contrary, her adventurous life is full of industry and hard work. Although she plays the adventurer's confidence game, she doesn't forget for a minute that a solid reality lurks under the mask of appearances. In fact, Moll is an expert at decoding appearances, like those Puritan divines, her ancestors, who were also great decoders, able to calculate the precise degree of perdition or grace in every human deed. But Moll's sense of grace or perdition is more concrete. It depends exclusively on money, which turns out to be another word for honor, self-respect, and social standing, the aim of life being to earn much of these advantages and spend little. Moll is an example of the adventurer as monk. As such, she enables us to understand the unique genius of the French *aventuriers*. Moll's morality is safer than Casanova's. When her career ends, she is rich, careful, and titled. Casanova did not operate that way. He had opportunities to earn a stable fortune, but his trust in adventure required that he risk everything all the time. The past and the future were ominous to him. Only today, in the innocence of good clothes, good company, and good health, could a man be sure he was alive. "Since nothing in life is real but the present, I enjoyed it fully, refusing images of the past and abhorring the shadows of the ever frightful future, for it brings with it nothing certain but death."

By the mid-eighteenth century, Venice had become a relic of the past. Its social rituals still functioned; its reputation for sumptuous living continued to be deserved. But history had passed it by. Like the royal court of France, the oldest republic in Europe had become a living antique, magnificent but useless. Nothing characterized the Venice of the eighteenth century better than its yearly carnival, when the wearing of black face masks was allowed. During these weeks, whores and wealthy patricians, criminals and their judges, discarded their identities and adhered to a democracy of masks. The Venetian carnival is a parable of European high society before the Revolution. The masked man or woman was not burdened with a past. He could not store up credit for future days. He was no one at all if he could not impose himself immediately through his sheer power as a man or a woman. When he stopped winning or losing spectacularly at the gaming tables, when he stopped talking, when his strong presence disappeared from a room, he became no man. The masked man was insulated from responsibility and rank. He had no place established for him in the world. The mask and black cape were like a death—that other great equalizer—which freed him from the entanglement of habits and choices which had long since closed off the alternative lives men dream of. But as a masked man, he could pursue the alternative lives. And nothing he did was irreversible.

Giacomo Casanova was born in Venice in 1725, the son of an actress named Zanetta Farussi. From the start he was an outsider in Venetian society, with nothing but his talents to advance him. But the world he grew up in taught him quickly that mere talent was valueless, that the appearance of talent was often more effective. Did a talent even exist apart from its appearance?

The carnival mentality said no. In later life, Casanova never seemed to distinguish between the success of a good sham, and the more complicated pleasures one supposes to accompany "real" success. On the contrary, he could act the part of anyone his caprice told him to; and once he chose a role, he was rarely unmasked. As he tells it, he was such a convincing actor that even he forgot that he was playing a part. He was always a masked man, and he believed his masks.

An episode when Casanova was only nineteen illustrates his protean gift. He tells how he stopped in Bologna on his way back from Rome, where a scandal had already ruined his prospect of a brilliant career in the Church. Wondering what to do next, he decides to become a military officer. As he writes: "Caprice led me to metamorphose myself into an officer." As usual, caprice was his oracle. But the word "metamorphosis" is important, too. For how does one become an army officer? Pay for a commission? Perhaps, but Casanova had no money. Besides, what army did he want to join? Venice, Austria, Spain? In fact, these are minor questions, for Casanova knew how to short-circuit the labor of becoming. Having made up his mind, he doesn't contact a recruiting officer, but a tailor. "When I had explained to him how I wanted my uniform made, and had chosen the cloth, he took my measurements, and by the next day, I was transformed into a disciple of Mars. I furnished myself with a long sword. With my beautiful cane in hand, a well-shaped hat with a black cocarde and a long faked tail, I went out and walked around the town." Now that he is a new man, Casanova moves to the best hotel in Bologna. He visits the expensive cafes, where his imposing air and long silences amaze the local gentry. Before long the whole town is talking about him, and he is thoroughly pleased by his performance.

At one point, a priest he had met in Rome the previous year recognizes him. Casanova tries to convince the man that he is mistaken. When that fails, he implies that there are secret political reasons for his disguise. Appropriately intimidated, the man holds his tongue. All his life, Casanova was able to impose his vision of himself on others. His self-confidence worked magic on his friends as well as his enemies, enabling him to manipulate situations with the most casual ease. As in the Bologna episode, he had a talent for beginning his life over again. Ecclesiastic, army officer, financial wizard, industrialist, royal spy, historian, poet, mining expert, colonial consultant, professional gambler, enthusiastic lover. At one time or another, he was all of these things. And each time, as in Bologna, the change belonged to the realm of metamorphosis. It was not an act of learning, but an act of personal magic.

At the age of thirty-five, after ten years of the wandering which characterized his life, he still arrives in a new town—in this case Grenoble—as if it were a world to conquer, repeating the litany of his irrepressible self-confidence: "Perfect health, in the strength of my years, with no obligations, no need to make plans, provided with lots of gold, dependent on no one, lucky in gambling, and well received by the women who interest me." On the verge of each new adventure he will repeat this litany, like a declaration of independence, wiping clean the slate of the past.

Casanova's passion for beginnings remained curiously infantile. He refused the "adult" need to create a self that is made of work and responsibility, a self attached to the world by the history of its needs and limitations. Like Walt Whitman, or Melville's confidence man, he needed to be all the selves. Money was useless to him, if he could not be free to squander it. "I have loved women to madness," he writes, "but I have always preferred to them my own freedom." Time after time, his freedom was forced upon him by angry creditors, disgruntled husbands, nosy policemen, or the rumors of public opinion. He never seems to have settled anywhere for long, before the prod to move on was applied by a suspicious world. But Casanova doesn't leave unwillingly. A few tears, a hasty farewell, and he packs his bags, as if in some way he were an accomplice of the society that perpetually sniped at him. A scandal in Rome, a prison break in Venice, a resounding business failure in Paris, an illegal duel in Poland, rumors of bad checks and cardsharping everywhere. In a curious way, the scandals served his purpose. They created the circumstances for his lifelong odyssey, cutting him loose whenever the weight of "reality" became too heavy to bear. Most of the rumors about Casanova's dishonesty were unfounded, according to the Casanovists, but that merely makes the scandals more interesting. Casanova bred the expectation of scandal like a protective air; it helped to preserve his innocence by turning his life into a series of episodes connected only by flight and the passion for pleasure.

Nowhere is Casanova's episodic nature more in evidence than in his abundant love life. He courted women, squandered money on them, risked his life for them. In each case, the love he inspired was a kind of silent applause. The *History of My Life* is, in part, a monument of gratitude to several dozen women: noblewomen of all sorts, nuns, chambermaids, actresses, middle-class daughters, prostitutes, and fellow adventurers. For Casanova, love was democratic. In an afternoon he could, typically, go from a shabby room, where several whores entertained him with group sex, to visit the daughter of the richest banker in Holland. He could fall in love with a Roman princess or a shoemaker's daughter. Love was the absolute adventure. Over and over, he swears eternal devotion to a woman. He throws himself at her feet. He spends his last penny on clothes, rents luxurious apartments to entertain her. To a lady in Milan whom he has showered with gifts, he admits: "I want to enjoy your beautiful surprise. Such pleasant shocks are my passion." Every detail of love had to be supervised with exquisite care. In his anxiety to please an erotic nun, Marie Madelaine, he takes a private apartment near the Piazza San Marco in Venice and hires the best cook in town. Having instructed the cook in every detail of the dinner he wants served, he sets an evening and comes at the agreed-on hour, but alone. He has decided to rehearse the meal through beforehand, in order to test the cook's talents. The next night, the dinner, the wines, and the sex, were perfect.

Many times he swore to marry his beloved, and probably believed it. Somehow it never worked out, and little by little

Casanova came to acknowledge that he wasn't made for marriage. Wherever possible, he managed almost comically to handpick a good husband for his beloved, a last gift from a generous lover. To hear him tell it, few women suffered at his hands. On the contrary, to give of his body, his pocketbook, and his emotions seems to have been Casanova's strategy in love. Upon splitting up with Marcoline, a beautiful lesbian he traveled with in France, Casanova writes: "My only consolation was to know that I had made her fortune, as with several other women who had lived with me."

No wonder that he had so much success with women. He was, of course, a good-looking man and claimed remarkable exploits in erotica. But he was also remarkably gentle, and women appear to have been reassured by his attentions. Casanova loved good talk, and good companionship. Sex plays only a small part in the story he tells of his romance with Henriette, which has inspired so many novelists. He was charmed by her grace and wit, moved to tears by her talent as a cellist. Without talk, the erotic pleasures were muted. Casanova complained that lovemaking was boring in countries where he didn't know the language.

Casanova appears to have been a veritable anti-Don Juan. There is no aggression in his love pursuits; no crowds of angry lovers cursing him. The power he longed for was not so much to possess as to please. The use of trickery or force was impossible, because he needed the tender consent of the beloved. Consent not only to his strong body or his cleverness, but to his entire being which he threw wholeheartedly into the moment of love. He writes: "The man who loves and knows that he is loved considers the pleasure he is certain to give the loved object more highly than the pleasure which that object can give him in fruition."

Casanova lived theatrically. His identity was a gift which he received from others, and the world was his audience. But an actor is not a liar, and he is not coldhearted. To a very real extent, he becomes the part he plays. Casanova was an actor of sorts, with this difference. There was no safe identity he could retire to when the play was over. All he had was the play, which acquired, thereby, an almost desperate intensity. The confidence game he played was the game of life. He avoided solitude as if it were a death. He cultivated his personal magnificence. Where he could, he acted generously, or startlingly, or even scandalously, because he needed to be visible, just as the older adventurers of myth and epic needed to be visible in the songs they sang about their adventurous deeds.

Naturally his love life was theatrical too. What he gave sexually, he needed to receive back again in all the small signs of womanly wonder. Each time he fell in love, it was a new theater of action, and he was a new lover. That is why he never compares his women, or makes judgments on them. Even as an old man, each love affair he remembered had an air of absoluteness. It was a small eternity, a step outside of time, for which he remained grateful. He expressed his gratitude in the memoirs by creating lively portraits of the women he loved. Dona Lucrezia, Henriette, Marie Madelaine, Esther, La Dubois, La Charpillon and countless others are recreated with a novelist's art. Perhaps that is why the many erotic passages in the memoirs remain so unpornographic, despite Casanova's frankness. Sex, for Casanova, never has the machinelike quality of Victorian pornography. On the contrary, there is a great deal of tenderness and humor in his erotica. Each woman's sexuality becomes part of an intimate portraiture which is frank, and yet not indiscreet.

Casanova needed to see his women; he needed to avoid the impersonality of sexual conquest, because he wanted to get something back from the women he loved. He wanted their gift of praise, their applause. Commenting on a Latin proverb, *Sublata lucerna nullum discrimen inter feminas* ("When the light is out, all women are the same"), he writes: "A true saying insofar as it regards material pleasures, but false and very false concerning the affairs of love." Material pleasures meant as much to him as to any man, and he was not averse to occasional raids on the whorehouse. But love was another question entirely. Love was a conversation of bodies and words mingled together. In love, time began over again as a pure adventure. It was an epitome of the episodic life. That is why Casanova had to love so many women. His inconstancy was part of the absolute passion he needed to declare over and over again. Love, for Casanova, could not be reconciled with the long story of a lifetime. On the contrary, love abolished that story to replace it by the many shorter, more luminous stories he tells in the memoirs.

In Apuleius' tale of Cupid and Psyche, the girl, Psyche, is visited each night in pitch darkness by a splendid lover she has never seen and must never see. At last, she can no longer bear the anonymity of her night pleasures, and so she schemes to shine a light when her lover arrives. Her scheme succeeds, she sees Cupid, and he is beautiful. But her lamp suddenly spills and burns him. He runs away, angry and terrified. After that Psyche undergoes years of persecution, until finally the gods and Cupid are placated, and the two are wedded face to face. The difficult marriage of erotic triumph and full human personality is accomplished; the pleasures of the night and the pleasures of daylight are reconciled. For Don Juan, the pleasures of the night sufficed. For Casanova, the pleasures of daylight were equally necessary. He is like Psyche, attuned to the needs of woman, because his role—to please—is feminine, too. Like the ancient adventurers, Casanova can cope with women because he has awakened his own feminine nature; he knows his adversary as well as he knows himself.

Perhaps this accounts for Casanova's extreme rage at an adventure which befell him one year in Switzerland. He had decided to settle for a while in the town of Soleure, playing the part of a wealthy gentleman—it is around this time that he began to call himself the Chevalier de Seingalt. As usual, when he had money, he rented a fine country house, hired servants, and managed to impress the local gentry, who were flattered that such an important personage had chosen to pass the season among them. As usual, too, it was not long before he was hopelessly in love with a beautiful townswoman. The woman unfortunately is married to a wealthy notable sufficiently devoted to his wife to make Casanova's advances difficult. Nonetheless, Casanova manages a rendezvous, and the woman, who responds to his advances, suggests that he invite her with her husband to spend a weekend at his magnificent country house. The guests arrive, along with Mme. F., an ugly prude, who has insisted on being of the party. After a delightful day, Casanova arranges to sneak into one of the anterooms of his beloved's apartment to spend the night with her, while her husband sleeps behind a thin partition in the bedroom. At last the hour comes:

I go to open the door of the apartment in which my angel was; but I find it open, and it does not occur to me to ask why. I open the door of the second antechamber, and I feel a grip. The hand she puts over my mouth tells me I must not speak. We let ourselves fall on the wide couch, and I instantly attain to the height of my desires. . . . Her furies, which seemed to exceed mine, raised my soul to heaven, and I felt certain that of all my conquests this was the first in which I could rightly take pride.

The next morning, Mme. F., the prude, abruptly takes her leave. After breakfast, Casanova and his beloved are strolling in the garden when she turns to him angrily and asks why he had kept her waiting all night. In a moment of unspeakable horror, Casanova understands what has happened. Mme. F., having guessed Casanova's intentions, had managed to take his beloved's place in the darkness of the outer antechamber. He has been the victim of a ghastly bed-trick:

I am left with the horrible certainty that I have spent two hours in the company of a monster from hell, and the thought which kills me is that I cannot deny having felt happy. This is what I cannot forgive myself, for the difference between the one woman and the other was immense and subject to the infallible tribunal of all my senses. . . . Touch alone should have sufficed me. I cursed Love, Nature and my own cowardly weakness in consenting to receive into my house the monster who had dishonored my angel and made me despise myself. At that moment I sentenced myself to death. . . .

Who would not be horrified at such a moment? But Casanova had perhaps more reason than most, for the very ground of his life had been challenged. As an erotic adventurer, he needed the paradisiac beauty of his beloved. Without her face, he could receive the pleasures of the body, but not the grace of the emotions. Elsewhere in the memoirs he admits: "I did not need women to satisfy my physical needs; I needed to love them and to recognize in the object of my feelings an abundance of merit for her beauty as well as for the qualities of her soul." The bed-trick at Soleure forced him to see how fragile was the fantasy which he pursued, how much the world and his own male nature threatened the fable of innocence in which he needed to believe. Soleure is the first crack in the pure youthfulness which Casanova kept so remarkably intact until he was an old man.

When he looked back over his life, Casanova remembered only the talking, the conspiring, and the loving. The memoirs reveal a man continually on the move, except for the enforced leisure of a prison cell, or a sickbed while he was recovering from one of his innumerable bouts with gonorrhea. According to his story, he managed never to be alone with his thoughts and never to settle down—above all, never to find himself locked into any sort of romantic isolation. Again, Rousseau comes to mind, as a perfect antifigure for Casanova. Yet even a casual reading of the memoirs makes one suspect that Casanova was a more complicated person than he makes himself out to be. He was, for example, enormously erudite. He kept up with the work of the *philosophes,* and knew the modern and classical poets thoroughly. His familiarity with law, medicine, and history seems to have been ample. Above all, he possessed the elements of the occult tradition well enough to impress even Mme. d'Urfé, who owned one of the finest occult libraries in Europe. Obviously he must have done a great deal of reading, though one would never know it from the memoirs. He does mention a library now and then and alludes occasionally to his activity as a writer, especially in later years. But for the most part he keeps his solitude to himself. Not, I suspect, because there was any secret about it, but because he felt that it was hardly worth mentioning. Only the result of his learning counted, not the experience of the mind at work which the *journal intime* would explore a decade later in the writing of Benjamin Constant, Maine de Biran, and others. In this sense, Casanova was an old-fashioned man. The private adventures of the mind, the glamour of the writer as hero, did not interest him in the slightest.

Yet mingled with Casanova's life of adventure one often divines another, quieter life in which nothing much "happened"; a life composed of reading, of the low-key days that most of us know. One glimpses occasionally a sort of inward preoccupation which Casanova tucks out of sight almost before it is seen. One day in Switzerland, for example, he climbs all day along a wild mountain path, until a group of stone buildings looms unexpectedly in the distance. He is surprised to discover the famous Abbey of Einsiedeln, set in the isolation of the Swiss Alps. As he visits the monastery, his mood begins to change. The quiet of the high mountain slopes, the austere gray buildings, the muted conversation of the father superior have a strange effect on him. Suddenly, he feels a powerful longing to abandon his career of adventure. Looking around him, he writes: "I thought I saw that I was really in the place where I could live happily until my final hour, escaping once and for all from the sway of Fortune. . . . To be happy, I thought I needed only a library." Casanova's hidden self momentarily overwhelms his public self, and he cries out: "It was then that I first felt a desire to become a monk." An unlikely thought for a man like Casanova, and of course it doesn't last. A week later he becomes infatuated with a woman he meets at his hotel, and the monastery is forgotten. But for a moment we have glimpsed Casanova's secret life, which inevitably disappoints our modern curiosity, for it is not dark and sexual, as we have come to believe all human secrets are. On the contrary, Casanova's sexuality is gloriously public. Only the monk in him is cloaked in darkness, perhaps because it offered no hold to Casanova's memory which seized hungrily on events and situations but let the inward life slip by unnoticed.

One aspect of Casanova's vast learning, however, is often on display in the memoirs. Casanova was famous throughout Europe as an expert in the occult sciences. He knew a great deal about alchemy, magic, Rosicrucian dogma, various oracles, including his personal favorite, Paralis, who spoke conveniently into his ear on many occasions. Whenever conversation turned toward the occult, as it often did during the eighteenth century, Casanova was in his element. The philosopher's stone held no secrets for him. Metempsychosis, the transmutation of the sexes, and other fashionable mysteries were at his fingertips. In the memoirs, he claims that his occultism was only a glorious joke. He enjoyed preying on the superstition of dupes, partly because dupes deserved their fate, and partly because occultism, properly handled, filled his pockets with money.

Casanova's favorite trick was a system of number permutations which he called his "cabbala." By working changes with pyramids of coded numbers, he could produce messages which answered any question put to him, claiming that the answer was spoken by his captive spirit, Paralis. By means of this "cabbala," Casanova gained the lifelong friendship of a Venetian nobleman, Bragadin, who was like a second father to him. Bragadin never made an important decision without first consulting Casanova's oracle. In return, he supplied Casanova with money and protection and continued to bail him out of trouble even after Casanova had been exiled from Venice.

On one occasion, during a trip to Amsterdam, Casanova made a public display of his number system to impress the great banker Thomas Hope and his daughter Esther. It is characteristic of the man that he had to include a genuine risk in the confidence game he played, so when Hope asked him if a certain ship, lost at sea, would ever be found again, instead of producing an obscure response to a question he clearly couldn't answer, Casanova impulsively came out with a date by which word of the ship's safety would be heard. By this time, Hope had so much confidence in Casanova's spirit voice, that he went out and bought the lost ship's cargo at a huge discount, believing that he would make an enormous profit when the ship turned up. At first, Casanova was terrified that he would be responsible for ruining Hope and humiliating himself. But the ship actually turned up a week later, according to the memoirs. Hope made a million on the deal and cut Casanova in for a large percentage. Whether or not this particular story is true, it is revealing. Casanova was obviously far more intrigued by his occult tricks than he liked to admit. Paralis may have been a con man's prop, but here was one case, according to Casanova, when he told the truth. This ambivalence fascinated Casanova, and he seems never to have made up his mind whether occultism was the fraud he claimed it to be or a mysterious power which he was privileged to manipulate. The problem is an old one. It is well known that shamans and medicine men use tricks and fake props in their ceremonies, without a trace of cynicism. Apparently, fraud and divine power can go hand in hand, when the occasion is right.

In another famous episode, Casanova convinced the crazy duchess Mme. d'Urfé that he could help her to be reborn as a man. He carried on this project for several years, in the course of which he milked Mme. d'Urfé of several hundred thousand well-spent dollars. His description of the incredible ceremonies he invented for her benefit are hilarious, and she must have been mad indeed to have believed them for a minute. But one reason for her gullibility was surely Casanova's convincing expertise. As much as she knew about the occult, he knew more. When he mumbled the names of demons and drew magic circles on the ground, he did it according to the rules. A charlatan maybe, but he knew what he was talking about.

As an old man, writing his memoirs, Casanova comes down hard on these "foolish superstitions." By the 1790s, the Enlightenment had established its cooling influence. Reason had become as fashionable as alchemy had previously been. Casanova prefers to remember occultism as a trick he played on others, not on himself. But the Casanovists have proved that his expertise was not only genuine, it was remarkably extensive. So many hours of study, so many bizarre episodes scattered over a lifetime, point to an interest which was surely less cool and rational than he makes it seem in the memoirs.

Magic was, of course, extremely fashionable in France during the eighteenth century. The growing interest in science by wealthy dilettantes who set up miniature laboratories in their homes only spread the craze, however paradoxical that may seem. An amateur whose main interest was to be amused did not see any crucial difference between a chemist's enterprise and that of an alchemist. Both mixed powders, lit lamps, and pounded unusual substances in mortars. Nonetheless, occultism must have had a particular fascination for a man of Casanova's temperament. It is a veritable science of adventure, for its aim is to control the relationship between human actions and the hidden designs of fate. Toward the end of the memoirs, with the epic of his life spelled out before him, Casanova comes close to a confession:

In the principal events of my life, unusual circumstances combined to make my poor mind somewhat superstitious. I am humbled when, reflecting on myself, I recognize this truth. But how can I deny it? It is natural that fortune does to a man who abandons himself to her caprices what a small child does to an ivory ball on a billiard table, pushing it from one side to another so as to laugh when he sees it falling into a pocket. . . . This fortune, which I ought to despise as a synonym of chance, makes herself respectable, as if she wanted to appear as a goddess to me in the most important events of my life. Her game is to make me see that she is not blind as they say she is; . . . It seems as if she wanted to exercise absolute power over me, simply to convince me that she thinks, and that she is the mistress of all things; to so convince me, she used startling means, all designed to force me into action, and to make me understand that my will, far from demonstrating my freedom, was merely an instrument which she used in order to do with me whatever she pleased.

The only hardhearted mistress Casanova knew was Lady Luck. All his life, he courted her, heard her wishes, and obeyed them whenever he could, abandoning career, wealth, and security over and over again for her sake. Whenever he acted on a whim, luck acted through him. Whenever he let himself be guided by impulse, he felt that he was in tune with the unwritten laws of fate. Like Odysseus, Gilgamesh, and Sir Gawain, Casanova was not only an adventurer, he was a lover, and the two careers are one. Every erotic triumph was the miniature of another triumph he pursued all his life, over the queen of lovers whose wishes became his wishes, especially when he wished impulsively, irrationally.

Thus, when Casanova pretended to have a genie named Paralis, who spoke private oracles to him, his pretense camouflaged a conviction that was solidly rooted in his character. Freud believed that the lies we tell reveal more about us than we know. This was surely the case with Casanova. Although he played confidence games with magic and laughed at the credulity of his victims, he believed in his games more than he liked to say. As a manipulator of human situations, he was fascinated by the possibility that he could also manipulate the invisible world of luck.

There are many examples of such "foolish superstition" in the memoirs. After Casanova's escape from the Leads, he tells of a masterful ruse he employed to throw off his pursuers. Walking into the house of a local police chief, he asks for hospitality, making up an implausible story to explain his torn, out-of-season clothing. Incredibly the ruse works, and Casanova comments on his luck:

It is inconceivable that I went into that terrible house, which both reason and nature told me to shun. I went straight to it, and I know for a fact that I did not go to it on purpose. If it is true that we all have a beneficent invisible being who guides

*us aright, as happened, though rarely, to Socrates, I must believe
that what made me go there was such a being.*

According to Casanova, Paralis, the false oracle, had an invisible
twin who spoke true. This was the voice Casanova listened to
each time he threw himself into an adventure. "I thought I was
simply doing what God willed whenever I carried out some
unpremeditated idea which came into my head from nowhere."
As an occultist, Casanova simply worked to make his inner
voice more audible, more predictable. However "foolish" or
"superstitious" this attitude may be, it is clear from a number
of incidents that Casanova took it seriously. Throughout the
memoirs, he alternates unpredictably between charlatan and
sorcerer, never distinguishing clearly between one and the
other.

A last example of Casanova's ambivalence toward the occult
occurs in the course of a particularly flamboyant adventure.
During his travels in Italy, he meets up with a man who claims
to know about a fabulous treasure buried many fathoms deep
in the earth on a farm near the town of Cesena. Casanova is
amused at the fellow's credulity, and decides to take advantage
of it. He convinces the man that he is a renowned sorcerer,
whose specialty is charming buried treasure to the surface.
After dickering about terms, Casanova agrees to come to Cesena,
where he meets the owner of the farm, who turns out, naturally,
to have a beautiful daughter. On the spot, Casanova devises a
complicated series of rituals whose main point is to get the
daughter alone and naked with him in the bedroom. The rituals
build for weeks toward the final day which will feature a
ritual deflowering of the daughter. Meanwhile the family sews
strange costumes, eats bizarre foods, and hangs on Casanova's
every wish. Casanova throws himself into these preparations
enthusiastically, not giving a thought to the inevitable failure
of his charade. At last the day comes. Dressed in a magician's
costume, Casanova starts to chant and mumble in the courtyard
of the farmhouse. He traces a magic circle on the ground and

dances around it three times, pronouncing bogus cult words, while the family looks on, awestruck. After a few minutes, he notices "a heavy black cloud coming up on the Western horizon." The cloud slowly expands until it fills the sky. Casanova can't take his eyes off it. Despite himself, he is frightened, then terrified:

As all this [the appearance of the cloud] was perfectly natural, I had no reason to be surprised at it; nevertheless, a beginning of terror made me wish I were in my room, and I began to shudder when I heard and saw the thunder and lightning which were following one another with the greatest rapidity. The flashes, which were all about me, froze my blood. In the terror which overtook me I persuaded myself that if the flashes of lightning I saw did not strike me down, it was because they could not enter the circle. For this reason I did not dare leave it and take to my heels. . . . The force of the wind, its frightful howling, my fear, and the cold combined to set me shaking like a leaf. My philosophical system, which I thought was proof against any assault, was gone. I recognized an avenging God who had lain in wait for me there to punish me for all my misdeeds and thus end my unbelief by death. What convinced me that my repentance was of no avail was that I absolutely could not move.

Casanova cowers inside his magic circle until the cloudburst passes. By then he is so disconcerted that he rushes upstairs to pack his bags, where he is terrified even more by the sight of the daughter waiting in bed for him, for now she appears to to a part of God's terrible vengeance. The Cesena incident expresses perfectly the mixture of mummery and genuine awe which characterized Casanova's fascination with the occult.

Indeed, Casanova's involvement with magic and occultism provides an important insight into his character. He believed firmly that the will functioned as a sort of personal sorcery. A wholehearted wish, mobilized by an undivided will, could not be resisted, he felt, as if the will tapped powers that were more than simply human. Casanova's memoirs are fascinating precisely because of the ubiquitous pressure of his will, tirelessly molding situations, projecting desires into the external world, where they take root and obey him, and make others obey him. "I've always believed that when a man gets it into his head to accomplish something, and if he thinks of nothing but that, he must succeed, in spite of all difficulties." His temperament as an adventurer gave him an edge in battles of the will. Most people live in a halfway house between past and future. Their desires are hedged by caution, because the present, however engrossing, can rarely make us forget the long haul of future moments. But Casanova lived only for the present. His wishes focused purely and simply on the situation at hand. Because he could risk everything, he was often able to win everything.

An incident in the memoirs illustrates Casanova's uncanny ability to manipulate situations by the sheer versatility of his will and quick-wittedness. After escaping from the Leads, he travels to Paris where the Abbé de Bernis, an important government official, offers to help him get established on a solid footing. Bernis arranges an appointment with the minister of finance, informing Casanova that if he can devise a scheme to raise money for the king's treasury, his fortune in France will be made at a single stroke. Casanova is understandably nervous, because he knows nothing at all about government finances. Nonetheless he is introduced to the finance minister as a fiscal expert, with a project to raise important sums for the royal treasury. Invited to attend a meeting of experts, he arrives without an idea in his head. Yet by the time the meeting ends, he has managed to convince the group that someone else's plan to create a royal lottery had actually been his own plan all along. Although he has said little during the course of the evening, he has given the impression that he knows what people will say before they say it. His performance is so convincing that he is named director of the new lottery and becomes overnight a figure of importance on the Paris scene.

This sort of manipulation is indeed close to sorcery. When Casanova prays, as in the Cesena episode, his intent is not entirely Christian. "People who say that prayer is useless don't know what they're talking about. I know that after I've prayed to God, I always feel stronger; and that's enough to prove its usefulness." Such a passage foreshadows Baudelaire's definition of prayer as self-invocation. More than that, it reiterates the common insight of nineteenth-century occultism, as it was formulated by the famous Magus Eliphas Levi, for whom "the Great Work is the regeneration of the Ego." The work of the occult, for Casanova, was the work of personal regeneration. The mystery of the world was also the mystery of the will, and Casanova's fascination with the occult was simply a way of interpreting the evidence of his own willful character.

Ever since Rousseau and the nineteenth-century Romantics, our culture has been enormously curious to know the secrets of the individual, as if we believed that a man's true character were expressed not by what he did or said but by what he held back. According to the modern "psychology of secrecy," as Malraux has called it, we are not what we do, but what we hide, especially if we do not know we are hiding it, because then our concealed identity bears the original imprint of the "id," the "true self," or the "natural man." The pleasure we take in a good novel is due, at least in part, to our knowing more about a character than he knows about himself.

With this in mind, it is easy to see why the reputation of Casanova's memoirs has been marginal until now. Casanova placed such a high value on stories, that he devoted all of his considerable talent to making his life worth talking about. Few men have mastered so thoroughly the art of turning wishes into actions, character into events. As a result, his memoirs are too public for our modern taste; he has no secrets to tell.

Nonetheless, we can understand the form of Casanova's life in the memoirs. It was a life devoted to a "bagatelle," a life for which this bagatelle, as he says, was "the most serious of affairs." Yet the *History of My Life* is not a frivolous book. Frivolity and the bagatelle composed a style of possibility for Casanova, perhaps the only style which could express the demands he made upon himself, and on the world. Living in a culture increasingly riddled with "explanations"—the Enlightenment —increasingly governed by an ethos of practical reason, where could a man turn when his character drove him to a life of action, if not to this airy stage on which heroism, audacity, and the taste for risk mingled disconcertingly with poltroonery and inconsequence? Casanova's world was frivolous, but for that very reason it was a world in which action and adventure were properly valued. Born fifty years later, the uniform he tried on with such pleasure as a young man might have been Napoleon's, and the occasion it offered might have been more heroic than a playful stroll through the streets of Bologna. Born still later, he might have resembled Stendhal's portrait of Julian Sorel, who was condemned to an exalted suicide because his impulsive nature could find no outlets in the calculating society of nineteenth-century France. Casanova's luck, and his limitation, was to have discovered, in the peculiar values of his century, a place for the adventurous life he needed to live.

PART THREE

CHAPTER

10

The Great Escape

WHEN Candide abandoned adventure for a garden, when Robinson Crusoe clothed himself in a "second nature" of walls and fortifications, each created for his century an image of moral freedom which would come to haunt it. It is not too much to say that two hundred years of bad dreams germed innocently in the soil of Candide's garden. The very notion that freedom—the Enlightenment's cherished discovery—required a sort of voluntary imprisonment, was filled with incipient drama. Not that Defoe or Voltaire intended anything quite so complicated. The parable of the Prodigal Son for one, the quietism of the Stoic for the other, supplied a conventional morality for their tales. But the Enlightenment was ready to make new use of old conventions. It is surely one of the ironies of history that the century which discovered "freedom" should also have discovered the "garden" of domesticity. Traditional values to the contrary, Voltaire and Defoe argued, adventure was servitude and action a courting of disaster. The man who wanted to be "free" worked valiantly to replace the mossy walls of tyranny by other more exigent walls: the walls of domesticity; what Nietzsche, a century later, called "the moral world order."

For the *philosophes*, human nature was luminous and balanced. Original sin had been disproved, restoring the natural Eden of the self, whose freedom lay in obedience to perfect laws. As we know, this vision did not last, nor was it, perhaps, ever more than a wishful fantasy of deists and philosophers. The walls of Candide's domestic ground darkened as the century aged; the reedy growth of Robinson Crusoe's fortress became heavy with compulsion and self-punishment. Voltaire dreamed of walls that would be the form and substance of wisdom. But the eighteenth century had another dream of walls, a nightmare whose fascination grew as the century passed. By a twist of the moral imagination—which knows that opposites are one—the garden walls became prison walls; the boundary marks of privacy and property sealed themselves shut. Not only did they keep out the stranger, they kept in the individual whose privacy became a prison. Defoe probably expressed a fundamental fear of his century when he described how closely action and crime resembled each other. The deeds by which urban man defined his presence in the world resembled transgressions which had to be secretly expiated in the prison of the lonely self.

The eighteenth century gave rise to an important literature of imprisonment: *Gulliver's Travels, Moll Flanders,* Diderot's *La Religieuse,* Sade's *Justine,* to name only a few of the better-known works. But these are only signs of a deeper fascination with helplessness and self-inflicted pain which found its characteristic form in the Gothic novel. Here the dream of freedom exposed its wormy underside; the newly discovered power of the individual revealed an equal and opposite terror of impotence. The Gothic castle is Candide's garden gone to seed; it is Robinson Crusoe's fortress become malignant and oppressive. It is an image of the tyranny in all social forms, but especially the tyranny from within, which the "free" man wields against himself. Out of guilt for the "crime" of individuality? In a losing battle to reconcile the "freedom" of his nature with the walls of domesticity? The fact remains that late eighteenth-century England, France, and Germany were obsessed by images of helplessness and obedience, self-inflicted pain and innocence destroyed. The principal character in these dramas of defeat is not human at all. It is the castle,

dark and complex, ruined but all-powerful; the work of man's hands, now turned against him, threatening his frail psyche, and defeating it.

The Gothic novel plays an important part in the history of adventure. It dramatized a problem which the new adventure literature of the nineteenth century would attempt to answer, with its dark heroes. Vautrin, Pym, Ahab, Maldoror, Marlow and Kurtz, and countless feuilleton adventurers like Rodolphe in *The Mysteries of Paris*, or Ponson du Terrail's Rocombole found in the experience of adventure an exaltation or a deferred suicide; and all were haunted by the essentially Gothic nightmare of impotence. While the novel, in the hands of Richardson, Jane Austen, and Flaubert, explored the newly discovered landscape of domesticity—the subtle variety of life in the "garden" of society—Gothic romance, in rough, agonized language, explored the opposite conviction that life in society was no life at all; that the complex dramas of "sensibility" were merely groans of boredom and defeat. In the domestic novel, society had become a field of tragic triumphs; in Gothic romance, society, and the individual who had tamed his energies enough to live in it, represented a failure of spirit. There was a current of *ressentiment* in the Gothic novel which perhaps accounts for the crudeness of its insights. But the *ressentiment* spoke convincingly to vast numbers of people, who were all too ready to acknowledge the tyranny of the castle and the darkness of the family drama.

When Horace Walpole wrote down a dream he had about a supernatural helmet and a gloomy castle, he didn't know how closely he had touched upon the nightmare of his age. *The Castle of Otranto*, published in 1764, was a literary afterthought for Walpole, inspired by his antiquarian tastes and the magnificent etchings of Piranesi. It is not a very good book, even by Gothic standards, which are low. *The Monk, Melmoth, Vathek*, even *The Mysteries of Udolpho* are far more satisfying. But Walpole had the advantage of pure creation. At a single stroke, he devised a language and a genre that changed the shape of modern literature. During the forty years following the publication of *The Castle of Otranto*, thousands of novels were written about villainous noblemen in ruined medieval castles, who persecuted helpless women, only to be destroyed by the oppressiveness of their own fortress walls. The stories were absurd and conventional, the characters crude, the castles regularly alike, and the books extremely long. In most histories of literature, the Gothic novel represents a nadir after the brilliant accomplishments of Defoe,

Richardson, and Fielding earlier in the century. From a purely literary point of view, one cannot quarrel with this judgment. Nothing in the Gothic novel, not even a relative masterpiece like *Melmoth*, can be compared to *Pride and Prejudice, The Red and the Black,* or *Vanity Fair.* Yet Gothicism profoundly influenced the art of storytelling. Great writers of the nineteenth century— Balzac, Flaubert, Dickens, Melville, Poe, Dostoevski, even James —found, in Gothic, a junkyard filled with treasures. Modern adventure writers like Conrad, T. E. Lawrence, and Malraux have directly Gothic ancestries. And I am not speaking simply of literary effects, such as the use of symbolic landscapes and richly charged language. I am speaking of a deep thematic affinity with Gothic.

The nineteenth century was obsessed by the fantasy of escape. The world itself was viewed as a prison to be probed relentlessly until a way out was found. The real and fictional heroes of the century—Napoleon, Byron, Julien Sorel, Ahab, Rimbaud —gave rise to a somber, quixotic literature, in which escape mingled with fantasies of self-destruction. When Ahab, in *Moby Dick*, says of the white whale, "How can the prisoner reach outside except by thrusting through the wall? To me, the white whale is that wall, shoved near to me," he describes the most powerful literary enterprise of his century. But the obsession to escape, the fever of imprisonment, the self-destructive willfulness which believes that life is a prison: these are Gothic themes. The adventure of escape belongs to the nineteenth century, but the prison is Gothic. And let us not forget the more recent developments of modernism. Its somnolent, almost voluptuous acceptance of claustrophobia as an essential human condition; its bitter laughter at action and adventure, its conviction that acts are lies, and that prison—the world of *No Exit* and *Nausea*, Proust's cork-lined room, Kafka's *Castle*, Joyce's Dublin—is the only reality: these themes define the weary genius of modernism, still, as one can see, in noticeably Gothic terms.

The contrast between the literary achievement of Gothic and its almost limitless influence is puzzling unless one grants that the Gothic novel of the late eighteenth century represents an entirely new sort of literary event. It is well known that during the eighteenth century large numbers of people learned to read, creating a vast audience for the written word, unlike any literate audience which had ever existed. Previously, the values of high culture had been formed by and for a small circle of educated readers. But now a new sort of reader emerged whose needs had not so long ago been supplied outside literature altogether, by popular theater, Sunday sermons, and professional storytellers. The Gothic novel spoke to this new audience as oral tradition had once spoken to it. Initially, therefore, Gothic was not literature at all, and wasn't meant to be. It was entertainment in the unchanging sense that Homer's poems were entertainments. Its aim was to transport, to trigger the listener's inward mobility, as storytellers had always done.

Freed by stories from the limitations of secular life, a people discovers the community of its images. The tales of oral tradition form a sort of mythology, as if, in its stories, a people were dreaming out loud. Needless to say, such stories have always been "raw material" for the more elaborate artistry of literature. Neither Homer, classical tragedy, nor medieval European romance can be conceived without the saga material they drew upon. The Gothic novel, too, represents an outburst of dream language, a thrust of irresistible storytelling which, for the first time in history, took a written form. The stories were meant to erupt and disappear and reappear, as stories always have. Instead they wait depressingly in the long stacks of libraries where we read them and groan, forgetting that we judge literarily what was never quite literature at all.

In a sense, Gothic was the folklore of the new literate classes. As such, it supplied a vision of anxiety and imprisonment on the epic scale, which writers of the nineteenth and twentieth centuries would elaborate into a great literature. The opposite side of the satanism of the nineteenth-century Romantics is the dream of helplessness which emerges in the Gothic novel. The claustrophobic atmosphere elaborated *ad nauseam* by Gothic fantasy reflects the same traumatic energies which fed the outbursts of the French Revolution, as at least one late Gothicist, William Godwin, would argue in his novel *Caleb Williams*. The anecdote about the Marquis de Sade inciting the people of Paris to revolt from his window at the Bastille has a perfectly Gothic logic.

Gothic novels, therefore, do not tell stories of adventure; they tell stories that long for adventure. Their situations call for adventurous exploits, which fail miserably. The flood of Gothic anxiety results from actions not accomplished, adventures deflated by ineptitude, heroes crushed helplessly by dark powers. These are stories of "creatureliness," to use Rudolph Otto's expression for a feeling of naked dependence on forces beyond the human scope. Gothic romance is filled with incipient Jobs and ridiculous tyrants, for the atmosphere of ineptitude in Gothic mystery affects not only the victims, but the victimizers. In a sense, there are only victims in Gothic. The castle alone triumphs.

The adventurers of the nineteenth and twentieth centuries emerge from this atmosphere with the clarity of knights-errant. They dissolve the anxiety of the Gothic prison by reasserting the ancient priorities of courage and solitude. Their exploits are crimes against the penitentiary morality of the Enlightenment, which the Gothic novel dramatized remorselessly.

It was Horace Walpole's genius, in *The Castle of Otranto*, to have composed at one sitting the entire repertory of Gothic effects. However flawed it may be as literature, *Otranto* is a fascinating road map of the new folklore, a sort of of Gothic handbook. At the center of Walpole's story stands the castle itself, tentacular and mysterious. At every turning point the castle speaks its will, through portents, apparitions, and prophecies. The human characters struggle to accomplish their destinies, but they are little more than puppets, manipulated by the cavernous presence of the castle. One thinks of Piranesi's ruins: dark, hulking shapes which dwarf the human figures clustered at their base. Walpole's "machinery" of ghosts and the supernatural is crude, but it achieves its effect: throughout the story the castle is not simply a setting, but an active, articulate presence. The great helmet, the ambulatory portrait, the bleeding statue, the giant knight express what the castle has on its mind: to avenge the crime committed by Manfred's grandfather, who usurped his title to the castle by murdering its rightful prince.

Walpole's story attempts to create an Elizabethan grandeur by weaving family passion and affairs of state into one fateful pattern. But the politics of *Otranto* are vague to say the least. As with most Gothic tales, the larger world of the story is pieced together haphazardly out of popular history. Otranto, although ostensibly in Italy, is really no place, and at no time. As J. M. S. Tomkins has noted, the authors of Gothic tend to write best about families and family crimes, reflecting perhaps the bewilderment which the late eighteenth century had begun to feel at the demands of the nuclear family.[1] Neither *Lear* nor *Macbeth* can properly be described as domestic dramas. The nature and principles of power are at the heart of these plays. *Otranto* aspires to a similar stature, but, like most Gothic novels it is really about fathers and sons, mothers and daughters. Its crimes are incest, adultery, and infanticide; its virtue, filial obedience; its failure, a broken home.

The children of the story—Isabella, Mathilda, Theodore—try in different ways to escape the castle, but they fail. There is no exit for them. Mathilda is stabbed by her own father. Isabella and Theodore are condemned to a loveless marriage. Bitterest irony of all, Theodore, making good his ancient claim as rightful heir of Otranto, is once more imprisoned by the castle, this time as its melancholy ruler. Even this "happy ending" is tainted with sadness, emphasizing the helplessness of the characters, their inability to make anything happen at all.

This failure, I would argue, is the principle theme of *Otranto*. All of its human characters have a genius for ineptitude. When decisive acts are called for, they lunge about and make a mess of things. The children hurry enthusiastically toward disaster like rabbits into a headlight. The fathers—Manfred, the monk Jerome, Frederic the good knight—are bunglers. Hippolyta, the

mother, is so desperately obedient that she seems to call down her husband's abuse, and deserve it.

The story, in its main lines, is quite simple. Manfred, prince of Otranto, has one obsession: to perpetuate his reign over the castle. To do this, according to ancient prophecy, he needs a durable male heir because his own wife, Hippolyta, has become sterile. Like an Elizabethan Machiavelli, he schemes to marry off his one sickly son, Conrad, so as to get a healthy grandson before he dies. When Conrad is killed too soon by the mysterious helmet, Manfred decides to divorce Hippolyta and marry his future daughter-in-law, Isabella, who until now has been like a daughter to him. Meanwhile, a sudden turn of events complicates his plan. A mysterious knight arrives to challenge his title to Otranto. A local peasant boy turns out to be a descendant of good king Alphonso, the murdered prince. In the midst of these events, Manfred schemes away furiously, to little effect. As a Machiavelli, he is passably fearsome and evil, but not very gifted. The only actual blow he strikes is a mistake: he stabs his own daughter. That is the way the story goes. The castle weaves its spell, while fathers and sons and wives and daughters blunder after each other murderously. Father Jerome's clever maneuver to save Theodore (his son, as yet unknown to him), almost causes the boy's head to be chopped off. When Theodore comes to Isabella's rescue, he assaults her father and almost kills him. When the good prince Frederic finally stands up for himself, he infuriates Manfred into blindly stabbing his own daughter. In the end Manfred, the evil tyrant, is no less a victim than Hippolyta, his wife. *The Castle of Otranto* resembles a dream many of us know: we try to open a door, but the knob keeps slipping out of our hand; we try to run, but we keep falling down. That is why there is no release in the book. Actions never come to discharge the anxiety the story is bathed in. The dungeons, the dead-end passageways, the bulky castle walls create a spirit of viscous impotence which reigns throughout.

I may be accused of making *The Castle of Otranto* seem better, and more complex, than in fact it is. What I have attempted to convey is not so much Walpole's accomplishment as a storyteller—it is indeed modest—but the power of the convention he created. In crude, antiquarian language, Walpole expressed a widely felt anxiety that institutions were by nature overwhelming and alien; that the individual, despite his passion for "freedom," was an accomplice in his own downfall; that individuality itself was a

burden too heavy to be borne, because its demands were limitless, haunted by the anxiety of failure. With its machinery of
antique settings and conventional characters, Gothic expressed
a potent set of emotions which it could not refine. That would be
the work of the new Romantic literature and the new political
philosophy of the nineteenth century. In the Gothic fairy tale
itself, the terrors grow more acute and the prisons more ghastly;
the victims conspire more servilely toward their fate. Strains of
morbid fantasy emerge with real literary power in works like
The Monk, where imprisonment, sadism, and necrophilia fester
brilliantly, as in this passage where Antonia, the beautiful victim,
tells of her confinement in the dungeons of a nunnery:

*Far from growing familiar with my prison, I beheld it every
moment with new horror. The cold seemed more piercing and
bitter, the air more thick and pestilential. My frame became
weak, feverish and emaciated. I was unable to rise from the bed
of straw, and excercise my limbs in the narrow limits to which
the length of my chain permitted me to move. Though exhausted,
faint and weary, I trembled to profit by the approach of sleep.
My slumbers were constantly interrupted by some obnoxious in-
sect crawling over me. Sometimes I felt the bloated toad, hide-
ous and pampered with the poisonous vapours of the dungeon,
dragging his loathsome length along my bosom. Sometimes the
quick, cold lizard aroused me, leaving his slimy track upon my
face, and entangling itself in the tresses of my wild and matted
hair. Often have I at waking found my fingers ringed with the
long worms which bred in the corrupted flesh of my infant. At
such times I shrieked with terror and disgust; and while I shook
off the reptile, trembled with all a woman's weakness.*[2]

In such passages, Lewis attains a level of pathology which Sade
and the dark Romantics would explore more fully.

As much as the encyclopedic diligence of the *philosophes,* the
Gothic novel belongs to the achievement of the eighteenth century. Its feudal atmosphere, its antiquarian decor, and its mood
of gross superstition created a disguise—what could be less "serious" than the medieval crudities of Gothic?—behind which the
Enlightenment began to dream out loud. Michel Foucault has

argued that the "classical age" was also the age of the great enclosure.[3] Its massive insane asylums, jails, and hospitals were the price which had to be paid for the Enlightenment's sanity. "Deviant" citizens had to be eliminated from the body politic, so that the cogs of the law could turn more smoothly, more airily. If man, as Pope would have it, was to be the proper study of mankind, certain wild species had to be uprooted from the garden of society. The "enclosures" which changed the shape of agricultural England produced as equal and opposite forms these other human enclosures which purified the leaven of the city. But the Gothic dream expressed an uncomfortable discovery. In order to accomplish the great enclosure, the citizens of the "moral world order" had to build in each separate self another enclosure. If the disorders in the city were to be suppressed, the disorders within had also to be suppressed, or "repressed." In the world of law, each separate citizen is sentenced for life. As the folklore of the great enclosure, Gothic literature reveals the internal logic of the "classical age." It is the equal and opposite darkness of the Enlightenment's faith in reason and domesticity.

A final mutation of Gothic occured during the 1790s, which crowned its achievement, as the French Revolution simultaneously crowned the eighteenth century's plea for individual freedom. After thirty years of tearful impotence, the spectacle of innocence betrayed began to pale. Fascination with helpless captives and obedient victims underwent a subtle change, best illustrated by Matthew Lewis's masterpiece, *The Monk.* Although we feel for Agnes and Antonia, we are forced to admire the torrential genius of the monk Ambrosio, who destroys them. The monk is wracked by passions, unable to control his massive sexuality. His vast egotism persuades him that a desire creates its own legitimacy, a wish legislates its fulfillment, justifying any deceptions and cruelties which accompany it. After having lived for thirty years as a good monk, Ambrosio decides that the "moral world order" and its Gothic caricature, the monastery, are frauds, for his egotistical nature cannot believe in laws, even perfect ones. To obey them, therefore, would be illegitimate. That, all along, had been the concealed morality of the Gothic novel. But "Monk" Lewis makes a qualitative leap in his rendering of it. Ambrosio, selling his soul to the devil, expresses a belief that the criminal is the only free man. Passions were created to be fulfilled, as Sade would argue a few years later, remembering *The Monk*. God, if He existed, would love a criminal.

Ambrosio cuts through the viscous atmosphere of earlier Gothic by fulfilling its wish for action. When he reaches for the doorknob, it does not slip out of his hand, the door is ripped from its hinges. When he perceives an obstacle, it does not loom agonizingly before him, he attacks it passionately, though cunningly. He does not calculate *à froid*; his dissimulation swells with impatience masterfully restrained, and hunger momentarily checked. The monk is the demonic rebel which the Gothic novel longed for; he is the criminal who knows that the "moral world order" can be neutralized only by cunning and adventure. To vanquish the castle, one must take a step beyond Walpole's Manfred. The idea is not to become a tyrant, for that is to accept the limits of the castle. The idea is to manipulate the castle, to possess it as a means, not an end. Ambrosio uses the "moral world order," not in order to gain power, but in order to fulfill his desires. He exploits the morality of the castle with passionate cynicism, and we are left puzzling over his death, which Lewis describes in several extraordinary pages:

Headlong fell the monk through the airy waste; the sharp point of a rock received him; and he rolled from precipice to precipice till, bruised and mangled, he rested on the river's banks. Life still existed in his miserable frame: he attempted in vain to raise himself; his broken and dislocated limbs refused to perform their office, nor was he able to quit the spot where he had first fallen. The sun now rose above the horizon; its scorching beams darted full upon the head of the expiring sinner. Myriads of insects were called forth by the warmth; they drank the blood which trickled from Ambrosio's wounds; he had no power to drive them from him, and they fastened upon his sores, darted their stings into his body, covered him with their multitudes, and inflicted upon him tortures the most exquisite and insupportable.

The eagles of the rock tore his flesh piecemeal, and dug out his eyeballs with their crooked beaks. A burning thirst tormented him; he heard the river's murmur as it rolled beside him, but strove in vain to drag himself toward the sound. Blind, maimed, helpless, and despairing, venting his rage in blasphemy and curses, execrating his existence, yet dreading the arrival of death destined to yield him up to greater torments, six miserable days did the villain languish. On the seventh a violent storm arose: the winds in fury rent up rocks and forests: the sky was now black with clouds, now sheeted with fire: the rain fell in torrents; it swelled the stream; the waves overflowed their banks; they reached the spot where Ambrosio lay, and, when they abated, carried with them into the river the corse of the despairing monk.[4]

Is this a spectacle of retribution and defeat? Does the monk pay agonizingly for his bargain with the devil? Or are we witnessing the dark changes of eternal nature, the metamorphosis of one form of energy into another through the ceremony of death? This culminating passage implies that the way down may also be a way out, as Sade and Baudelaire would argue; that death is also an episode in the cycles of life. Even in death, perhaps, the monk triumphs demonically over God and the devil.

Lewis's monk is the hero which the Enlgihtenment did not dare to proclaim, although Rousseau and Adam Smith conspired, bizarrely, to educate him. If Robinson Crusoe embodies a myth of order and civilization, the monk embodies an opposite myth of instinctual freedom, and the two myths, unexpectedly, are one. Thus the ideology of reason which had undermined the traditional values of adventure prepared new ground for them to spring from again.

A remarkable pamphlet written by the Marquis de Sade during the French Revolution demonstrates with perfectly Gothic logic how the ideology of law can transform itself into a paean of egotism and *jouissance*. The pamphlet was called *Français Encore un Effort, Si Vous Voulez Etre Republicain,*[5] and was originally published as a disgression in the *Philosophie dans le Boudoir*. Sade is such a remarkably Gothic figure, and this pamphlet such a curious example of his seriocomic logic, that it is worth including among the founding texts of the nineteenth century's literature of adventure.

The pamphlet begins by describing the danger to the Republic of a partial revolution. If men are to be freed from the tyranny of kings, Sade argues, not only the monarchy, but the Church, too, must be dismantled stone by stone, for all the tyrannies of the *ancien régime* emanate from this central despotism over men's souls:

A republican should not grovel at the knees of an imaginary being, or a vile imposter; his only gods now should be courage and liberty. Rome vanished when Christianity was allowed to preach there, and France will be lost if Christianity is still reverenced.[6]

The argument might be Diderot's or Voltaire's, and Sade develops it with conventional republican verve: down with the Church in the name of secular morality; down with superstition in the name of freedom and reason. Until this point in the argument, therefore, there is nothing new, and nothing especially Sadian. Even the fervor of the style belongs more to the inflated rhetoric of the Revolution, than to any personal animus.

In the second part of the pamphlet, Sade addresses himself to a more complex problem. Now that the reign of tyranny has been destroyed, the time has come to question the structure of morality on which the authority of the *ancien régime* had been founded. With a logic worthy of Plato, Sade points out that an authoritarian society creates a set of habits and customs which influences the very character of the individual. A free society, therefore, requires a new morality in order to create a new sort of man. Sade's arguments are cool and procedural, as if logic were speaking with its own voice. But a subtle ambush has been laid.

First of all, Sade argues, a republic must outlaw religious persecution as a violation of individual freedom. Capital punishment must be abolished, too, but for a different reason. Although

individuals may assault and kill each other in the heat of argument, the law, by nature cold and premeditated, must never
do so, for cold-blooded murder, even by law, is a crime against
nature. This resembles some modern arguments against capital
punishment. Sade knows how to imitate the forms of reason,
with a sort of genius. But he has sowed a principle on which he
intends to collect interest: passion justifies an act, he argues,
reason and purpose do not.

Next, Sade proposes to investigate the code of values by which
some acts are considered crimes. According to the method of
"natural philosophy," he divides crime into four categories:
calumny, theft, indecency, and murder. Must these sorts of act,
condemned under tyranny, he asks, also be condemned in a
republic of free men? Consider calumny. Calumnious allega-
tions are either true or false. If true, they are not calumnies at
all, but warnings against a previously undetected scoundrel. If
false, the insulted party is obliged to prove his innocence. His
excellence is made public, and he is appropriately honored. He
may even work harder at being good, to make the calumny seem
more undeserved. The result: calumny apparently does more
good than harm and cannot be considered a crime.

The next crime to be considered is theft. Sade argues here
from historical precedent:

> *If we consider antiquity, we will see theft permitted, rewarded
> in all the republics of Greece; Sparta . . . encouraged it openly;
> some other peoples considered it a warlike virtue; it clearly
> promotes courage, strength, skill, virtues useful to a republican
> government, and therefore to ours. I dare to ask, without preju-
> dice now, if theft, which equalizes riches, is a very great fault
> in a government whose goal is equality? Obviously not; if on
> the one hand it promotes equality, on the other it encourages the
> individual to protect his property.*[7]

Thus theft, too, must be revalued by republican morality. In a
thieving society, the individual becomes lean and hard; he
learns to value life, attacking others and defending himself with

skill. Since the strength of a revolutionary republic depends upon the accrued strength of its citizens, according to Sade, the limited warfare of theft introduces a homeopathic ferment into the body politic, making it apt for the rigors of patriotic combat.

A larger question has gradually been raised, and Sade does not hesitate to confront it in the same procedural manner. Under the reign of kings, morality had been the keystone of public order. Obedience to the concentric authorities of God, Pope, and King had created a strict code, touching not only on matters of public violence, but also on private matters such as sexuality. Since the old moral code represented a form of obedience to the principle of tyranny, what should be the attitude of men whose revolution is the most glorious disobedience in the history of the world; a disobedience, moreover, which must defend itself against the hostility of its neighbors by the most "immoral" of all means, warfare?

Now I ask how it can be shown that in a state whose obligations are immoral, it is essential for the individuals to be moral? I will go further: it is good that they not be moral. The lawmakers of Greece understood perfectly well the need to infect the members, so that their moral dissolution, having a useful influence on the body itself, would cause an insurrectional state always useful to a government like the republican government which must necessarily provoke hatred and jealousy all around, if it is to be happy. These wise lawmakers knew that insurrection is not a moral condition; yet it had to be the permanent condition of a republic; it would therefore be absurd and dangerous to require that those who must sustain the perpetual immoral upheaval of the body should themselves be very moral, because the moral condition of a man is one of peace and tranquility, while his immoral condition is one of perpetual movement resembling the necessary insurrection which the republic must lead against the government it belongs to.[8]

Sade's argument is in full stride now. The "perpetual movement" of immorality is not simply a form of disorder, it is an expression of revolutionary energy; it is the influence of the revolution on the inward character of the citizen. To Plato's list of socio-psychological types—the man of tyranny, of aristocracy, of democracy—must be added another type, the most integrally free, the highest political specimen of them all: republican man, the man of revolution, in whom a revaluation of all values has taken place. For republican man, calumny, theft, and murder are not simply allowed, they are required as signs of his internal revolution. And that is not all. Adultery, rape, incest, sodomy, and prostitution become republican man's field of accomplishment, perpetuating his inflamed nature in which passion has replaced reason as the governing ideal; or rather, in which reason has logically transformed itself into its opposite: unreason. That is Sade's tour de force. Enlightenment, according to its own principles, has become darkness; virtue has become evil; order has become disorder. The values have been revalued not by some devilish fiat, but from within. The "moral world order," and its rule of law, have self-destructed into an ideal of antinomian freedom. The criminal and rebel as hero is born. The adventure of revolt and the politics of revolution—puritanically separated by Saint Just, Robespierre, and all subsequent political revolutionaries of the nineteenth and twentieth centuries—are shown, by Sade's perverse logic, to be dimensions of a single enterprise.

The New Mythology of Adventure: Edgar Allan Poe

I
N a beautiful passage, Spengler describes European history as a progressive democratization of time. During the Middle Ages, time was the property of monks who kept count of the days for the purposes of religious celebration. Steeple bells distributed time into the world of the seasons. Then time passed into secular hands. Public clocks made it available on town squares and principal streets. By the seventeenth century, the wealthy were able to share the monopoly of time, by means of pendulums, in the privacy of their homes. Two centuries later, clocks distributed time to everyone, from store windows, on mantlepieces. Wristwatches and fobs made it portable. Time became a free commodity. Europe bathed in it. By the nineteenth century, literature had acknowledged the reign of time with the advent of the novel. The novel describes the history of memories which measure time; the transformations of character and destiny which are time's flesh and blood. Life in the shadow of the clocks, measured out upon the vast grillwork of time, which now belongs to all and possesses all: that is the element of the novel, as Paul Valéry jokingly proposed, with his famous first sentence for the eternal novel: *La marquise sortit a cinq*

heures. Robinson Crusoe ticking off the days of his solitude on a dry stick is the metronome the novel will move to.

Here, too, the Gothic novel is a conduit for the mythology of modern times. Along with so much else, the nineteenth century learned the value of unified plot from the Gothic novel. In *The Castle of Otranto*, the story has a coherence and a tautness which novels of the eighteenth century rarely tried for. Walpole sustains the reader's interest by constantly delaying the solution of a riddle, so that an element of suspense overshadows the complexity of the action. The loosely connected incidents of picaresque are replaced by a feeling of inevitability. Events have a deadly momentum, which subordinates individual scenes to the sequence of the plot. As Wilhelm Dibelius remarks of Ann Radcliffe's work:

The action is very full, indeed too full, and one finds a strong effect on every page; but it is extraordinarily unified, much more integrated than in any earlier author. . . . This is one of the decisive turning points in the history of the novel. The world learned from Walpole, and especially from Mrs. Radcliffe, that a novel could be organized artistically and suspensefully throughout all its small individual scenes.[1]

In the loosely organized novels of the eighteenth century, as in earlier epic romance and in picaresque, time was a neutral medium, a stage on which the action occurred, but unconcerned by it. The stage did not tremble with the pathos of the play. But in the Gothic novel, time is charged with anguish and suspense. Time conceals, and only time reveals. The readers and characters of Gothic are prisoners of the irreversibility which has seized hold of them, taunting them with hints of a resolution, tantalizing them with delays. The visible walls of the castle are complemented by the invisible walls of time, from which there is no exit. Just as the castle, in Gothic, is active and willful, so time binds events into a sequence which must run its course before there can be any release.

Artistically, of course, one grasps the enormous advance

which this represents. A coherent medium becomes possible for
the novel. Aristotle's requirement for the unities of storytelling:
inevitability, involvement and denouement, reversal and recognition, become charged with complex energy. The transition
from an eschatological to a secular drama of fate is achieved.
Now men can have destinies not only in relation to God, but to
each other. Time has completed its spread from the monasteries
to the humble cottages of private life. In this transition, the
Gothic novel, as folklore of the new urban mentality, acts the
role of midwife. Again the Gothic novelists saw crudely what
later masters of the novel would grasp as an entirely new possibility for narrative form. From being a conventional setting,
like the landscape in a quattrocento painting of the Madonna,
time enters into the internal logic of character; it becomes the
element of destiny.

But Gothic time is not simply a cruder version of novelistic
time. It belongs integrally to the Gothic atmosphere of anxiety
and confinement. What Gothic calls for, and fails to provide, as
we have seen, is a hero who can breach the castle walls. The
artistic unity of plot, in the Gothic novel, reflects the helplessness
of its central characters, their inability to smash the fatal sequence
of events. Gothic time, therefore, is negative; it measures impotence. The dream implicit in Gothic time is of a hero who
can overcome the irreversibility of events, a hero who can vanquish time. The ambivalence of Ambrosio's fate in *The Monk*
causes the reader to wonder. Has Ambrosio's time come at last,
or, on the contrary, has he leapt outside time's irreversible sequence into the eternal rhythms of life itself?

Like Ambrosio, the adventurers of the nineteenth century
will be rebels and criminals. Their passion will be to break
through the inscrutable walls which have been thrust up close
to them. They will be rebels against time, too. As the *Pequod*
sails into the vast calm of the South Seas, it enters into a timeless
realm "which even in these modern days still preserve[s] much
of the ghostly aboriginalness of earth's primal generations, when
the memory of the first man was still a distant recollection. . . ."[2]

Marlow, in *Heart of Darkness*, travels the same road, on his way to meet Kurtz: "Going up that river was like traveling back to the beginnings of the world." [3] The irony which Marlow's adventures have taught him is that time, however important it may seem "novelistically," has no real hold on the shapes of destiny. The heart of darkness at the upper end of the Congo also looms over London and the Thames, as it loomed there 2,000 years ago, when the Roman legions first explored Britain. Marlow sits in the deepening dusk of the Thames estuary, telling his story to a group of London businessmen, his friends, who are visible only as blots of shadow, occasional coughs and scrapes. They don't even have names, nor does anyone else in the story, besides Marlow and Kurtz, who have earned their baptism of identity by journeying outside the walled city, into the timeless darkness of the psyche, and the exigent darkness of adventure. "Novelistic" time, the time of domesticity, has brought only titles to the businessmen. They are, for Marlow and for us, the Accountant, the Director of Companies, the Lawyer. Conrad has subtly reversed the novelistic assumption that identities are measured with the pulse of domestic time, the time that measures work, pay, age, and change. Only at the frontier between the raw power of existence, and the laborious routines of the "moral world order," is a true identity possible: on the fine line between eternity and the murmur of the clocks. Marlow represents this equilibrium of timelessness in the midst of time. Several times in the story, we see him sitting cross-legged in the lotus position, his face lean and yellow: "He had sunken cheeks, a yellow complexion, a straight back, an ascetic aspect, and, with his arms dropped, the palms of hands outwards, resembled an idol." [4] Marlow ceased, and sat apart, indistinct, and silent, in the pose of a meditating Buddha." [5] Marlow's Oriental calm has been earned on the borders of society; it represents the wisdom which only adventure can teach to those it does not destroy. One recalls an identical insight at the end of *Gilgamesh*, represented first by Utnapishtim, the happily married immortal, and then by Gilgamesh's decision to return to Uruk and the works of domesticity, no longer as a victim, but as a wise man who will engrave the lesson of his adventures on the walls of the city.

By Conrad's time, the classic novels of the nineteenth century had been written. For a hundred years, the subject of adventure had survived in odd corners of the narrative art which he could not but have known: Grimm's fairy tales; the vast popular production of the French *roman noir;* Walter Scott and James Fenimore Cooper; Kipling and, above all, Robert Louis Stevenson. In Conrad's hands, adventure became a- lever to be used against the traditional framework of the novel. In the process, a subtle criticism of the novel and of adventure emerges in the form of Conrad's dense irony and his relentless Gothic pessimism.

Earlier in the nineteenth century, however, writers like Poe and Melville, even Cooper and Scott, do not so much criticize the novel, as they ignore it. The virtue of artistic unity escapes them. Cooper never could write viable dialogue. Poe and especially Melville are remarkably careless, from a novelistic point of view. The first quarter of *Moby Dick* is almost a separate book. Ishmael, its central character, all but disappears from the story after that, only to reappear at the very end as sole survivor of the *Pequod.* The humor of the early chapters is forgotten, replaced by florid Gothic imagery. Obviously Melville began to write one book and then changed his mind, never bothering to harmonize his two separate intentions. Jane Austen, Flaubert, even Stendhal would have been scandalized, but Melville never noticed. Nor, in fact, do we. The same holds true for Poe's all but forgotten adventure masterpiece, *The Narrative of Arthur Gordon Pym,* which falls into several disconnected parts, each with a different tone and a different narrative stance. Poe's errors of continuity are obvious. Yet the book sustains itself despite, perhaps even because of, these "faults."

The disregard for novelistic time is even more flagrant in the French derivative of Gothic: the vast feuilleton novels which attained such enormous popularity in France during most of the nineteenth century. Eugène Sue, Frédéric Soulié, and Ponson du Terrail created a vast new reading public which made even Balzac pensive with jealousy, and influenced Dickens in his later feuilleton novels. Works like *The Mysteries of Paris, The Wandering Jew, The Memoirs of the Devil,* and *Rocombole* were published in weekly newspaper installments, often appearing for several years at a time. In order to hold the reader's interest from week to week, the writer created a quantity of subclimaxes within the larger story, so that each installment could have its share of cliff-hanging. Long-range coherence was less saleable than excitement. Errors of continuity passed unnoticed, since the reading public had before it not a bound book, but a sheaf of episodes. The *roman noir* tended to recreate some of the conditions of oral epic. As with the Homeric poems, the feuilleton audience experienced the story as a perpetually unfolding present, whose past was blurred and partly forgotten, whose future had not yet been created. Week by week, the novel appeared, and week by week it disappeared. Its essential medium was episodic, not out of disregard for the values of artistic unity, but out of the necessity of the form itself. There is, no doubt, a "story" in *The Mysteries of Paris.* The identity of Rodolphe, the mysterious nature of his relationship with certain characters, his inexplicable anxieties, and above all the reason for his relentless warfare against the forces of evil, make the reader aware of an intention which guides the weekly episodes toward a final denouement. But the "plot" of the story, like its pious morality, contributes surprisingly little to the vigorous growth of kidnappings, murders, thefts, and other events which sprout so thickly out of the story's central trunk, so as to obscure it completely. The reader starts each episode secure in the knowledge that every situation, however unlikely, will reveal a side plot of adventure; that every character evolves in a medium of surprise. From beginning to end, the reader is plunged in a density of anecdotes, which creates a sort of eternal present. Formlessness becomes the medium of the *roman noir.* Like any viable form, it makes possible the articulation of an experience to which it is necessary; here, the experience of adventure, the perpetual leap out of time and continuity into a dreamlike world of risk and violent action. The effect is not unlike that of the *Arabian Nights,* where the Ur-plot, concerning the fate of Scheherazade, is submerged by the proliferation of stories sprouting out of each other endlessly, until the reader is lost in a forest of interlocking tales.

The episodic form of the adventure story becomes an artistic strategy which writers like Poe, Melville, and Sue develop more or less instinctively, and which corresponds to the adventurer's escape from time. The condition of adventure is not development, but repetition, not coherence but illumination. The adventure story does not move principally from beginning to end, but from peak to peak, reflecting an order of values different from that of the novel. The most grandiose formulation of this order of values will be Nietzsche's conception of the "eternal return," as I will attempt to show in Chapter 12. The "eternal return" describes, at a high level of abstraction, the adventurer's cosmology, his experience of plenitude in repetition. Nietzsche's injunction to "live dangerously" aims at recreating the antique unity between the philosopher and the adventurer, which was embodied in the Homeric poems by the figure of Odysseus. The Nietzschean philosophy of adventure culminates a development which started with the Gothic novel and Sade, passed in the margins of Romantic literature, to emerge reflectively in the work of the German philosopher.

Before entering into the difficulties of Nietzschean interpretation, I would like to look more closely at Edgar Allan Poe's archetypal adventure novel, *The Narrative of Arthur Gordon Pym,*[6] which offers a remarkable example of the nineteenth century's mythology of adventure.

The Narrative of Arthur Gordon Pym, published in 1838, never achieved the popularity of Poe's more condensed stories. In particular, the novel has been overshadowed by *Moby Dick,* which developed a similar sort of sea myth on a grander scale. It is probable that Melville not only knew Poe's story, but was influenced by its use of adventure as the principle of a symbolic fable. The white figure rising out of the Antarctic mists at the

end of *Pym* has obvious affinities with the symbolic whiteness in
Moby Dick. But Poe's story is more simply a tale of adventure
than Melville's. The book moves swiftly from climax to climax,
in a gathering fantasy of violence which caused W. H. Auden
to call it "an object lesson in the art" of "pure adventure."

The novel begins as Pym, a boy in his early teens, stows away
aboard a merchant vessel, the *Grampus*. The arrangements have
been made with the help of his best friend, Augustus, whose
father is captain of the ship. Shortly after leaving New Bedford,
there is a mutiny. The ship is taken over by a murderous faction
of the crew who plan to become pirates. After a series of adventures, during which the mutineers kill each other off, Pym,
Augustus, and two sailors manage to regain possession of the
ship which a violent storm has turned into a hulk. A series of
horrible episodes ensues, culminating in a savage ritual of cannibalism. This crescendo of horrors creates a dreamlike atmosphere which is exploded finally by its own excess in the cannibal
episode. Later, the survivors—Pym and a half-breed Indian, Dirk
Peters—are rescued by a ship, the *Jane Guy*, and the nightmare
of the mutiny closes behind them: "Both Peters and myself re-
covered entirely from the effects of our late privation and dreadful suffering, and we began to remember what had passed rather
as a frightful dream from which we had been happily awakened,
than as events which had taken place in sober and naked reality." [7] The notion that intense horror can generate another sort
of reality—a notion common to all of Poe's stories—dominates the
first part of the narrative. When the horrors end, Pym and Peters
return to "sober and naked reality," as if from a shamanistic
journey.

In the second part of the novel, Pym and Peters cruise with
their rescuers on a prosaic voyage of trade and exploration, in
the fashionable style of nineteenth-century travel literature. Poe
salts his account with ample doses of geography and maritime
lore, including a description of seal hunting on the island of
Tristan da Cunha, and other sorts of accurate or mock-accurate
data gleaned from actual travel books. The tone is soberly fac-

tual, making the adventures of the first part of the novel seem all the more phantasmagoric.

After months of cruising, Captain Guy, of the *Jane Guy*, decides to sail south into the Antarctic, in order to verify the location of a group of islands reported by previous navigators. Here, insensibly, the narrative takes a turn. As the *Jane Guy* proceeds further and further south, strange signs appear: a veil of clouds is seen far toward the south; the water becomes inexplicably warmer; an unknown variety of white sea animal is discovered. The Antarctic ice barrier disappears and the *Jane Guy* enters an empty gray sea, farther south than any recorded voyage ever made. This section, too, is told with the reassuring verisimilitude of the middle chapters, but a change has taken place. The *Jane Guy* has entered into a subtly different reality. Some days later, the captain sights land. He sails toward it and casts anchor in a natural harbor where the ship is greeted by several canoes filled with natives "about the ordinary stature of Europeans, but of a more muscular and brawny frame. Their complexion [was] a jet black, with thick and long woolly hair. They were clothed in skins of an unknown black animal, shaggy and silky, and made to fit the body with some degree of skill, the hair being inside, except where it was turned out about the neck, wrists, and ankles. Their arms consisted principally of clubs, of a dark, and apparently very heavy wood." [8] The canoes contain black, egg-shaped stones; even the teeth of the savages are black. Furthermore, the natives are strangely terrified when they encounter any pale-colored objects, "such as the schooner's sails, an egg, an open book, a pan of flour." [9] The verisimilitude of Poe's style is so convincing, in this section, that one hardly remarks details like these which emerge unobtrusively. Later, when the crew explores the interior of the island, they make surprising discoveries. The water, for example, resembles no liquid ever before known:

Upon collecting a basinful, and allowing it to settle thoroughly, we perceived that the whole mass of liquid was made up of a number of distinct veins, each of a distinct hue; that these veins did not commingle; and that their cohesion was perfect in regard to their own particles among themselves, and imperfect in regard to neighboring veins. Upon passing the blade of a knife athwart the veins, the water closed over it immediately. . . . If, however, the blade was passed down accurately between the two veins, a perfect separation was effected, which the power of cohesion did not immediately rectify. The phenomena of this water formed the first definite link in that vast chain of apparent miracles with which I was destined to be at length encircled. [10]

The natives, too, are puzzling in a subtle way. Their language of clicks and hisses is suggestively serpentine, and they appear to be familiar with several varieties of huge snake, "of a formidable aspect." All the objects in their environment are overwhelmingly black. Their eating habits are repellent, dinner consisting "of the palpitating entrails of a species of unknown animal," which they "devour yard after yard." [11] When finally the savages spring a devastating ambush which destroys the entire crew, except for

Pym and Peters, we understand what these physical details have meant. In Poe's Antarctic realm, the moral and the physical, the natural and the supernatural are one. The black complexion of the natives corresponds to their moral blackness. Their black furs and black birds and black stones, the blackness of the entire island, have been signs to be "read," not merely to be observed scientifically. Despite their "diabolical" cunning, the natives had, indeed, been an open book which only travelers from the "real" world could have failed to understand. Later Poe carries this principal of legibility much further. The landscape of the island becomes bizarrely suggestive:

The place was one of singular wildness, and its aspect brought to my mind the descriptions given by travelers of those dreary regions marking the site of degraded Babylon. Not to speak of the ruins of the disruptured cliff, which formed a chaotic barrier in the vista to the northward, the surface of the ground in every other direction was strewn with huge tumuli, apparently the wreck of some gigantic structure of art; although, in detail, no semblance of art could be detected.[12]

A network of signs invests the very land. The imprint of biblical evil sprawls in the jumbled rocks and cliffs. After surveying the desolate landscape, Pym and Peters climb down into a series of dusty chasms, which twist and turn in peculiarly ungeological fashion. Later, Pym traces a map of their exploration, which the "editor" of *Pym* analyzes in a scholarly appendix. The lines of the map, "when conjoined with one another in the precise order which the chasms themselves presented," turn out to "constitute an Ethiopian verbal root . . . 'To be shady'—whence all the inflections of shadow or darkness."[13] Pym and Peters have stumbled upon the original signature of creation, stamped cleanly into the crust of the earth. Here is the seal of God's intention: that His works should be legible; that the book of the world, as Renaissance theologians had argued, should extend and supplement the book of the word. Pym's adventure leads him to rediscover the ancient world of signs and correspondences, which had been effaced by the seventeenth century's discovery of the rule of law. The clinching marvel of the chasms, however, is found on the far wall of the last cave, where Peters notices some pieces of broken rock scattered on the ground, and a pattern of gouges in the wall, apparently the result of an ancient earthquake. This too, the scholarly editor remarks, yields a meaning, for the gouges resemble a combination of Ethiopian and Arabic letters. Properly read, they signify: "I have graven it within the hills and my vengeance upon the dust within the rock." Here then is the handwriting on the wall, the legislating script of the earth's curse, which is also cried aloud by flocks of seagulls wheeling overhead, and by the natives who make a cry resembling, "Tekelili-li," echoing the biblical handwriting on the wall: *Mene, Mene, Tekel, Upharsin.*

The Narrative of Arthur Gordon Pym ends on a mysterious note, as Pym and Peters escape from the island and drift southward toward a curtain of white mist billowing silently on the horizon. The sea too whitens and becomes warm. A spirit of drowsy peace overwhelms the voyagers until, days later, at the edge of the silent cataract of mist, they look ahead of them:

And now we rushed into the embraces of the cataract, where a chasm threw itself open to receive us. But there arose in our pathway a shrouded human figure, very far larger in its proportions than any dweller among men. And in the hue of the skin of the figure was of the perfect whiteness of the snow.[14]

The story concludes with these enigmatic, never explained words.

Although the three parts of the narrative do not seem to hang together, they achieve a sort of obsessional unity by force of repetition. Poe offers a veritable polyphony on the theme of mutiny and betrayal. The revolt aboard the *Grampus* is the most evident. But minors and variants of mutiny play throughout the narrative. Augustus plots against the authority of his father, Captain Barnard, by smuggling Pym aboard the *Grampus* in the first place. When Pym broaches the subject of a sea voyage to his family, they predictably turn a deaf ear: "My father made

no direct opposition; but my mother went into hysterics at the bare mention of the design; and, more than all, my grandfather from whom I expected so much, vowed to cut me off with a shilling if I should ever broach the subject to him again."[15] Pym's obsession with the adventurous life leaves him no choice. He mutinies in secret. He even assaults his grandfather when he meets him by chance on a foggy street one night, as he is hurrying to sneak aboard the *Grampus*. The interplay of mutiny and deception is at the heart of *Pym*. Even the prosaic cruise of the *Jane Guy*, the second part of the novel, is transformed by degrees into a mythic journey by a sort of mutiny, or subversion of authority. In this case, one perceives a conflict between narrative probability and the obsessional coherence which the story slowly acquires. As the *Jane Guy* proceeds on its way, with Pym and Peters gratefully aboard, Pym begins to gain a sort of ascendancy over the good Captain Guy. When the captain sensibly wants to turn back out of the Antarctic seas, Pym feels himself "bursting with indignation at the timid and ill-timed suggestion of our commander. I believe, indeed, that what I could not refrain from saying to him on this head had the effect of inducing him to push on." [16] The captain "was exceedingly sensitive to ridicule . . . and I finally succeeded in laughing him out of his apprehensions." It is hard to believe that a ship's captain would be quite so sensitive to the opinions of an adolescent castaway. Surely Poe is being novelistically careless here. Or is he simply giving free reign to his obsession with authority? The captains and fathers in *Pym* exist to be undermined or betrayed. Even when the narrative substance of the story does not provide the proper leverage, they fall under the pressure of Poe's thematic persistence. From this point of view, the grandiose betrayal by the natives, in part three, forms a pendant to the mutiny on the *Grampus* in the first part. The devils of Tsalal express the mutiny in the human heart.

As an adventurer, it is Pym's destiny to violate the rule of law. His life depends upon transgression and provokes transgression. The "moral world order," and its fathers, cannot contain him. Thus, Poe's narrative inconsistencies reveal, at another level, a profound thematic unity. The story proceeds through modulations of revolt and mutiny. As the fathers fall, Pym drifts ever closer to the mysteries of the far south. The concluding half dozen pages of the book present a problem in this respect. The notations are dreamlike and laconic. Mutiny and revolt are left behind, their work accomplished. The sea progressively whitens, inducing Pym and Peters into a narcotic daze:

The wind had entirely ceased, but it was evident that we were still hurrying on to the southward, under the influence of a powerful current. And now, indeed, it would seem reasonable that we should experience some alarm at the turn events were taking—but we felt none. The countenance of Peters indicated nothing of this nature, although it wore at times an expression I could not fathom. The Polar winter appeared to be coming on— but coming without its terrors. I felt a numbness of body and mind—a dreaminess of sensation—but this was all. . . .
The white ashy material fell now continually around us, and in vast quantities. The range of vapor to the southward had arisen prodigiously on the horizon, and began to assume more distinct-

*ness of form. I can liken it to nothing but a limitless cataract,
rolling silently into the sea from some immense and far-distant
rampart in the heaven. The gigantic curtain ranged along the
whole extent of the southern horizon. It emitted no sound.*[17]

The drift to the south which began the night Pym smuggled himself aboard the *Grampus* in New Bedford ends in an atmosphere
of hypnotic stillness, as the white-shrouded figure rises up from
"the embraces of the cataract" to receive them. The style and
the mood of these concluding pages are so different from the
rest of the book that they almost seem tacked on. For that reason, Henry James felt that the conclusion of *Pym* was a failure.

Artistically, these pages do present a problem. Thematically,
however, they have the dreamlike coherence which *Pym* so
often achieves. The white-shrouded figure, rising from the embraces of the white sea, becomes a sort of dream mother.
Passive, hugely feminine, she bathes the world with her narcotic
milk. Driven by his obsession with adventure, Pym has breached
the walls of the father; he has obeyed the mutiny in his soul.
Now, beyond the outermost wall, beyond reality itself, he discovers the form toward which his destiny has hurried him from
the first: the white mother, the same element of mystery to
which Odysseus, Gilgamesh, and Beowulf had also been drawn.
An incestuous myth guides Pym's destiny as an adventurer. The
obsession which drove him beyond reality, into a realm of
"legible" mysteries, is the same obsession which drove Oedipus
to his doom. No wonder Pym's mother became "hysterical" when
he first proposed going to sea. Like Jocasta, she knew that it
was better to leave well enough alone.

This reading of the "shrouded human figure," is confirmed by
a study of Poe's sources for *Pym*. When Poe was a boy, an
imaginative ex-soldier named Symmes published a manifesto
which began: "I declare the earth is hollow and habitable within
. . . that it is open at the poles." An expedition managing to
reach the North Pole, or rather "hole," would find "a warm and
rich land stocked with thrifty vegetables and animals, if not
men. . . ." Symmes's theory was ridiculed for a quarter of a cen-

tury, but not forgotten. A writer named Adam Seaborn published a novel based on it, which relocated the hole in the Antarctic and peopled it with a race of dazzling white natives. A friend of Poe's, Jeremiah N. Reynolds, was a staunch defender of Symmes. In the issue of *The Messenger* which carried the first installment of *Pym*, Poe wrote an article praising a speech by Reynolds.[18] Obviously Poe knew Symmes's theory and Seaborn's novel. Obviously, too, he used and transformed their eccentric materials in the conception of his own adventure tale. Mingled with Poe's fantasy of a vast maternal figure rising out of the milky sea is Symmes's and Seaborn's original conception of a hole penetrating the earth and giving access to a realm of magical fertility. Pym's adventure is enlarged into a fantasy of cosmic incest. The mystery he penetrates is the mystery of the earth itself. Having violated the "moral world order," he discovers, in himself and in the world, another order, no less extraordinary than the one Odysseus found in the magic countries of the Aegean.

I mentioned earlier how often and easily Pym is terrified by unexpected events. This is important to the story in a number of ways. Terror is not what one might call a personal emotion. On the contrary, it obliterates personality. We remember terror as an interruption of our personal histories; in terror, we are out of our minds, and out of our selves. In this sense, terror is a form of ecstasy; like ecstasy, it provides glimpses into another order of experience, akin to that of dreams. In *Pym* the capacity for terror becomes a shamanistic trait, opening a breach in reality through which Pym will plunge steadily onward, until he reaches the southern realm.

The scenes of terror in the novel are alike in certain important respects. Invariably Pym is scared by something he sees. In his panic, he takes it for an eruption of the supernatural. Upon a closer look, however, the event turns out to be quite ordinary, if not actually harmless. Pym's infernolike dream in the hold of the *Grampus* is a typical example:

I stood naked and alone, amid the burning sand plains of Zahara. At my feet lay crouched a fierce lion of the tropics. Suddenly his wild eyes opened, and fell upon me. With a convulsive bound he sprang to his feet, and laid bare his horrible teeth. In another instant there burst from his red throat a roar like the thunder of the firmament, and I fell impetuously to the earth. Stifling in a paroxysm of terror, I at last found myself partially awake. My dream, then, was not all a dream. Now, at least, I was in possession of my senses. The paws of some huge and real monster were pressing heavily upon my bosom—his hot breath was in my ear—and his white and ghastly fangs were gleaming upon me through the gloom.[19]

The hellish beast turns out to be his dog Tiger, let down into the hold by Augustus to keep Pym company. Pym's terror has resulted from ignorance. The supernatural apparition was, in fact, an illusion caused by hysterical fear, nothing more. And yet how vividly it is portrayed. Invariably, Poe outdoes himself in such scenes. The mysteries accumulate so convincingly that the reader, too, is sure that Pym has seen a ghost. Logic and reality have momentarily lost their power to explain; they are obliterated by terror.

Another such episode takes place at the very opening of the book. Pym and Augustus are running helplessly before the wind in the sailboat *Ariel*,

. . . when suddenly, a loud and long scream or yell, as if from the throats of a thousand demons, seemed to pervade the whole atmosphere around and above the boat. Never while I live shall I forget the intense agony of terror I experienced at that moment. My hair stood erect on my head—I felt the blood congealing in my veins—my heart ceased utterly to beat, and without having once raised my eyes to learn the source of my alarm, I tumbled headlong and insensible upon the body of my fallen companion.[20]

Here too the demonic apparition is "really" a ship looming out of the darkness, about to ram them. Frightening, yes, but not supernatural. In such scenes Poe appears closer to the Gothicism of Ann Radcliff than to that of Walpole and Monk Lewis. Instead of real ghosts and devils, Poe creates frightening illusions which turn out, finally, to be explainable in rational terms.

Yet the scenes themselves are so convincing. For a moment, illusion or not, we are in the world of devils and ghosts. The "mistake" which haunts us is tantalizingly vivid. So much so that, for a moment, reason, logic, and causality appear not as principles of explanation, but as weapons to fend off the ambient horror which erupts whenever "reality" loses its hold on us. The world of facts and laws, in *Pym*, functions as a bulwark against the supernatural. Ignorance, therefore, gives rise not simply to a "mistake," but to a glimpse of the demonic realm rushing in to fill a gap in the chain of causality. Pym's propensity for terror signifies his fragile connection to the world of laws. He is inwardly mobile, passing easily into the demonic realm and back again.

In the first part of the book, the supernatural erupts into factual reality in the wake of an emotion: fear, which Poe exploits in the Gothic manner. Poe here reflects the conventional attitude of his century, which believed, after Rousseau and the early Romantics, that strong emotion contained a power of revelation; that emotion itself could become an adventure—perhaps the only one left in a world which science had "explained" away. De Quincey's *Confessions of an English Opium-Eater*, Baudelaire's *Paradis Artificiels*, Rimbaud's "*raisonné déreglement de tous les sens*" will pursue the experience of inward adventure, preparing the way for the twentieth century's proliferation of drug epics. Poe is a master of such Gothic effects, but his originality in *Pym* lies elsewhere, in the use he makes of them as initiatory adventures. What Pym, in the first part of the novel, experiences in the romantic mode of terror, he experiences in the third part as a mythic voyage, a displacement not inward into the realm of personal intensities, but outward into the supernatural. Here is where Poe takes his place among the masters of adventure literature. The novelistic incoherence of *Pym* conceals a powerful symmetry. Pym's voyage toward the south is doubled by his voyage into terror. Only after he has mastered this double voyage does he enter the "legible" realm of adventure.

Through a dialectic of action and ecstasy, *Pym* recreates the epic world of the *Odyssey* and *Beowulf:* a world in which acts speak for themselves, more powerfully than words. In a culture which had begun to believe that sensibility and not action was the true field for spiritual accomplishment, Poe reverses the current. In *Pym*, emotion loses its purely psychological quality, becoming a pathway into a world in which actions are still possible.

CHAPTER

12

Nietzsche: The Philosophy
of Adventure

WHEN Nietzsche wrote that the philospher should "live dangerously," he meant by it a number of things. He meant that the philosopher should expect to be out of tune with the reigning conceptions of his time; that he should welcome the hostility which "untimely reflections" inevitably cause. He also meant that the philosopher should accept the internal dangers of self-knowledge, shucking off shallow but comforting notions even when this makes him inwardly vulnerable and puts him in danger. At the same time, the phrase contains a provocation, for it is not normally used to describe the reflective life. Bandits and warriors "live dangerously," not philosophers, and they seem to be Nietzsche's model: "Believe me, the secret of the greatest fruitfulness and the greatest enjoyment of existence is: to *live dangerously*! Build your cities under Vesuvius! Send your ships into uncharted seas! Live at war with your peers and yourselves! Be robbers and conquerors, . . . you lovers of knowledge!" [1] Passages like these are at the heart of Nietzsche's idiom. Repeatedly he insists that "knowledge" cannot be obtained through Cartesian detachment. The philosopher who shuts out all of his senses and meditates in the darkness of his intellect may discover that he thinks, and therefore is. Like Kant, he may parlay this cold certainty into a number of speculative conclusions. But how much closer will he then be to understanding the drives of nature, and of human nature? Socrates, that cunning dialectician, had a more complicated notion of what it meant to "know thyself." For one thing, Socrates and Plato knew that philosophy was a kind of warfare:

Nothing is less Greek than the conceptual cobweb-spinning of a hermit, amor intellectualis dei, *in the manner of Spinoza. Philosophy in the manner of Plato should rather be defined as an erotic contest, as a further development and inward intensification of the old agonal gymnastics and their presuppositions. . . . What finally emerged from this philosophical eroticism of Plato? A new artistic form of the Greek agon, dialectics.*[2]

Socrates and Plato may be the villains who banished Homer but the form of their philosophy inherited Homer's view of struggle as the central human event. Philosophy, for the Greeks, was the knowledge of struggle, the arbiter of struggle, and was itself a struggle, albeit sublimated into a sort of contest, or *agon*, which they called a dialectic. When Zarathustra preaches that "wisdom . . . loves only a warrior,"[3] when Nietzsche exclaims in *Twilight of the Idols* that "The man *who has become free—* and how much more the *mind* that has become free—spurns the contemptible sort of well-being dreamed of by shop-keepers, Christians, cows, women, Englishmen and other democrats. The free man is a *warrior*,"[4] he indicates how completely he has taken this Greek idea into his own thought, aiming it in particular against the German tradition of speculative philosophy, but also against the modern—one might say "novelistic"—values of domesticity.

In order to make this point, Nietzsche was not content simply to argue, although he does so often and well. He created a stylistic medium, using the language of epic and high adventure, which the novel had relegated to the badlands of popular literature, in order to dramatize the agonistic quality of knowledge, his view that intelligence without courage or willpower was not attuned to the energies of life, and therefore could make only pale discoveries. Zarathustra speaks the characteristic Nietzschean idiom: "Have you never seen a sail go over the sea, rounded and taut and trembling with the violence of the wind? Like the sail, trembling with the violence of the spirit, my wisdom goes over the sea—my wild wisdom." [5] Elsewhere Nietzsche invokes Odysseus to characterize the personal agon of the philosopher: "I too have been in the underworld, like Odysseus, and I shall yet return there often; and not only sheep have I sacrificed to be able to talk with a few of the dead, but I have not spared my own blood." [6] Any reader of Nietzsche recognizes the imagery as well as the hint of provocation in these passages. Both are constant elements of Nietzschean style, and the crux of the difficulty he has presented to his interpreters. For the violence in Nietzsche's language is often overstated, even misleading. Walter Kaufmann points out an example of this in Nietzsche's introduction to *Twilight of the Idols,* where he speaks of philosophizing with a hammer. The image, properly read, is not that of an iconoclast smashnig idols into pieces, as has often been believed, but that of a musician who makes music by playing upon the idols with a felt-padded hammer. One need only read the image in its context to grasp its unwarlike meaning. Yet the mistake is easy to make. The character of the phrase itself seems to transform the musician into a warrior before one's eyes, against the grammar of the sentence, that is, against the meaning which Nietzsche carefully assigns to it. Kaufmann warns against such passages, pointing out how Nazi apologists made all too good use of them to deform Nietzsche's philosophy. One must distinguish, Kaufmann argues, between Nietzsche's rhetoric, which often runs away with him, and his thought, which is always rigorous and precise. As a corrective to the image of Nietzsche which Nazism had made popular even in America, Kaufmann's argument was indispensable. One must, nonetheless, hold Nietzsche responsible for his words, especially when they indicate a coherent style which he remained faithful to in all his writing from the youthful fragment, "Homer's Contest," to the works of his last year of sanity.

When Zarathustra declares that wisdom . . . loves only a warrior," he is not merely ironizing on the sedentary image of the philosopher. He is expressing a definite idea about the nature and function of reason:

What, indeed, does man know of himself! Can he even once perceive himself completely, laid out as if in an illuminated glass case? Does not nature keep much the most from him, even about his body, to spellbind and confine him in a proud, deceptive consciousness, far from the coils of the intestines, the quick current of the bloodstream, and the involved tremors of the fibers? She threw away the key; and woe to the calamitous curiosity which might peer just once through a crack in the chamber of consciousness and look down, and sense that man rests upon the merciless, the greedy, the insatiable, the murderous, in the indifference of his ignorance—hanging in dreams, as it were, upon the back of a tiger. In view of this, whence in all the world comes the urge for truth? [7]

In such a state of affairs, the sensible man should not waste his intelligence on speculative activities; he should learn, as best he can, to stay on the tiger's back, even if this means learning the arts of the tiger and, in part, becoming one. To the extent, therefore, that philosophy must reflect the nature of life, in order to teach the art of living, it must be tigerish and murderous; it must live close to the tiger's claws.

Nietzsche's greatest praise for the Greeks in "Homer's Contest" was that they were clear-minded and courageous enough to acknowledge the "inhumanity" in human nature, the nihilistic furor which underlay the flowering of human acts. In the pre-Homeric beginning, he writes, had existed, "a life ruled only by the children of Night: strife, lust, deceit, old age and death." [8] Although the world of the *Iliad* seems brooding and cruel to the "modern" sensibility, it is flooded by the light of artistic achievement which "raises" nihilistic strife into a limited, but expressive form: the agon, the contest. This, for Nietzsche, was the essential accomplishment of the Homeric poems: to express the primitive energies of hatred and cruelty, while creating an integral human form which transmutes their nihilistic power. The culminating act of the *Iliad* is not Achilles' beserker rage, but the funeral games which placate the "children of Night," by giving them free rein in the form of an agon. Homer's irony, for Nietzsche, is the healthy irony of Greek culture itself. From Homer, the Greeks learned that strife, regulated but vigorously expressed, had the power to reconcile. Just as Greek philosophy, in the dialectic, took the form of an agon, so the greatest artistic achievement of the Greeks, the tragic theater, was presented each year at a contest or agon. Strife nobly expressed enhanced culture; above all, it protected the Greeks from the "pre-Homeric abyss," with its "terrifying savagery of hatred and the lust to annihilate." [9] Instead of simply condemning barbaric traits like those reported by Thucydides, the Greeks recognized in them a form of human necessity which they had to cope with and transform:

When the victor in a fight among the cities executes the entire male citizenry in accordance with the laws of war, and sells all the women and children into slavery, we see in the sanction of such a law that the Greeks considered it an earnest necessity to let their hatred flow forth fully; in such moments crowded and swollen feeling relieved itself: the tiger leaped out, voluptuous cruelty in his terrible eyes. [10]

For Nietzsche, this was the essential difference between the Greek world and the modern. The aim of Greek morality was to transform warfare, at every level, into an agon. Law, for the Greeks, was essentially regulatory. Its goal was not to outlaw strife, but to lay down rules for it, and to diversify its objectives. Nothing, according to Nietzsche, could be further from the modern conception of morality and law whose aim is not to regulate struggle, but to eliminate it; to refuse it any legitimate place among the arts of man. The goal of individual excellence has been replaced in modern times by that of group survival, he argues. When the "herd instinct" triumphed in the democratic ideal and the "slave morality" of Christianity, intelligence was detached from its root in action:

Insofar as the individual wants to preserve himself against other individuals, in a natural state of affairs he employs the intellect mostly for stimulation alone. But because man, out of need and boredom, wants to exist socially, herd-fashion, he requires a peace pact and he endeavors to banish at least the very crudest bellum omnium contra omnes *from his world.* [11]

Twenty years later, in the *Genealogy of Morals*, Nietzsche's argument had not essentially changed. "To accept any legal system as . . . a *weapon against struggle* . . . is an anti-vital principle which can only bring about man's utter demoralization." [12] The preoccupation with struggle guided Nietzsche's thought from his early fascination with Greek culture to his mature vision of the "overman," whose existence would be a "transvaluation of all values," because in him struggle would have become the highest form of health. This "higher type" of man would seek, "not contentment, but more power; not peace, but war; not virtue, but proficiency (virtue in the Renaissance style, *virtu*, virtue free of moralic acid)." [13] Like the Greeks, he would master the "children of Night," by creating a culture in which peace would be only the warrior's repose.

The epic tone of Nietzsche's writing is not due merely to his provocative temperament. It reflects his unwavering belief that man is made of conflict, and made for conflict. The "transvaluation of all values" which was implicit in the Gothic novel's nightmare of impotence, which Sade had crudely proposed in his revolutionary tract, which creators of mythic adventure like Poe and Melville had dramatized in fiction, Nietzsche established as the central work of his philosophy. The modern ideal of domesticity was superseded, for Nietzsche, by the "higher" ideal of adventure; the "civil servant mentality" [14] of modern man, by a spirit which would accept the old "chivalrous and aristocratic valuations," which "presuppose a strong physique, blooming,

even exuberant health, together with all the conditions that guar-
antee its preservation: combat, adventure, the chase, the dance,
war games, etc." [15] If Nietzsche had so remarkably little to say
about the novel (surely the most complex art form of his century), it was because he felt a profound distaste for the redefini-
tion of subject matter which the novel accomplished. He had
only contempt for the values of domestic activity: for the glorification of work, security, and duty. "To make society secure
against thieves and fireproof and infinitely comfortable for every
trade and activity . . . these are low, mediocre, and not at all
indispensable goals. . . ." [16] As for "work," it was a form of
pseudoactivity, an anti-action whose material necessity had been
parlayed, by the "slave" morality of modern times, into a moral
necessity:

*Behind the glorification of "work" and the tireless talk of the
"blessings of work" I find . . . the fear of everything individual.
At bottom, one now feels when confronted with work—and what
is invariably meant is relentless industry from early till late—
that such work is the best police, that it keeps everybody in
harness and powerfully obstructs the development of reason, of
covetousness, of the desire for independence. For it uses up a
tremendous amount of nervous energy and takes it away from
reflection, brooding, dreaming, worry, love and hatred; it always
sets a small goal before one's eyes and permits easy and regular
satisfactions. In that way a society in which the members continually work hard will have more security: and security is now
adored as the supreme goddess.* [17]

Work may have saved Robinson Crusoe; it may have seemed
to Candide to be the activity of a wise man. But Nietzsche saw
clearly that the business of work was to build walls, and that
salvation at such a price was not worth having. For Nietzsche,
as for the mythology of the Gothic novel, the space within the
garden of society was a negative space. The walls of the garden
were dark and oppressive. Life in the garden represented a failure
of nerve, bordering on nightmare.

Just as the atmosphere of the Gothic novel called for a man of action to shatter its spell of impotence, so the "decadence" of modern times called for a new transgressor who would step nonchalantly over its sacred barriers and violate its life-denying codes. In Nietzsche's typology, the criminal is a prelude to the "overman." His character bears the negative imprint of his society; his very existence challenges the claustrophobic ideals of the modern world:

The criminal type is the type of the strong human being under unfavorable conditions, a strong human being made sick. What he lacks is the wilderness, a certain freer and more perilous nature and form of existence in which all that is attack and defense in the instinct of the strong human being comes into its own. His virtues have been excommunicated by society; the liveliest drives within him forthwith blend with the depressive emotions, with suspicion, fear, dishonour. But this is almost the recipe for physiological degeneration. He who has to do in secret what he does best and most likes to do, with protracted tension, caution, slyness, becomes anaemic; and because he has never harvested anything from his instincts but danger, persecution, disaster, his feelings too turn against these instincts—he feels them to be a fatality. It is society, our tame, mediocre, gelded society, in which a human being raised in nature, who comes from the mountains or from adventures of the sea, necessarily degenerates into a criminal.[18]

With incomparable logic, and an assist from Dostoevski (whom he acknowledges further on in the passage), Nietzsche once again formulates, analytically, what the adventure myth of the nineteenth century had previously dramatized in fiction: that the edifice of obedience and guilt represented by the "moral world order" had not eliminated the adventurer, but had turned him into a rebel and a criminal. Since the rule of law was endowed with full authority over the moral and physical worlds, the adventurer had no choice but to create an "underworld" in the interstices of authority, in the dark corners of the city and the psyche.

When Zarathustra speaks to the "pale criminal" he does not reproach him for his crime, but for his pallor, caused by guilt.

The criminal has not understood his own act. He thinks he wanted to kill and rob when, in fact, he wanted to free the strife in his nature which the "moral world order" had buried so deeply that only an explosion could release it:

But I say unto you: his soul wanted blood, not robbery; he thirsted after the bliss of the knife. His poor reason, however, did not comprehend this madness and persuaded him: "What matters blood?" it asked; Don't you want at least to commit a robbery with it? To take revenge?" And he listened to his poor reason: its speech lay upon him like lead; so he robbed when he murdered. He did not want to be ashamed of his madness.[19]

The criminal's violence is equal and opposite to the repressive moral code which divides him against himself until he resembles "a ball of wild snakes, which rarely enjoy rest from each other: so they go forth singly and seek prey in the world." [20] Like Lewis's monk and Raskolnikov, Nietzsche's criminal remains trapped in the Gothic nightmare. Because he cannot value himself, he cannot fully accede to the transvalued morality which he announces. This will be accomplished by a "higher type" of man, who will be to the criminal what the criminal is to the "civil servant": a superior negation, the negation of a negation, neither obedient nor disobedient, neither good nor evil. A man who will shake loose from "bad conscience," and "earth-calumniating ideals." To accomplish that aim, however, "different minds are needed than are likely to appear in this age of ours: minds strengthened by struggles and victories, for whom conquest, adventure, danger, even pain, have become second nature. Minds accustomed to the keen atmosphere of high altitudes, to wintery walks, to ice and mountains in every sense. Minds possessed of a sublime kind of malice, of that self-assured recklessness which is a sign of strong health." [21] The morality of the "overman" will no longer be a "weapon against struggle," but a regulator of struggle, a humanizer of struggle. Nietzsche's "overman" is a profoundly epic conception, in the tradition of Gilgamesh, Odysseus, and Beowulf.

His advent will lay open to man the "pre-Homeric abyss" of his inhumanity; it will humanize the inhuman.

It is clear now that the figure of the adventurer is at the heart of Nietzsche's critique of modern values. Not the moralized hero, whose actions are a form of obedience—to the state, to God, to an ideal—but the adventurer whose life is, at the highest level, a *bellum omnium contra omnes*. Nietzsche's "great man," or "over-man," or "higher type," understands that a self-creating act must be done for its own sake. "Oh my friends," says Zarathustra, "that yourself be in your deed as the mother is in her child—let that be *your* word concerning virtue!" [22] Value must arise from the deed, as the child from the mother. Action must be at once a mothering and a fathering, a terrain of androgynous, self-delighting values. Virtue and *virtu*, goodness and proficiency, reason and action—separated by the domestic morality of modern times —must again become one, as they were in the world of "chivalrous and aristocratic valuations." Robinson Crusoe preserved his sanity by discovering that he was in fact never alone. Even at the ends of the earth, he had God, and his father, to converse with; above all, he had society indelibly inscribed in his psyche. To the joy of imperial England, Robinson Crusoe discovered that the sun never set on Yorkshire and the "middle station of low life." But Nietzsche's "higher type" must now learn to see the world in a new way because, properly understood, "there are a thousand paths that have never yet been trodden—a thousand healths and hidden isles of life. Even now, man and man's earth are unexhausted and undiscovered." [23] In order to rediscover solitude and the joy of self-delighting acts, he must undo the authority of the "moral world order" which Robinson Crusoe found so comforting. He must recreate the world of adventure in which "there is no eternal spider or spider web of reason," in which meanings are delivered from "their bondage under Purpose." " 'By Chance,'—that is the most ancient nobility in the world," the nobility of adventure (*ad venio*, whatever chance brings.) Like Gilgamesh, Odysseus, Beowulf, and the adventurers of medieval romance, the "overman" must seek himself in loneliness; he must undo the spirit of obedience ("reverence") which seeks from a distance to impose its meaning upon the acts and enterprises of men:

Truthful I call him who goes into godless deserts, having broken his revering heart. In the yellow sands, burned by the sun, he squints thirstily at the islands abounding in wells, where living things rest under dark trees. Yet his thirst does not persuade him to become like these, dwelling in comfort; for where there are oases there are also idols.

Hungry, violent, lonely, godless: thus the lion-will wants itself. Free from the happiness of slaves, redeemed from gods and adorations, fearless and fear-inspiring, great and lonely: such is the will of the truthful.

It was ever in the desert that the truthful have dwelt, the free spirits, as masters of the desert; but in the cities dwell the well-fed, famous wise men—the beasts of burden.[24]

Nietzsche's critique of "reason" and "morality" is by no means that of an irrationalist, or an immoralist. He establishes clearly in *Zarathustra* that to organize "meanings" and values is man's characteristic activity. To be sure, values and meanings differ from people to people and are often at war with one another. It is even essential to a people's integrity to establish such warfare with their neighbors: "No people could live without first esteeming, but if they want to preserve themselves, then they must not esteem as the neighbor esteems."[25] It is characteristic of Nietzsche that he should argue for a relativity of values, but not for tolerance. Man, he argues, is "the esteemer": "He alone created a meaning for things, a human meaning." By this act, he set himself in contention with other esteemers: "Never did one neighbor understand the other; ever was his soul amazed at the neighbor's delusions and wickedness." To contend and to create, to struggle and to value: in these central activities, "man" forges his identity.[26] Nietzsche's philosophic crusade against the values of the "herd" is merely an episode in the age-old contention of the great esteemers. His virulent style restores to the activity of esteeming its nobility as the central warfare of man. To be an esteemer in the highest sense—to be a creator of meanings, a philosopher—one must be, like Odysseus, "skilled in all ways of contending"; one must be an adventurer.

Nietzsche's quarrel, therefore, is not with reason, but with a certain hubris of reason, which made it into a universal principle of explanation. In "modern" times, he argues, reason has been separated from its role in the struggle of esteeming and placed in the service of world order. The rule of law, in its speculative dimension (Spinoza, Leibnitz, and others), or as a founding principle of science (the Enlightenment's "natural philosophy"), supposes that what is unknown or unpredictable appears so only through ignorance, for reason is the key to all the secrets of existence. If everything were known, there would be no contradiction and no disorder in the world. This is fundamentally wrong, Nietzsche argues. Reason is a precarious human faculty which must be constantly exercised in the struggle of esteeming. It is not a lawgiver, but a weapon. Contention is its element. The notion of a rational world order, crowned and supported by "Providence" (belief that "law," moral or scientific, will prevail, is a form of belief in Providence), weakens the human faculty of reason, by encouraging a passive attitude; it is therefore antirational:

In the great whirlpool of forces man stands with the conceit that this whirlpool is rational and has a rational aim: an error! The only rational thing we know is what little reason man has: he must exert it a lot, and it is always ruinous for him when he abandons himself, say, to "Providence." [27]

From the point of view of world order, human reason is not an active faculty. At best it discovers the "laws" implicit in nature and conforms to them. Reason in this sense is a form of "reverence." To be reasonable and to be "virtuous" become the same thing: both are matters of obedience, both refer to a world governed by a cosmic equivalent of common sense. For Nietzsche reason must not obey—quite the opposite. To the extent that reason belongs to the activity of esteeming, and to the warfare which defines values, it is a creator. The same holds true for virtue, the moral by-product of reason. "A virtue has to be *our* invention, *our* most personal defense and necessity: a virtue merely from a feeling of respect for the concept 'virtue' . . . is harmful."[28]

Far from being an irrationalist, Nietzsche seeks to free reason from its role as universal explicator, to restore its vigor as a human faculty, a dimension of the precarious skill which the "great man" deploys to affirm his existence. The difference, once again, is between the reason of speculative philosophy and the reason of the adventurer; between passively established meanings which, because they do not arise from combat, can believe themselves absolute and "epic" meanings, which arise from the struggle to humanize the inhuman. In short, between the values described by systems and the values described by stories.

The two most controversial ideas of Nietzsche's mature philosophy—the will to power, and the eternal return—finalize the morality of adventure which Nietzsche had been concerned with since his earliest writings. I cannot enter here into all the complexities of these concepts, nor can I address the enormous difficulties they have presented, and continue to present, to Nietzschean interpreters. I would like simply to point out how closely both concepts are linked to the elements of adventure as Nietzsche perceived them in his theory of the "great man," or "overman."

The will to power conceptualizes Nietzsche's lifelong belief in struggle as the central human event. The Enlightenment's structure of moral and natural laws is replaced for Nietzsche by a field of conflicting energies. From highest to lowest, all the forms of life are interlocked in a massive combat, with victory and defeat succeeding each other endlessly. The mutability of nature, like the mutability of human affairs, reflects the fortunes and disasters of this warfare: "It is of time and becoming that the best parables should speak: let them be a praise and a justification of all impermanence."[29] Change is the element of the will, and all change, for Nietzsche, implies creation. Zarathustra answers the Gothic nightmare of imprisonment with these words:

Whatever in me has feeling, suffers and is in prison; but my will always comes to me as my liberator and joy-bringer. Willing liberates: that is the true teaching of will and liberty—thus Zarathustra teaches it. Willing no more and esteeming no more and creating no more—oh, that this great weariness might always remain far from me! In knowledge too I feel only my will's joy in begetting and becoming; and if there is innocence in my knowledge, it is because the will to beget is in it.[30]

By acknowledging his will, man takes his place in the vast warfare of existence, seeking no longer to rise above nature, but to be victorious within nature. In the section on "Self-Overcoming," one of the highlights of *Zarathustra*, Nietzsche develops the idea that all relationships are forms of obedience or command:

That the weaker should serve the stronger, to that it is persuaded by its own will, which would be master over what is weaker still: this is the one pleasure it does not want to renounce. And as the smaller yields to the greater that it may have pleasure and power over the smallest, thus even the greatest still yields, and for the sake of power risks life. That is the yielding of the greatest: it is hazard and danger and casting dice for death.[31]

Instead of a great chain of being, or a structure of interlocking causalities, Nietzsche proposes a field of battle, a *bellum omnium contra omnes*, ruled over by "chance." From minute to minute, a cast of the dice changes the order of the world. Adventure is the mode of relationship of each to each, with the strongest, the "great men," casting their dice against death. In the epic struggle of "great men" seeking to humanize the inhuman, the highest level of the struggle occurs when men contend with death, refusing to acknowledge the modern world's humiliating conception of "natural death," an externally imposed, impersonal limit to the accomplishments of the will. A few years later, in the *Twilight of the Idols*, Nietzsche develops this idea further: "One perishes by no one but oneself. Only 'natural' death is death for the most contemptible reasons, an unfree death, a death at the *wrong* time, a coward's death. From love of *life* one ought to desire to die differently from this: freely, consciously, not accidentally, not suddenly overtaken." [32] We have seen that the adventurer's fascination with risk—as a warrior, a lover, a gambler—is a way of contending with death; a will to make of death an adversary. Every risk successfully run is a triumph over death, a "self-overcoming," to use Nietzsche's phrase.

In its broadest definition, the will to power becomes identified with "the unexhausted, procreative will of life" itself. [33] The cycles of nature, the observable phenomena of birth and death, result from its activity: "Where there is perishing and a falling of leaves, behold, there life sacrifices itself—for power." [34] In the human world, the will to power does not manifest itself only in acts of moral or physical violence. The warfare Nietzsche describes takes place at every level of human accomplishment. Indeed, that is the crux of Nietzsche's philosophy of adventure. The "blond beast" is not merely an Aryan warrior whose "health" depends upon unrepressed brutality. Here again Nietzsche's provocative vocabulary proves misleading. For even philosophy can be accomplished in the mode of the blond beast. Even the "will to truth" describes a form of heroic contention:

> *"Will to truth,"* you who are wisest call that which impels you and fills you with lust?
> A will to the thinkability of all beings: this I call your will. You want to make all being thinkable, for you doubt with well-founded suspicion that it is already thinkable. But it shall yield and bend for you. Thus your will wants it. It shall become smooth and serve the spirit as its mirror and reflection. That is your whole will, you who are wisest: a will to power—when you speak of good and evil too, and of valuations. You still want to create the world before which you can kneel: that is your ultimate hope and intoxication. [35]

In the sphere of meanings and values, the will to power gives rise to a ferment of self-willed, self-destined acts, governed not by "law" but by chance; by the confrontation of opposing wills, and self-opposing wills. The resultant "health" is brought about by an interplay of self-interests, akin to that proposed by Adam Smith's theory of "liberal" economics. What Smith proposed for the economic sphere, Nietzsche proposed for all the activities of the natural and human worlds. When Nietzsche argues for the creativity of warfare, he is using his characteristic epic idiom to describe the "higher" mode of all human activity, and its connection to the vast order/disorder of nature.

It is on this crucial point that one distinguishes Nietzsche's philosophy of adventure from Sade's formulation in *Français Encore un Effort*. Nietzsche did not intend to prescribe warfare, or even individual combat, as the "healthiest" human activity. He meant to offer combat as a model for the more complex activities of culture. In terms of epic contention, he meant to propose an agonistic vision of culture, and of life itself. Nietzsche's philosophy restores the adventurer to the place he had occupied in traditional cultures: no longer an outcast or a criminal, but, like Odysseus or Gilgamesh, a source of values, expressing the essentially human adventure of man engaged in the economy of struggle which is the world.

The second of Nietzsche's culminating ideas, the doctrine of the eternal return, is never described systematically. It emerges in *Zarathustra* as an impassioned teaching, closely tied to the will to power, indeed a crucial complement to it. Again, I do not mean to enter exhaustively into the problems presented by the doctrine of "recurrence." The accepted interpretation of it as a complement to Nietzsche's *amor fati* makes crucial sense, I think, as the ecstatic songs in *Zarathustra* demonstrate abundantly:

Have you ever said Yes to a single joy? O my friends, then you said Yes too to all *woe. All things are entangled, ensnared, enamored; if ever you wanted one thing twice, if ever you said, "You please me, happiness! Abide, moment!" then you wanted* all *back. All anew, all eternally, entangled, ensnared, enamored —oh, then you* loved *the world. Eternal ones, love it eternally and*

evermore; and to woe too, you say: go, but return! For all joy
wants—eternity.[36]

The eternal return represents an act of love, an ecstatic appetite
which declares: I wholly embrace this moment, its pains and its
joys, its ebullience and its failures. I embrace the best in it,
which means that I must also embrace the worst, for any holding
back tilts the moment into an endless flow of unsatisfied moments, which is time. *Amor fati* is the love which holds nothing
back. The moment becomes a fulcrum which pivots the lover
out of time, for he has entered into the fullness of repetition.
There is a mystic quality in Nietzsche's conception, but also a
stoical morality of acceptance. Dinoysus, the god of recurrence,
is both an ecstatic god and a god of courage.

Walter Kaufmann is surely right to connect this experiential
quality of the eternal return to its "scientific" aspect. According
to Nietzsche, if one considers time without beginning or end,
within which finite combinations of matter occur, then every
combination, every moment, has already occured, and will occur
again. The cycles of the world repeat themselves in a monotony
of pain and pleasure, disasters and miracles. In such a welter of
meaningless energy, only the higher man, capable of complete
love, can embrace his life. Only *amor fati*, with its power of
courage and self-acceptance, can will the return, by willing each
moment to flourish, saying: come again.[37] However question-
able Nietzsche's cyclical theory of nature may be, it projects the
sense of a new heroism which Nietzsche proclaims throughout
his later work: the heroism of praise, of *amor fati*. Only in these
terms can we understand the sweeping declaration which culminates *Twilight of the Idols*: "I, the last disciple of the philosopher
Dionysius—I, the teacher of the eternal recurrence." [38]

It is Nietzsche as storyteller who suggests a connection between the philosophy of adventure and the culminating wisdom
of recurrence. The idea is first presented in *Zarathustra*, as a
riddle to a crew of sailors of whom Zarathustra says: "There

was much that was strange and dangerous to be heard on this ship, which came from far away and wanted to sail even farther. But Zarathustra was a friend of all who travel far and do not like to live without danger." [39] Recurrence, for Nietzsche, is attuned to adventure, and to the "courage which attacks." Later, in the incantatory celebration ending Part III, Zarathustra strengthens his statement of the bond between adventure and recurrence:

> . . . *if that delight in searching which drives the sails toward the undiscovered is in me, if a seafarer's delight is in my delight; if ever my jubilation cried, "The coast has vanished, now the last chain has fallen from me . . . !" Oh, how should I not lust after eternity and after the nuptial ring of rings, the ring of recurrence?* [40]

> . . . *if I ever played dice with the gods at the gods' table, the earth, till the earth quaked and burst and snorted up floods of fire. . . . Oh, how should I not lust after eternity and after the nuptial ring of rings, the ring of recurrence?* [41]

Zarathustra's higher man must surmount his dependence upon the consolations of morality; he must recast himself as an adventurer, a thrower of the dice, a seafarer avid for unknown spaces.

Recurrence has always been a crucial theme for the adventurer, from Odysseus who organized his identity by returning into "trouble" over and over again, to Don Quixote wandering from episode to episode, in a manner we have come to call picaresque. The adventurer, like Nietzsche's higher man, is attuned to the "moment"; in the fullness of casting the dice, he pivots out of time; his life too is an agon, rising to peaks of action, subsiding in a *little death*, and then rising again. Repetition, not progression, is the sign of his identity; the "moment," not time, is the medium of his nature. The adventurer has no biography, because he is over and over again the child of his acts, a creature of beginnings.

With the doctrine of recurrence, as with the will to power,

Nietzsche broadens his lifelong preoccupation with struggle into a theory of adventure which unifies his thought and justifies the apparent excesses of his language. It was Nietzsche's genius to have conceptualized what previously had been a countercultural ambiance, a half-articulate hybrid of popular fantasy and demonic romanticism.

CHAPTER

13

Conclusion

IN the preceding chapters, I have defined adventure simply as a physical challenge, a confrontation with bodily risk. The adventurer has chosen to meet death as an enemy. With his action, the adventurer says: "Death, thou shalt die." He will have won, finally, more often than he has lost. In the fullness of his act, he will have proved that death is fallible; that a man, crippled by mortality, can nonetheless win out against the limits of his nature. In the *Iliad,* an Achaean warrior asks his companion why they are risking their lives in battle. The companion answers: we risk our lives because we are mortal; we choose combat because it is the fate of man to die. Because death's ambush incites him to caution and fearfulness, the warrior chooses to stalk the stalker. That is why his acts do not need to be explained or justified. On the contrary, in mythologies, epic, and folklore, they are the source of meanings. The warrior's duel with death provides culture with its essential tools, its founding myths, its knowledge of the world.

It is in these terms that we have approached the great works of adventure literature, and the act of storytelling itself. But the questions we ask of past traditions are different from those we ask ourselves. Because our lives have not yet arranged themselves into history, we feel a deep connection to whatever is unfinished, groped toward. The clumsy novel, the bad movie, the flawed poem, if they are contemporary, struggle with the same bulky meanings that we struggle with. Listening to them, we hear our own voice speaking, full of stumbles and rough tones, and we are caught up in its struggle. Now, when the storyteller sets up in the marketplace, we are the ones who squat around him in a circle, dragging our past and dragged by our future. Historically speaking, literature has been the unique footprint of adventure, its definitive trace, like Friday's footprint on the sand. But here suddenly is Friday, his body oiled and naked, and here are we, clothed in caution, obsessively social. We cultivate simulacrums of danger in the interstices of our lives. We remark the self-serving energies of certain men who provoke actions we admire but also resent, wondering what it would be like to experience our own lives under the aspect of adventure. It is true that we have our small dramas of escape: our love affairs, our exotic vacations. But we also have a sense that alternatives have gradually been sealed shut as years pass; that every commitment we make has bricked us into a familiar, often comfortable identity, but one we can no longer choose to leave. Our uneasy fascination with adventure grows as the domestic walls become smoothed by use, until finally they resemble a mirror. Beyond the mirror, as beyond the hillcrest of primitive legend, exists a world of encounters, a magic world we imagine but never reach. Yet we glimpse it now and then. It erupts without warning and recedes in a blend of excitement and terror: a near accident in a car; a chance meeting with an old lover; a robbery. The world beyond the mirror breaks in upon us, wounding our methodical but fragile surfaces; and before the wound can heal, we glimpse an abyss of possibilities, a pit of otherness which is dizzying or frightening, but unforgettable.

Sometimes we feel that we have paid too high a price for our comfort; that the network of relationships and names which we have become does not leave us room to breathe. The limits which define us for others then seem like prisons. And we suspect, momentarily, that we live in exile from the best part of ourselves.

Conclusion

It is to this suspicion that adventures appeal. We daydream them, watch them in movies, follow them in newspapers, hear about them from friends, and tell our own modest stories under the guise of adventures. We allow ourselves this small measure of "irresponsibility," because we know that we have no choice. We need to find a defense against continuity. Adventure, we suspect, is our secret failing, as it was for Robinson Crusoe and Candide; it represents our inability simply to be ourselves; our "childish," illicit, but definite need also to be someone else, at least in our dreams. This is not simply a "literary" matter. Indeed, "serious" literature, as we have seen, does not encourage this vein of fantasy. Instead we must rely on our "bad taste" to let in pulp magazine stories, second-rate movies, sports events; or else, in another register, fast cars, gambling casinos, hikes in the wilderness: small vertical escapes from the chain gang of our days; parentheses of unreal intensity, which later seem dreamlike. Yet these side ventures have a reality of their own, an aura of released energy which is joyful even if it can be terrifying. These are our adventures: our "frivolous," necessary moments, like brief myths, which descend upon us, transposing us into their wholeness and vanishing.

Yet the scope of these daily adventures often seems fleeting and private; our bubbles of grandeur form and burst without applause, in a thin medium scarcely able to sustain our tall tales and our gossip. They are not adventures to sing about or live by, but to entertain in a minor key. Like Defoe, we have domesticated adventure. It has become a fillip for our identities; a wash of exotic color in our lives. Where in the modern world must we look, then, to witness the Nietzschean confrontation which Conan Doyle's romantic hero mused about in *The Lost World:*

> . . . it is only when a man goes out into the world with the thought that there are heroisms all round him, and with the desire all alive in his heart to follow any which may come within sight of him, that he breaks away as I did from the life

he knows, and ventures forth into the wonderful mystic twilight land where lie great adventures and great rewards.[1]

What answer do we have for Conan Doyle's earthy newspaper editor, who objects: "I'm afraid the day for this sort of thing is rather past. . . . The big blank spaces in the map are all being filled in, and there's no room for romance anywhere."[2]

A few years before, Marlow, in *Heart of Darkness*, had told of his childhood fascination for those "white spaces" on the map. There were not many of them left by the end of the nineteenth century, but those that remained evoked a sense of mystery and confrontation with the unknown which Conrad conveyed with passionate skill. When another English writer, Charles M. Doughty, made his way into the Arabian desert, in the 1880s, it was, he said, to revive the splendor of the English language, by discovering a subject matter worthy of the high style. The result, *Travels in Arabia Deserta*, is a classic of adventure literature. Doughty devised a baroque style which transformed the desert into a world of heightened perceptions, like the magic countries of the *Odyssey*, or Gilgamesh's land of Faraway. For Doughty as for Conrad, the power of imagination and the resources of style were able to transform distance once more into an ontological fact.

Conan Doyle's hero in *The Lost World* sets out for the Amazon jungle, but, in fact, he travels further, into a fantastic valley inhabited by Stone Age tribes and prehistoric monsters. In Conan Doyle's popular idiom, the "blank spaces" were not merely undiscovered portions of the earth; they were gateways into another order of experience. The same was true for the French novelist, Pierre Benoit in his famous romance, *L'Atlantide*. For Benoit, the unexplored Hoggar mountains in the southern Sahara became a slate wiped clean of geographical perceptions, in which his vision of lost Atlantis could arise, as if by the natural motion of reality itself. The unknown still flourishes in the interstices of the known. Even in the twentieth century, distance can acquire a supernatural dimension and become a proper scope for adventure.

But as the mysteries of geographical distance have been solved by camera safaris, tourist cruises to the Antarctic, and the grim banalities of jungle warfare, the measure of distance has changed. Its horizon has come increasingly to exist in the emotional style of the adventurer, not in the "white spaces" which the map no longer contains. Already in *Heart of Darkness*, it is Marlow's narration which turns the Congolese jungle into a mythic wilderness. He sees it as a place of demonic confrontations, and he conveys his vision with dense language which describes not so much a place as a way of experiencing. The substance of adventure has been displaced inward, so that *Heart of Darkness* must also be read as a precursor of modernism, and Marlow's voyage up the Congo River as a voyage into the depths of the psyche. As Robinson Crusoe discovered that shipwreck and a desert island could not remove him from his mind, which held to the "middle station of low life," so our modern sense of adventure has discovered that an exploit's interior face contains its true potency.

This discovery prepared the way for several possibilities. The adventure story, which Mérimée, Robert Louis Stevenson, and Kipling had trimmed to a swift, bouyant genre, became slow and atmospheric; action swam in an elaboration of imagery and extreme emotions which became the architecture of a highly literary genre. The complex resources of style were devoted to myth-building of a new sort. Now, the magnifications of myth lay not in the framework of great exploits, but in the interior rhythm which the adventurer imposed upon the world of his experience. Instead of epic clarity, we had baroque developments of language. Instead of narrative swiftness, we had Gothic amplifications of atmosphere, a mythicization not of events but of sensibility. The classic adventure stories of this new genre present an unexpected anomaly: they tell tales of splendid courage and exotic actions in a style which secretes complexity and slowness, until the actions recede and become a background for the elaborate frescos of style. The greatest example of this new epic stylization is, of course, *Moby Dick,* in which the grandeur of the action is conveyed through an elaborate ground-swell of digressions and stylistic asides. Doughty's *Travels in Arabia Deserta,* Conrad's early novels and stories, T. E. Lawrence's *Seven Pillars of Wisdom,* much of Malraux's work, especially *The Royal Way,* Genet's prose in *Thief's Journal,* are other examples of the genre.

The case of T. E. Lawrence is especially interesting to consider, from this point of view, because we have what amounts to two separate portraits of his career: one a product of the popular imagination, transmitted by newspapers, heightened by eyewitness accounts of famous people who knew him well; the other buried in the involute prose of his masterpiece, *Seven Pillars of Wisdom.*

The outward facts of his career are as simple as they are fascinating. Lawrence played a crucial role in a minor episode of World War I. While historic massacres were taking place in the trenches at Verdun and elsewhere, the British Arab Office in Cairo organized a campaign of harrassment against Germany's Middle Eastern ally, Turkey. The idea was to encourage a nationalist uprising in the Arab territories of the old Ottoman Empire. The enterprise might well have gone unnoticed, if an American journalist, Lowell Thomas, had not come across the Arab campaign and written a series of dispatches about a small, blue-eyed Englishman, who wore an Arab bridal costume, and out-bedouined the Bedouins on excruciating raids across the desert to blow up Turkish railway stations and destroy bridges. Suddenly this unimportant backwater of the Great War was news, and "Lawrence of Arabia" became a hero larger than any created by Kipling or Conrad.

It is hard now for us to imagine the enthralled atmosphere in which Lawrence's legend thrived. Crowds came regularly to hear Lowell Thomas lecture in London. For years after the war, newspapers were filled with rumors of new exploits and dark manipulations. Indeed, every colonial disturbance in the world during the 1920s seems to have been connected to Lawrence, who had conveniently disappeared from view. During the time of his legend, Lawrence enlisted as a recruit in the air force, under the assumed name Shaw, and he spent the rest of his life in a provocative sort of half-concealment, as an enlisted man in the armed forces. This private, almost invisible quality of Lawrence's post-Arabian years left the public free to create a troubling fantasy, which was never trimmed to size by real acts committed by the real man. The legend billowed in public, while Private Shaw kept half in and half out of his anonymous shelter in the armed service, like a secular monk, at least partly guilty of the Augustinian sin of pride at his excessive humility.

The popular craving for adventure reached an extraordinary peak during the 1920s and 1930s, in pulp magazines like the Doc Savage series, in Westerns, in the soaring cult of movie stars, in the creation of instant legends around figures like Rupert Brooke and Lawrence in England, and Lindbergh in the United States. Perhaps the catastrophic scope of World War I had something to do with it. The course of the war had been so vast and machinelike, and its results so paltry, that a certain conception of national life became suspect. One was eager to admire the heightened figure of heroes, but war, the traditional field for heroic endeavor, inspired horror. One wanted destiny scaled to the will of individuals, not cataclysms which made a joke of individuality, however brave or reckless. Also, one wanted to reaffirm an ancient sense of the unmediated struggle with fate, the primitive face-to-face between the Homeric hero and the god, between Beowulf and the monster: the demonic short circuit by which the heightened man swept aside religion, language, and morality, stepping beyond them into a sphere of solitary challenges. In this sense, adventure represents a sort of "Protestantism" of action, as opposed to the mediated, institutionalized bravery of heroes. But World War I had tarnished the mediating ideals; it had wounded the very notion of bravery. Death in such vast, faceless numbers could no longer be an adversary; it became a plague, a dissemination of poisons. Lawrence himself understood the problem, when he called the strategies of the European theater "murder war" and defined his own aims in terms which we have since come to identify as guerrilla warfare: an extended, minimally organized version of individual combat, on the model of medieval romance. By his own account, Lawrence stood in the shadow of Saladin, not Napoleon; his measure was legendary, not military. Even his military strategy, which the British military historian B. H. Liddell Hart particularly admired, presented a chivalric model: "Every enrolled man should serve in the line of battle and be self-contained there. The efficiency of our forces was the personal efficiency of the single man. . . . Our ideal should be to make our battle a series of single combats, our ranks a huge alliance of agile commanders-in-chief."[3] Against the backdrop of trench warfare, Lawrence's desert tactics, as he describes them in *Seven Pillars of Wisdom*, represent a sort of adventure war. We will never know how much of Lawrence's theorizing was done in the midst of the action, as he claims it was, and how much during the early 1920s, when he wrote three versions of his book, against the never-mentioned background of his immense fame. In any case, Lawrence identified unerringly the quality of solitary conflict, of "antinomian"[4] fluidity, which made his venture so appealing to the British public.

Lawrence's antinomian aura was not limited to his conception of military tactics. It was essential to the legend which magnified his obsessive personal qualities into a demonic portrait, owing as much to Gothic fantasy as to actual fact. Lawrence was perceived not only as a hero and a patriot, but as something of a monster: a homosexual, an uncontrolled killer, a masochist, a sadist, a cool manipulator. There is a certain comic-book exaggeration in the fascinated distrust, as well as the worship he inspired. Indeed, one genuine mystery is the extraordinary variety of opinions he fostered around him: Intellectuals like Robert Graves and George Bernard Shaw thought he was an excellent writer; Winston Churchill thought he was a great diplomat; Liddell Hart believed him to be one of the great military innovators of all time; the Arab warrior, Auda Abu Tayi, called him "the world's imp"; Allenby, the British commander-in-chief in the Middle East, suspected he was a "charlatan"; the French military attaché in Arabia, Colonel Bremond, thought he was a psychiatric case; many Arabs thought an "aurens" (their pronunciation of Lawrence) was a tool for blowing up trains. Perhaps the most troubling impression is one he relates in *Seven Pillars of Wisdom*. An old Bedouin woman, staring at him for a long time, marveled at his "white skin and the horrible blue eyes which looked, she said, like the sky shining through the eye-sockets of an empty skull."[5]

There is a question, itself part of the Lawrence legend, as to how much Lawrence was an accomplice in fostering these variously skewed impressions. He tells, in the *Seven Pillars,* of his genius for manipulation. Sitting one night around a tribal fire, he and his men preach the ideology of revolt:

After dark we gathered around Auda's hearth, and for hours I was reaching out to this circle of fire-lit faces, playing on them with all the tortuous arts I knew.[6]
Our conversation was cunningly directed to light trains of their buried thoughts; that the excitement might be their own and the conclusions native, not inserted by us. Soon we felt them kindle: we leaned back, watching them move and speak, and vivify each other with mutual heat. . . . They turned to hurry us, themselves the begetters, and we laggard strangers: strove to make us comprehend the full intensity of their belief; forgot us; flashed out the means and end of our desire. A new tribe was added to our comity.[7]

What he practiced with the Arabs, he seems to have practiced compulsively, perhaps even consciously, with everyone, always interposing a willed impression between himself and his interlocutors. As he writes: "I must have had some tendency, some aptitude, for deceit, or I would not have deceived men so well."[8] After Lawrence's initial notoriety was established, it is surely this element of refracted vision, as if the man had too many faces, too many shapes, for one to be sure he had any of them, that kept him in the public eye. He seems to be a man with too many biographies for us to believe he had any biography at all.

It is perhaps at this point that popular legend and Lawrence's involute self-portraiture intersect: The demonic voluptuary of pain, capable of extraordinary suffering and of inflicting extraordinary suffering, serving his country, and yet, perceptibly, making his country serve his own compulsive needs; providing an image of epic proportions to ignite the patriotism in the English soul, yet icily detached from the community of passions which the war drew upon, devoted only to his cruel privacy. All of this, like a page from a Gothic novel, made Lawrence the complicated, somewhat sinister figure of which England was both proud and afraid.

The impression we get from *Seven Pillars of Wisdom* is not entirely different. Indeed, the public and the private Lawrence are profoundly linked to one another, but there is a shift in emphasis which makes *Seven Pillars* an extremely curious book. It is, in some ways, an epic without any action; an elaborately crafted structure of impressions scaled to the stature of myth, within which the Arab revolt and Lawrence's reckless exploits proceed almost invisibly, as traces of feeling, modifications of the landscape. One sees why the Bloomsbury group was so interested in Lawrence. *Seven Pillars* is a book which Virginia Woolf might have written; its ability to mythicize the feelings of a very complicated man is oddly Proustian, too. Lawrence is by no means a master of his instrument as were these writers, but the resemblance of intention is striking. Precisely what made him so visible to the English public, his warrior qualities, blends in the book with the elaborate experience of the desert itself, with portraits of self-inflicted pain and troubled conscience, so as to be present only in the most elusive way.

Let me take a central example from the book. The march to Akaba is a turning point in the Arab revolt. Its daring conception and execution put the Turks on the defensive once and for all, and projected Lawrence into a central role in the war. By crossing hundreds of miles of impenetrable desert, by creating an army as he went from nomad tribes who distrusted each other almost as much as they hated the Turks, by drifting unnoticed behind the Turkish defenses, like a "gas" as he describes it, and then coalescing at the proper moment to carry the assault, Lawrence overturned the balance of power in Arabia. He demonstrated to the English that an irregular force using the desert the way pirates use the ocean, and held together by the fervor of an ideal, could do what no regular army could have done. Liddell Hart, a connoisseur in the matter, considers the Akaba expedition to be one of the important pages in the history of military strategy. In any case, it made Lawrence famous in Arabia and gave him almost unlimited credit with the Arab commander, Feisal, whose advisor he was. Yet it is precisely this bold relief which is missing from Lawrence's description of the Akaba expedition. The crucial actions of the march and its goal are present, in a sense, only as negatives, shadows cast against the densely colored atmosphere of the desert which Lawrence evokes on page after page in all its intricate variation:

. . . *we re-entered the volcanic ground. Little pimply craters stood about, often two or three together, and from the spines of high, broken basalt led down like disordered causeways across the barren ridges; but these craters looked old, not sharp and well-kept like those of Ras Gara, near Wadi Ais, but worn and degraded, sometimes nearly to surface level by a great bay broken into their central hollow. The basalt which ran out from them was a coarse bubbled rock, like Syrian dolerite. The sand-laden winds had ground its exposed surfaces to a pitted smoothness like orange rind, and the sunlight had faded out its blue to a hopeless grey.*[9]

We marched on, over monotonous, glittering sand; and over those worse stretches, "Giaan," of polished mud, nearly as white and smooth as laid paper, and often whole miles square. They blazed back the sun into our faces with glassy vigour, so we rode with its light raining direct arrows upon our heads, and its reflection glancing up from the ground through our inadequate eyelids.[10]

These desert passages, modeled after Doughty, but surpassing him by far, call upon all of Lawrence's artistry as a writer. In some sense they constitute the true subject matter of his book. The desert becomes a locus of values for Lawrence, but also a vision, a place of epic clarities within which the soft monotony of the town is brutally pared away.

Lawrence's desert is as far from England as Gilgamesh's cedar forest from Uruk and Grendel's cave from Hrothgar's brightly lit halls. The desert is "elsewhere," it is the essential elsewhere, and the desert traveler, like the archaic adventurer, is for Lawrence a traveler between the worlds. There is a visionary energy in *Seven Pillars*. Like Marlow steaming up the Congo River, like Ishmael sliding through the South Seas, Lawrence describes his entry into an order of mythic reality. Often, in the course of the book, the desert warrior is offered as an antitype which fascinated Lawrence, and which he tried, throughout his years in Arabia, to become, even to the point of madness. The Bedouin, writes Lawrence, exist in a world of moral and spiritual certainties, as stark and as vividly wrought as the desert landscape itself:

They were a people of primary colors, or rather of black and white, who saw the world always in contour. They were a dogmatic people, despising doubt, our modern crown of thorns. They did not understand our metaphysical difficulties, our introspective questionings. They knew only truth and untruth, belief and unbelief, without our hesitating retinue of finer shades.[11]

Because values and their source in God stood about him like natural formations, a sort of divine geography, so to speak, the Bedouin nomad was not introspective or ceremonial; places were not sacred to him, domestic boundaries were merely conveniences to be erected and demolished; he was at home nowhere and everywhere, because each place he was and each place he wasn't was equally inscribed in the element of holiness:

The Bedouin could not look for God within him: he was too sure that he was within God. He could not conceive anything

234

which was or was not God . . . yet there was a homeliness, an everydayness of this climatic Arab God, who was their eating and their fighting and their lusting. . . . Arabs felt no incongruity in bringing God into the weaknesses and appetites of their least creditable causes.[12]

The desert, for Lawrence, was an epic medium, generating perfect actions as naturally as the fertile land generated agriculture. Lawrence saw the Bedouin warrior as a man of pure acts that were ends in themselves: acts without pattern or long-range goal. Wherever the Bedouin was, became his goal; his life was essentially picaresque. He was an adventurer from birth. This was the ideal Lawrence longed for and learned to imitate by a ferocious act of will.

Yet he never could lose his trapped self-awareness. When he considers the great Arab warrior, Auda Abu Tayi, it is from a distance, and the distance, he felt, measured his failure to become another self: "The epic mode was alien to me, as to my generation. Memory gave me no clue to the heroic, so that I could not feel such men as Auda in myself. He seemed fantastic as the hills of Rumm, old as Mallory."[13] Lawrence drove himself to feats of endurance. He outdid the Bedouins in rough living, in ferocity, in the stealth and canniness of the desert. He planned and executed raids with all the skills of old Auda himself. He tried, too, to remake himself from within: to simplify the knot of "introspective questionings" which locked him into his European self ("The war held for me a struggle to side-track thought"[14]) and made him strangely exterior to the epic self for which the Arabs mistook him. But he could never succeed in this effort, and the failure became an obsession. A sense of his fraudulence plays through Lawrence's story like a leitmotif, paralyzing not so much his actions as his solidarity with them, his experience of being one with them. He felt that he was a put-up Bedouin. He apparently also guessed that the goal of Arab nationalism would be sold short in negotiations after the war, despite England's promises to the contrary. By serving Feisal he also betrayed him.

Lawrence's adventures, therefore, were tarnished by a bad conscience. By an extraordinary irony, Lawrence created in *Seven
Pillars of Wisdom* an epic world into which he had no entry.
His longing for action exhausted itself in the delineation of a
complex, stylistically dense "song" inhabited not by adventures,
but by his failure to have had any, except, perhaps, at certain
moments when a substitute for the Bedouins' naturally "thoughtless" nobility occured to him: pain, sheer mindless endurance
which Lawrence came to value as a joust against nature, an
essentially spiritual act. Suffering released him from doubts and
betrayals; it was a divine drunkenness, a berserker rage turned
inward. Suffering became a momentary access to the grandeur
of the epic world. If Lawrence had a flaw as a military commander, it was his inclination to undertake unimportant but ex-
cruciatingly painful missions; to throw himself into ordeals of
endurance for the sheer pain of it. His description of a violent
sandstorm conveys his sense of exaltation in suffering:

*By noon it blew a half-gale, so dry that our shriveled lips
cracked open, the skin of our faces chapped; while our eyelids,
gone granular, seemed to creep back and bare our shrinking
eyes. The Arabs drew their headcloths tightly across their noses,
and pulled the browfolds forward like visors with only a narrow,
looseflapping slit of vision . . . for my own part, I always rather
liked a khamsin, since its torment seemed to fight against mankind with ordered conscious malevolence, and it was pleasant to
outface it so directly, challenging its strength, conquering its
extremity.*[15]

Lawrence has been called a masochist. He is frank about his
erotic sensations when he was tortured at Deraa. But, in *Seven
Pillars*, pain becomes a back door into Auda's world, a form of
the adventurer's active passiveness, tinged by the longing for
death:

*Step by step I was yielding myself to a slow ache which con-
spired with my abating fever and the numb monotony of riding
to close up the gate of my senses. I seemed at last approach-*

*ing the insensibility which had always been beyond my reach:
but a delectable land: for one born so slug-tissued that nothing
this side fainting would let his spirit free.*[16]

Seven Pillars of Wisdom is penetrated by a passion for adventure, but also by a sense of the fraudulence of adventure for the
modern Englishman, condemned to a life of inner complexity. It
also presents, in a brilliant stylistic fresco, the paradox of the
modern adventurer: his actions ramify not into a story, but into
a portrait of his sensibility, an aggrandized mythology of his self-
awareness. The difference between the adventure story and the
modernist epic of sensibility dwindles, as the authenticity of the
adventurer's quest comes to lie not in the grandeur of acts themselves, but in the "form of experiencing" which encompasses the
acts from within. *Seven Pillars of Wisdom*, like *Ulysses, Rem-
brance of Things Past*, and *The Man Without Qualities*, creates
a constellation of inward space, a vast paralysis of style within
which Lawrence's actual exploits move imperceptibly, almost
irrelevantly.

Lawrence's eccentric prose embodies the paradox of our culture: its longing for great acts, combined with a sense of their
irrelevance. Action creates values, yet it is a fraud; it represents
the essential Nietzschean struggle, yet it is inauthentic, for authenticity exists only in the leisure of sensibility. What Lawrence
himself experienced as a double bind verging on tragedy, became,
a generation later, an intellectual passion, simplified eventually
into an ideology.

André Malraux and Jean-Paul Sartre divide Lawrence's paradox between them. For both, the values of the domestic world
seem false and confining. Claude Vannec, in Malraux's novel *The
Royal Way*, has no love for the penitentiary society he fled when
he came to the jungles of Cambodia:

*Although he was not naïve enough to be surprised by it, he had
thought, in former days, about the conditions of a civilization
which gives such a place to intellect that those who make a*

steady diet of it undoubtedly become overstuffed and are slowly brought to ever cheaper meals. Then what? He had no desire to sell cars, stocks, or speeches like those friends of his whose slicked-down hair signified distinction; or to build bridges, like those whose rough-cut hair signified science. What were they working for, if not to earn respect, but he hated the kind of respect they valued.[17]

In Sartre's *Nausea*, too, the world of social values and inherited gestures has become thin and scratchy, like the jazz record Roquentin listens to over and over again; each time it is played, the record becomes more deformed. For Roquentin, the community of shared words is no closer to the rich voice of the singer than this cunning imitation on the record player.

Yet, having judged the domestic world as severely as Nietzsche or Lawrence ever did, Sartre and Malraux draw opposite conclusions. Standing clearly in Lawrence's shadow, Malraux became not only a novelist, but a philosopher of adventure. In *The Royal Way*, we are told that Perken, an aging soldier of fortune, has carved out a fragile empire among the dissident tribes of Indochina. Behind Perken stands the legend of Meyrena, a nineteenth-century French adventurer, who made himself king over a confederation of jungle tribes. Both figures echo Lawrence's adventure in Arabia, and it is interesting that Malraux, only a few years ago, in *Antimemoirs*, should have retold the story of Meyrena in great detail, showing how much, even now, he is haunted by a vision of power and self-transformation of the kind Lawrence mythicized in *Seven Pillars of Wisdom*.

The central character in *The Royal Way*, Claude Vannec, is an intellectual and a student of history, like Lawrence himself. He has come to Cambodia to unearth valuable sculptures which he is sure adorn temples as yet undiscovered along the ancient royal way, deep in the Cambodian jungle. His plan is to steal and sell the sculptures, in order to buy his freedom from the domestic servitudes of a career. But Claude's quest in the jungle quickly becomes more real than any goal, more real than Europe or money. His adventure itself becomes the escape. When the carts loaded with sculpture are taken away by Moïs tribesmen, Claude has already forgotten them amidst the encroaching tragedy of Perken's death and Claude's own anguished insight into the cost, but also the necessity, of adventure:

These worn-out ideas of men who believed that their lives served the end of some salvation; the words they say in conforming their lives to a pattern: they were corpselike and dead, and what had he to do with corpses. The absence of a set goal in life had become a condition for action. Let others confuse this painful premeditation of the unknown, with a surrender to chance. All he wanted was to wrench his own images from a stagnant world. . . . "What they called adventure," he thought, "isn't a flight, it's a hunt: the established order does not yield to chance, but to the will to profit by it." [18]

Being killed didn't frighten him: he didn't care much about his own skin; even in defeat he would have found his combat. But to accept the vanity of his existence, like a cancer; to go on living with the lukewarm feel of death in his hand: that he couldn't do. . . . What was this need for the unknown, this temporary destruction of the relationship of master to prisoner, which those who know nothing about it call adventure, if not a defense against those very things? . . . To possess more than himself, to escape the dusty life of the men he saw every day. . . . [19]

Adventure, for Claude, is a struggle against the diminished values of the modern world; but it is also, as he learns from Perken, a struggle against time, against age, against solitude, against the physical humiliation of death. Adventure alone can restore values which have been worn thin by domesticity. As he penetrates into the fetid atmosphere of the jungle, Claude enters into a primitive confrontation with the burgeoning power of life, thrusting itself upon him in all its viscous formlessness:

As if into an illness, Claude sank into the fermenting forms that swelled, stretched, and rotted beyond the world where men count for something, and which divided him from himself with the force of darkness. . . . Now the oneness of the forest dominated; for six days, Claude had given up distinguishing beings and forms, life that moves from life that oozes; an unknown power bound fungus growths to the trees, made all those temporary things seethe over the ground like foam of the tide, in these steaming woods of the world's beginning. Could any human act have a meaning here? Could any will preserve its integrity? Everything ramified, softened, tried to adjust itself to a world that was both ignoble and fascinating, like the gaze of an idiot, assaulting the nerves with the same abject power as the spiders hanging between the branches, which it was so hard for Claude not to look at.[20]

The jungle has become the essential battleground, the element of life revealed to Claude in all its naked hostility. Against this "clenched fist,"[21] only a man of action can survive, returning blow for blow. As Claude strikes desperately at the stone wall of the temple, trying to detach the massive sculptures he has found, his act generates an ecstasy of pain; he flexes his very being against the forest, striking "almost unconsciously, the way a man walks when he is lost in the desert."[22] "He needed all the exaltation of his will to keep on going, to keep advancing against the forest, against men. . . ."[23]

To be sure, Malraux knows that a certain sort of adventure can be as fraudulent as the penitentiary morality from which Claude is escaping. Perken accuses Meyrena of having been a comic-opera figure, parading himself like a story, "a man intent on playing his own biography."[24] The captain of the ship which brings Claude and Perken to Cambodia formulates a judgment which Lawrence himself would have recognized: "Tout aventurier est né d'un mythomane," every adventurer starts out as a liar, a storyteller who wants to believe his own stories, and therefore needs to act them out. In this sense, the escape from culture becomes a coy act of culture, a dissimulated round trip; it is a going which is covertly a coming. The adventurer as *myth-omane* has, in fact, never let go. He has simulated the radical separation of the traveler, but he persists in sending back messages which are stepping stones across the demonic seas, in view of his own safe return. We have seen that this traditionally has been an integral part of the adventurer's act, but Malraux challenges the tradition, and creates an adventurer who is committed to silence, or rather to a total act which does not need to be told in order to leave its imprint on the map of reality. Unlike Meyrena, Perken does not want to be a king, he wants to leave a "scar on the map." [25] Neither Claude nor Perken tells his story. As articulate as they are to each other—*The Royal Way* often resembles an essay on adventure—they tell nothing to anyone else, and nothing to us, who learn the story from a conventional novelistic narrator. Having abandoned the comic opera of storytelling, Malraux's adventurer is locked into a solitary combat with the viscous element of the jungle, with the fever of decay which saps his body, with the irreducible solitude which constitutes *la condition humaine.* Only in the mode of combat is it possible to know these enemies and to acknowledge them, without the interposed veil of customs and conventions, without the false comfort of society.

In *The Royal Way*, Malraux has simplified adventure into an act of revolt, which is also an act of truth. In the process, the epic desire to humanize the inhuman, extending the net of language ever further into the demonic darkness, has altered its focus. The act of Malraux's adventurer is not accomplished for man, but for self, because the adventurer has learned that "man" does not exist, but only selves. Name making and home going are not intertwined, as they were for Odysseus, for Gilgamesh, and for Beowulf. Malraux's adventurer refuses to have a home. He is not willing to die like Homer's Odysseus, at his fireside in the peace of old age, but rather like Dante's Odysseus, in mid-Atlantic. Malraux's morality of adventure sets aside T. E. Lawrence's concern about the fraudulence of action. Adventure circumscribed by silence becomes a crucial answer, perhaps the only fully human answer, to the problem of existence.

In these terms, we approach the most moving critique of the adventure morality in our century: that of Jean-Paul Sartre, for whom Malraux appears to be the perfect antitype, a dark and opposite twin in the manner of Gilgamesh and Enkidu. Like Malraux, Sartre expresses distrust of the intricate deceptions which bind men into a language, a set of principles, a routine of acts: in short, into society. Like Malraux, he pronounces a desperate judgment upon the "bad faith" of conventional attitudes, which conceal from each of us the terrible simplicity of "existence." Little by little, the shell of artifacts, names, and ambitions peels away from Sartre's hero, Roquentin. Against his will, Roquentin breaks through into a fetid vegetative life which had always been there, concealed by the enormous prestidigitation of culture: "A confusion of soft, monstrous bulks were left—naked, frighteningly, obscenely naked." [26] "Everywhere budding, blossoming, my ears droned with existence, my very flesh trembled and opened; it surrendered to the universal flowering. . . ." [27] The language might be Malraux's in *The Royal Way*, describing the jungle that closes in upon Claude Vannec. But where Claude saw a "closed fist," and struck back with hammer blows, Roquentin sees a limp flow of "marmalade," filling everything with its "jelly-like collapse." [28] This elemental larva-life does not call for acts; it is not a closed fist, but a jelly, dissolving acts, making them ludicrous. On the contrary, Roquentin's illumination requires that he "not . . . make the least movement," [29] that he abandon himself to the overflow of a world without names, unmediated by acts and purposes. Instead of hammer blows, his response is "nausea" which is the bad taste of truth. As for the closed fist theory, Roquentin laughs bitterly:

Imbeciles talk to you about the will to power, and the struggle for life. Hadn't they ever looked at an animal or a tree? This plane tree with its layers of peeling bark, this half-rotted oak, I was supposed to take them for harsh young energies spurting toward the sky. And what about this root? Should I imagine it as a hungry claw, tearing the earth, ripping out its food?

I couldn't see things that way. Softnesses, weaknesses, yes. The trees floated; more like a collapse; from minute to minute, I expected to see the trunks become wrinkled, like weary rods, shrinking and falling to the ground in a soft, black, folded heap.[30]

This is not the only place in *Nausea* where Sartre seems to be answering Malraux. Indeed, if *The Royal Way* resembles an essay on adventure, *Nausea*, developing a similar insight into "existtence," resembles an essay against adventure, and against Malraux. The character of Roquentin counterpoints that of Claude Vannec. Like Claude he is an intellectual, and a historian; like Claude too, he has been to Indochina. When Roquentin was younger, we learn, he had longed for a life of action, but something happened in Indochina to bring about a change in his thinking. As a result, he has chosen to live in a claustrophobic little town, Bouville (literally "Mudville") in Normandy, where he is writing the biography of an early nineteenth-century figure named Rollebon, a Casanova-like character whose life was devoted to intrigue.

Although he does not yet know it, Roquentin has begun his retreat from "action" into "existence." From acts, he has withdrawn to a history of acts; from adventure, he has withdrawn into leisure, made conveniently possible by a modest personal fortune. Having begun his retreat, however, Roquentin finds that it has taken him further than he meant. For his provincial routine gives way suddenly to "nausea," which is Roquentin's entry into the raw leisure of "existence."

The same insight which plunged Claude Vannec into action immobilizes Roquentin with a profound conviction that action of any kind is fraudulent. Willful violence was Claude's answer to the fetid encroachment of existence, but Roquentin, looking at a roomful of busy people, thinks: "They each had their small personal stubbornness that kept them from noticing that they existed."[31] The personal stubbornness, the obsession which focuses their lives, serves only to mask existence, not to confront it. The notion that "it is best to act first, to throw oneself into things,"[32] is precisely the lie out of which culture is made. As for adventure, it is simply a more flamboyant example of the same lie. Roquentin had been proud of the dangers he had sought out in Hanoi, Morocco, and elsewhere. They were luminous heights, moments of "melody" which he valued. But now it seems to him that the quest for such moments is not essentially different from the "personal stubbornness" of the toothpaste salesman. Roquentin may have sought out danger, he muses, but:

I never had any adventures. Complications, events, incidents, anything you like. But not adventures. I'm beginning to see that it's not simply a question of words. Something was more important to me than all the rest, and I hadn't noticed. Not love, or God, or glory, or wealth, but . . . I had a feeling that at certain moments my life could take on a rare and precious quality. Extraordinary circumstances weren't necessary: all that I required was just a little discipline. There is nothing particularly brilliant about the life I'm leading: but from time to time, for example, when they played music in a café, I thought back, and said to myself: once in London, Meknes, Tokyo, I had fine moments, I had adventures. That's what they're taking away from me now. For no apparent reason, I've suddenly seen that I lied to myself for ten years. Adventures happen in books. And naturally, what they say in books can actually occur, but not in the same way. It was the way of occurring that was so important to me.[33]

At least one of Sartre's aims, in *Nausea,* is to discredit adventure as an alternative to the facile comforts of culture. If Malraux chose to express one side of T. E. Lawrence's paradox—adventure as a program of existence—Sartre, with the sorrow of a disappointed lover chooses the other: the fraudulence of adventure, its quality of a willed artifact.

Yet it is clear that Roquentin's adventurous past has a bearing upon his fall into existence. His travels, the longing to organize his life into a "melody," even his fascination with the episodic career of the adventurer Rollebon, express embryonically his inability to accept the essential "dishonesty" of culture, its perspective of goals and purposes which stares with outrageous self-confidence from the portraits of local notables in the Bouville art museum. For Sartre, in *Nausea,* adventure is not an answer; it is a symptom, a first delirium of the nausea to come. Roquentin, returned from Indochina, is Claude Vannec who has entered into a more desolate wisdom. From the standpoint of nausea, the escape into adventure is a doomed attempt to use the tools of culture against culture itself. Leaving a "scar" on the map is ultimately not a form of silence, Perken and Claude to the contrary. It is a braver, yet stagier way to make a book. For "existence" to be an enemy, it must be seen with the eyes of fever, as Claude and Perken still see it. Roquentin has moved beyond fever, into the massive indifference of a larva-world which presses in upon him without will or intention, no longer as an enemy, but as a presence.

When the Autodidact wonders timidly if he might one day be ready to have an adventure, there is poignance in Roquentin's anger, for adventure had represented his last illusion that a victory might be won. Without an enemy there can be no victory. In Bouville, the will to adventure has become Bovaryesque, a gesture of escape reeking of the prison. The adventurer, for Sartre, is John the Baptist in the desert, announcing the negative dispensation of existence, but unable to let go of the last comfort which culture can offer: the book of his exploits.

The adventure of sensibility, developed in various ways by Melville, Conrad, and T. E. Lawrence, self-destructs in the immense passiveness of *Nausea*. As the adventurer explores the labyrinth of his sensations, he discovers that the labyrinth is no jungle, but merely a ramification of culture, another cell in the vast prison of continuity from which he thought to escape. Sartre, more radically than Lawrence, against the magniloquence of Malraux, announces the dead end of adventure. Unlike characters in the classical novel, Roquentin's leisure exists not this side of adventure, but beyond it, in a sort of negative beatitude.

The inward complication of the adventure story belongs to what may be called a vast imperialism of the mind, culminating absurdly, if splendidly, in the culture of the twentieth century. Since Descartes and Montaigne, a new space has been proclaimed for the accomplishment of aims, situations, and events; a space as complex as the material world, and as unfathomable as the cosmos of the Greeks: it is the space of personal experience. Whereas older, more humble conventions taught men to interrogate their experience in order to learn the nature of the world which impinged upon them in the form of events and situations, now men interrogate their experience in order to develop an interior geography, which has become the only locus for essential moments. If the Greeks suspected, uneasily, that they were guests among the higher mysteries of the world, the modern suspicion is different; today we suspect, uneasily, that it is the world which intrudes as a guest among the higher mysteries of the mind. The inward has accomplished an imperial victory over the outward. That is why storytelling has become a quaint and minor art, offering an antiquarian sort of pleasure: the pleasure of recalling a more ancient time when the world existed, and men could read it, according to the lexicon of signs which today serve only as metaphors for our experience of ourselves.

Pascal's image of man perched at the balance point between two infinities has taken on a strange literalness for us. We live with the firm conviction of the roominess of our interior space. We believe it to be largely unexplored, perhaps even inaccessible. We are fascinated by attempts to clarify it. We admire a sort of "travel literature" which has sprung up describing daring descents into the unknown element, for which the oceans, the heavens, and the depths of the earth provide metaphoric analogies. Coleridge's *Kubla Khan;* De Quincey's *Confessions of an English Opium-Eater;* Baudelaire's *Poeme du Hashish* and his *Paradis Artificiels;* the Romantic association of insanity with a form of adventure: All of these literary idioms borrow the traditional expectations of adventure to express our most daring enterprise: the exploration of interior space.

The very movement inward, which undermined the traditional framework of adventure, created in its place the medium for a new exploit, and a new simplicity. Alongside our Proustian, our Freudian, and our existential complication, we have circled back to a level of primitive certainties. By blurring the distinction between inner and outer space, by reversing our standards of value and authenticity, we have returned once again to the shamanistic origins of adventure.

If shamanism can be understood as a system of techniques for mastering the insecurity of personal experience by organizing its "absences" into a story, then the tradition of hallucinatory fantasies from Gerard de Nerval's *Aurelia*, to Hesse's drug narrative in *Steppenwolf*, and the "interior voyages" which form a vigorous element of contemporary literature, reassert once again a shamanistic vision of the psyche. The divorce between inward and outward adventure, consecrated by epic literature and reiterated by the Western tradition of storytelling, has ended in the nineteenth and twentieth centuries, so that we are faced today with an archaic insight: Once again we believe that the collapse of human limits—in the psyche as well as in the world—is a nightmare from which man perpetually awakens, by turning his terror into a story.

While T. E. Lawrence and Sartre grappled with the vanishing authenticity of "action," another, more naïve tradition asserted itself, founded on the shamanistic premise that the mind offers a shortcut into the invisible world which the psychic adventurer, using drugs, dreams, or trance, is not afraid to take, because he possesses the skill of safe returns, the skill of storytelling. Raymond Roussel and the surrealists; Herman Hesse; Henri Michaux; William Burroughs; more recently Carlos Castaneda's Indian sage, Don Juan: All of these, and others, have given rise to an idiom of adventure which has had a profound influence upon our cultural attitudes. Divorced from "action" by the enforced leisure of his self-awareness, the modern adventurer enters boldly into "interior space." Whereas Gilgamesh opened the great cedar gate, and Odysseus slipped compulsively into unknown seas, the shamanistic hero charms open the gate in his mind. The way out of the Gothic confinement of Sartre's no-exit world and Proust's cork-lined room has become not "action" in the old sense, but "absence" in the still older sense.

Indeed, the escape from continuity has become our most powerful cultural idiom, not only in Thomas Pynchon's and Norman

Mailer's flirtation with adventure narrative, or in the immensely popular revival of medieval-style romance by Tolkien, but in the episodic sensibility of so much contemporary literature. The memorable works of fiction of the past decade have not been novels at all, but fragmentary forms, short stories, dream fantasies. I am thinking of Isaac Bashevis Singer's demonic tales; William Burroughs' *Naked Lunch* and *Nova Express*; Jerzy Kosinski's *The Painted Bird* and *Steps*; the pervasive influence of Borges; Norman Mailer's autobiographical journalism. It may be that William Faulkner was our last novelist. Since then, we have lost our interest in the extended metaphor of character which presides even over modernist novels like *Ulysses.*

One way to describe the change is this. The novel has traditionally set out to reassure the reader that a form exists in every life, giving it meaning and direction. The aesthetic wholeness of the novel, its beginning, middle, and end, make this meaning palpable. Every event in the novel, every emotion, no matter how seemingly arbitrary or spontaneous, has been kindled in advance by the impending satisfaction of an end, a palpable, inherently artistic conclusion.[34] What no man can grasp from within—the sense of an elaborate wholeness, a fully woven pattern—is offered comfortably, realistically, by the novel. Recently, however, we have begun to expect another pleasure from the stories we read. The spectacle of life's hidden form emerging from the vagaries of experience no longer warms our hearts. On the contrary, it chills us just a little, as if the form were a prison, and the novel's end-informed story the evidence for a failure of spirit. What Singer, Burroughs, and Borges express in their work are disruptive moments, flashes of illuminating intensity. It is not the end which is important, but the episode; not the form, of which the end is the final clarity, as when a sculptor unveils a statue, but the illumination itself, unruly and momentary, not casting a new light over what has been lived, but compressing life itself into its absoluteness, and bursting.

Robert Jay Lifton has written: "Such things as the drug revolution among the young, and their general stress upon intense experience, or upon what could be called experiential radicalism —whether in politics, art or life style—all these may well be quests for new forms of experiential transcendence." [35] Adventure, too, as we have defined it, is clearly a form of "experiential transcendence." In the midst of action, each move is dense with the weight of a lifetime, and is a lifetime, blazing with momentary intensity. Action fuses the moment into a separate whole, its parts powerfully compressed and interrelated, as in a dream. It is no surprise, therefore, that the popularity of episodic forms has been accompanied by a renewed fascination with adventure. The declining popularity of detective novels among the young is one evidence for the change. Whereas an older generation found its pleasure in the proposition that mysteries are puzzles which can be solved by "ratiocination," the young today show a marked preference for science fiction, or Tolkien-like fantasies; that is, for versions of romance, in which the mysteries exist not to be explained, but to be vanquished.

Perhaps the most interesting recent argument for the episodic has been made by Norman Mailer. In a sense, he is the historian of the change, and a main figure in it. Mailer became famous twenty-five years ago for exploiting the last subject matter in which a serious novelist and popular fantasy could meet: warfare. *The Naked and the Dead* is probably our last nineteenth-century novel, a kind of subspecies of *War and Peace*, and the final act of our nostalgia for novelistic wholeness. Ever since then, Mailer has floundered in and out of narrative, acknowledging his passion to tell a story, but recognizing, too, the campiness of "plot" with its mannered scenery, its characters busy doing nothing, its web of penitentiary relationships.

During those years, Mailer made an important discovery for himself. He discovered that he could no longer believe in the novelistic relationship between writing and life. The proposition that any man's existence, properly translated into language, could become a field of mysteries worthy of epic, was untrue, and worse, uninteresting. The net of syntax can be cast with intricate skill, but Leopold Bloom will still, ultimately, be a boring man, and Stephen Dedalus a sensitive but small-time aesthete.

The true "existential" exploit is not to make subject matter out of your life, but to make your life over and over again, into subject matter. In *Advertisements for Myself*, and *The Presidential Papers*, one sees a personality rising to the occasion of language, performing erratically, self-indulgently, because without the episodic heroism and the bizarre self-enlargements, he would not be subject matter; as if Mailer felt that to be the "hero" of a story, one had to be a hero in the archaic sense, the kind songs are sung about. Mailer's satisfaction as a writer resembles that of Odysseus at the feast in Phaiakia, when he tells the long story of his adventures. Mailer's public personality has been that of a man endlessly picking a fight: prizefighting has been his image of what it feels like to be a writer, but also of what it feels like to be a man. Who can forget the extraordinary description of Benny Paret's death in his fight with Emile Griffith? The climax of blows is hypnotic, like a sexual climax. It is Mailer's archetypal scene: a man facing death or humiliation, and therefore revealed in the fullness of his mystery.

A question is inevitably raised by this shift in the values of fiction. What adventures are there left to have? Where must one look to discover those gaps in the net of reality through which the adventurer slips? We know that forests are composed of ecological balances, not tree-gods and snake-spirits. We know that the horizon is not an ontological barrier. We know that all the places in the world are connected by lines of longitude and latitude, and most likely by politics, too. Yet the taste for adventure persists. Frivolous heroisms erupt when and where we least expect them. A man rows a dinghy across the Atlantic, or floats on a ship made of Egyptian papyrus from Africa to the Caribbean. Sir Francis Chichester sails alone around the world in a small sailboat. Mountain climbers scramble up a sheer cliff face, "because it's there." Young men and women hitchhike around the world, cross the Sahara, build primitive farms in remote areas of the Rocky Mountains, or hole up in isolated hamlets in Nepal.

The heroic explorations of Scott and Rasmussen, the muscular ambitions of Hemingway and Malraux, the intensities of Faulkner, appear even now to belong to a naïve age of belief, admirable but not wholly available to us. World War II seems to have been the watershed. Before then a residual confidence in adventure remained a firm part of the popular imagination, expressed in the old pulp magazines, in movies, in the sphere of political revolution, even in the fascination for great criminals like Dillinger and Al Capone. Since then, the world has gotten smaller and more businesslike. Even espionage and crime have become encased in the ordinary. James Bond amuses us precisely because we don't believe anything about him, because he is a kind of joke.

Mailer has said that he admires Hemingway and Malraux. He likes to imagine himself as a continuer of the tradition which they represent, the tradition of great adventurers. As a novelist, in works like *The Naked and the Dead, The American Dream,* and *Why Are We in Vietnam?,* he evokes the extravagant energies inhabiting moments of risk and extremity. But as his subject matter has intertwined itself with his own life, as Mailer has become the episodic hero of his "song," it has become clear that his personal exploits do not at all resemble those of Hemingway or Malraux. He does not go hunting in Africa, write battlefield reports from Indochina, or participate in revolutions. The heroism he builds in the interstices of his life and the extravagance of his style are elusive, often composed of a flirtation with ridicule. As if he earned rights to the heroic violence of his prose, by odds and ends of violence in his life, which are all that a "serious" man can manage these days.

Mailer's willful blundering describes the paradox of the episodic morality. Its exploits are not exotic journeys, crimes, even revolutionary violence. Its energy is aimless. Yet this is precisely what links it to the ancient energies of adventure, for the adventurer's quest must be its own goal. Like Odysseus, Gilgamesh, and the knights of medieval romance, the episodic heroes go nowhere in particular. The world may or may not harbor spacious possibilities, but the adventurer's magnificence lies in the going itself.

Notes

Chapter 1

1. Graham Greene, *The Ministry of Fear* (New York: Viking, 1952), p. 140.
2. *The Epic of Gilgamesh*, trans. N. K. Sondars (London: Penguin, 1960), p. 72.
3. *La Vie Surhumaine de Guzar de Ling Le Hero Thibétain*, trans. by Alexandra David-Neel and Soma Yongden (Paris: Editions ADYAR, 1931).
4. Mario Praz, *The Hero in Eclipse in Victorian Fiction*, trans. Angus Davidson (New York: Oxford University Press, 1956).
5. Joseph Conrad, *Lord Jim* (London: Penguin, 1957), p. 11.
6. Robert Scholes and Robert Kellogg, *The Nature of Narrative* (New York: Oxford University Press, 1960), pp. 6-7.
7. Ian Watt, *The Rise of the Novel* (Berkeley, Calif.: University of California Press, 1959), pp. 9-60.
8. André Malraux, *Le Temps du Mepris* (Paris: Gallimard, 1935).

Chapter 2

1. Charles H. Taylor, Jr., ed. *Essays on the Odyssey*, (Bloomington, Ind.: Indiana University Press, 1963), p. 40.
2. Ibid., pp. 39-40.
3. *The Odyssey*, trans. Robert Fitzgerald (New York: Doubleday Anchor Books, 1963), p. 440.
4. C. S. Lewis in Fitzgerald, *Essays on the Odyssey*, p. 41.
5. *The Odyssey*, p. 328.
6. *Essays on the Odyssey*, pp. 54-72.
7. Ibid., p. 55.

Notes

8. Ibid., p. 55.
9. Ibid., p. 60.
10. Ibid., pp. 60-61.
11. *The Odyssey*, pp. 188-89.
12. R. D. Laing, *The Divided Self* (London: Penguin, 1965), p. 110.
13. Dante, *The Inferno*, trans. John Ciardi (New York: Mentor, 1954), p. 223.
14. Eric Auerbach, *Mimesis* (New York: Doubleday Anchor Books, 1957). p. 4.

Chapter 3

1. *Beowulf*, trans. Burton Raffel (New York: New American Library, 1963), p. 6.
2. Ibid, p.5.
3. Ibid.
4. Ibid., p. 38.
5. Ibid., p. 7.
6. Ibid., p. 12.
7. Ibid., p. 14.
8. Ibid., p. 16.
9. Ibid., p. 59.
10. Georges Dumezil, *L'Heur et Malheur du Guerrier* (Paris: Presses Universitaires de France, 1969), p. 121.
11. Ibid., p. 121.
12. Ibid., p. 80.
13. Ibid., p. 97.

Chapter 4

1. Joseph Conrad, *Heart of Darkness* (New York: Dell, 1960), p. 92.
2. Ibid., p. 95.
3. Friedrich W. Nietzsche, *The Birth of Tragedy*, trans. Francis Golffing (New York: Doubleday Anchor Books, 1956), p. 29.
4. See Chapter Five, "The Flight from Women."
5. *The Epic of Gilgamesh*, trans. N. K. Sonders (London: Penguin, 1960), p. 60.
6. Ibid., p. 70.

Chapter 5

1. Lewis Mumford, quoted by Wolfgang Lederer (New York: Harcourt, Brace, Jovanovich, 1968), pp. 86-87.
2. *The Epic of Gilgamesh*, trans. N. K. Sonders (London: Penguin, 1960), p. 63.
3. Ibid., p. 63.
4. Ibid., pp. 64-65.
5. Ibid., p. 62.
6. Ibid., pp. 105-106.

Notes

7. Tacitus, quoted by J. L. Borges in *Essai sur les Anciennes literatures germaniques,* Coll. 16/18 (Paris: 1966), pp. 13-14.

Chapter 6

1. Miguel de Cervantes, *Don Quixote,* trans. J. M. Cohen (London: Penguin, 1950), p. 576.
2. John G. Neihardt, *Black Elk Speaks* (Lincoln: University of Nebraska Press, 1961), p. 23.
3. Meyer Levin, *Classic Hassidic Tales* (New York: Citadel Press, 1966), p. 82.
4. Ibid., p. 82.
5. I. M. Lewis, *Ecstatic Religion* (London: Penguin, 1971), pp. 188-89.
6. Mircea Eliade, *Chamanisme* (Paris: Payot, 1968), p. 153.
7. Ibid., pp. 237-38.
8. Ibid., pp. 186-187.

Chapter 7

1. Max Weber, *The Protestant Ethic and the Spirit of Capitalism* (New York: Scribner, 1964), p. 154.
2. Montaigne, *Complete Essays,* trans. Donald Frame (Stanford, Calif.: Stanford University Press, 1958), p. 600.
3. Daniel Defoe, *Serious Reflections During the Life and Surprising Adventures of Robinson Crusoe* (London: J. M. Dent, 1895), p. 2.
4. Ibid., p. 6.
5. Marshall Berman, *The Politics of Authenticity* (New York: Atheneum, 1970), p. 49.
6. Defoe, *Serious Reflections,* pp. xi-xii.
7. James Sutherland, *Defoe* (Philadelphia: Lippincott, 1938), p. 46.
8. J. T. Boulton, ed., *Daniel Defoe* (New York: Schocken, 1965), p. 130.
9. Ibid., p. 2.
10. Ibid., p. 131.
11. Defoe, *Serious Reflections,* p. x.
12. J. Paul Hunter, *The Reluctant Pilgrim* (Baltimore: Johns Hopkins Press, 1966); George Starr, *Defoe and Spiritual Autobiography* (Princeton, N.J.: Princeton University Press, 1965).
13. Starr, *Defoe and Spiritual Autobiography,* p. 93.
14. Quoted in Hunter, *The Reluctant Pilgrim,* p. 37.
15. Quoted in Starr, *Defoe and Spiritual Autobiography,* pp. 80-81.
16. Quoted in ibid., p. 57.
17. Quoted in ibid., p. 56.

Chapter 8

1. Georg Simmel, "The Adventure," *Essays on Sociology, Philosophy and Esthetics* (New York: Harper & Row Torchbooks, 1959), pp. 243-258.
2. Frank H. Ellis, ed., *Robinson Crusoe, Twentieth Century Interpretations* (Englewood Cliffs, N.J.: Prentice-Hall, 1969), p. 21.

Notes

3. Daniel Defoe, *Robinson Crusoe* (New York: Signet Classic, 1961), p. 72.

4. Ibid., p. 17.

5. Ibid., p. 57.

6. Ibid., p. 68.

7. Ibid., pp. 159-160.

8. Homer Brown, "The Displaced Self in the Novels of Daniel Defoe," *English Literary History*, 38:4 (Dec. 1971), 562-590.

9. Defoe, *Robinson Crusoe*, p. 112.

10. Defoe, *Robinson Crusoe*, p. 9.

11. John Milton, *Paradise Lost* (New York: Odyssey Press, 1962), Book X, 1. 209ff.

12. Milton, *Paradise Lost*, Book X, 1. 216.

13. Quoted in Ernst Cassirer, *The Philosophy of the Enlightenment* (Princeton, N.J.: Princeton University Press, 1951), p. 217.

14. Ibid., p. 213.

15. Ibid., p. 243.

16. Ibid.

17. Ibid., p. 9.

18. Ibid., p. 13.

19. Basil Willey, *Eighteenth Century Background* (Boston: Beacon Press, 1961), p. 20.

20. Ibid., p. 111.

21. Ibid., p. 52.

Chapter 9

1. Choderlos de Laclos, *Les Liaisons Dangereuses* (New York: Signet Classic, 1962), p. 55.

2. Ibid., p. 293.

3. Ibid., p. 177.

4. Quoted in J. Rives Childs, *Casanova* (London: George Allen & Unwin, 1961), pp. 101-102.

5. This and all other quotes from Casanova's writing are taken from Casanova, *History of My Life*, trans. Willard Trask (New York: Harcourt, Brace & World, 1968).

6. Jean Starobinski, *The Invention of Liberty* (Geneva: Skira, 1964), p. 14.

7. Ibid., p. 15.

8. Ibid., p. 16.

Chapter 10

1. J. M. S. Tompkins, *The Popular Novel* in England (London: Methuen, 1969).

2. Matthew G. Lewis, *The Monk* (New York: Grove Press, 1952), pp. 395-396.

3. Michel Foucault, *Histoire de la Folie* (Paris: Plon, 1961).

4. Lewis, *The Monk*, pp. 419-420.

Notes

5. De Sade, *Français Encore un Effort* (Paris: Pauvert, 1965). The translation of this, and the following passages from de Sade, are mine.
6. Ibid., p. 61.
7. Ibid., p. 97.
8. Ibid., pp. 102-103.

Chapter 11

1. Wilhelm Dibelius, *Englische Romankunst* (Berlin, 1910), vol. 1, pp. 316-317 (quoted in the manuscript of Joseph Frank's critical biography of Dostoevski).
2. Herman Melville, *Moby Dick* (New York: Bobbs-Merrill, 1964), p. 308.
3. Joseph Conrad, *Heart of Darkness* (London: Penguin, 1957), p. 67.
4. Ibid., p. 28.
5. Ibid., p. 125.
6. Edgar Allan Poe, *The Narrative of Arthur Gordon Pym* (New York: Hill & Wang, 1960).
7. Ibid., p. 120.
8. Ibid., p. 146.
9. Ibid., p. 149.
10. Ibid., p. 151.
11. Ibid., p. 156.
12. Ibid., p. 186.
13. Ibid., p. 197.
14. Ibid., p. 195.
15. Ibid., p. 16.
16. Ibid., p. 144.
17. Ibid., pp. 193-194.
18. Ibid.
19. Ibid., p. 24.
20. Ibid., p. 9.

Chapter 12

1. Friedrich W. Nietzsche, "The Gay Science," in *The Portable Nietzsche*, ed. and trans. Walter Kaufmann (New York: Viking, 1954), p. 97.
2. Friedrich W. Nietzsche, *Twilight of the Idols*, trans. R. J. Hollingdale (London: Penguin, 1968), p. 81.
3. *Thus Spoke Zarathoustra*, in *Portable Nietzsche*, p. 153.
4. Nietzsche, *Twilight of the Idols*, p. 92.
5. *Zarathoustra* in *Portable Nietzsche*, p. 217.
6. *Mixed Ofrious and Maxims* in *Portable Nietzsche*, p. 67.
7. *On Truth and Lie in an Extra-Moral Sense* in *Portable Nietzsche*, p. 44.
8. *Homer's Contest in Portable Nietzsche*, p. 34.
9. Ibid., p. 38.
10. Ibid., p. 33.
11. *On Truth and Lie* in *Portable Nietzsche*, p. 44.

Notes

12. Friedrich W. Nietzsche, *Genealogy of Morals*, trans. Francis Golffing (New York: Doubleday Anchor Books, 1956), p. 208.
13. Friedrich W. Nietzsche, *The Antichrist*, trans. R. J. Hollingdale (London: Penguin, 1968), p. 116.
14. Ibid., p. 116.
15. Nietzsche, *The Genealogy of Morals*, p. 167.
16. *The Dawn*, in *Portable Nietzsche*, p. 83.
17. Ibid., p. 82.
18. Nietzsche, *Twilight of the Idols*, p. 98.
19. *Zarathoustra* in *Portable Nietzsche*, p. 150.
20. Ibid., p. 151.
21. Nietzsche, *Genealogy of Morals*, p. 229.
22. *Zarathoustra* in *Portable Nietzsche*, p. 208.
23. Ibid., p. 189.
24. Ibid., p. 216.
25. Ibid., p. 170.
26. Ibid., p. 170.
27. *Notes (1874)* in *Portable Nietzsche*, p. 50.
28. Nietzsche, *The Antichrist*, p. 121.
29. *Zarathoustra* in *Portable Nietzsche*, pp. 198-199.
30. Ibid., p. 199.
31. Ibid., pp. 226-227.
32. Nietzsche, *Twilight of the Idols*, p. 88.
33. *Zarathoustra* in *Portable Nietzsche*, p. 226.
34. Ibid., p. 227.
35. Ibid., p. 225.
36. Ibid., p. 435.
37. Walter Kaufmann, *Nietzsche* (New York: Meridian Books, 1956), pp. 266-286.
38. Nietzsche, *Twilight of the Idols*, p. 111.
39. *Zarathoustra* in *Portable Nietzsche*, p. 267.
40. Ibid., p. 342.
41. Ibid., p. 341.

Chapter 13

1. Conan Doyle, *The Lost World* (New York: Berkley, 1965), p. 11.
2. Ibid., p. 12.
3. T. E. Lawrence, *Seven Pillars of Wisdom* (New York: Dell, 1962), p. 341.
4. Ibid., p. 197.
5. Ibid., p. 220.
6. Ibid., p. 402.
7. Ibid., p. 546.
8. Ibid., p. 550.
9. Ibid., p. 245.
10. Ibid., p. 254.
11. Ibid., p. 37.
12. Ibid., p. 40.
13. Ibid., p. 547.
14. Ibid., p. 448.

15. Ibid., p. 251.

16. Ibid., p. 451.

17. André Malraux, *La Voie Royale* (Paris: Livre de Poche, 1959), pp. 36-37 (all translations mine).

18. Ibid., p. 37.

19. Ibid., pp. 37-38.

20. Ibid., pp. 65-67.

21. Ibid., p. 49.

22. Ibid., p. 82.

23. Ibid., p. 92.

24. Ibid., p. 12.

25. Ibid., p. 60.

26. Jean-Paul Sartre, *La Nausé* (Paris: Livre de Poche, 1959), p. 180 (all translations mine).

27. Ibid., p. 187.

28. Ibid., p. 189.

29. Ibid., p. 180.

30. Ibid., p. 188.

31. Ibid., p. 158.

32. Ibid., p. 159.

33. Ibid., p. 58.

34. Frank Kermode, *The Sense of an Ending* (London: Oxford University Press, 1966).

35. Robert Jay Lifton, *Boundaries: Psychological Man in Revolution* (New York: Vintage, 1967), p. 28.

Index

261

Index

Arabian Nights, The, storytelling convention in, 84, 191

Ares (god), 54

Ariosto, Lodovico, 14

Aristotle, 93, 187

Army recruitment posters, hero figures and, 48

Arthur, King (legendary figure), 64

Aruru (goddess), 72

Astronauts: as heroes, 35; response to, 46

Asvin (god), 45

Athena (goddess): intervention in Trojan War by, 54, 55; as representative of new patristic religion, 77; wanderings of Odysseus and, 20

Atlantide, L' (Benoit), 226

Auerbach, Erich, 21, 31–32

Augustine, Saint, 141

Aurelia (Nerval), 88, 247

Austen, Jane, 12, 170, 189

Autobiography: adventure as form of, 114; Casanova's History as, 139–140, 141; spiritual, Robinson Crusoe similar to, 108, 110–111, 112

Autolycus (Greek mythology), 25

Balzac, Honoré de, 12, 14–15, 171, 190

Baudelaire, Charles, 163, 180, 202, 246

Beckett, Samuel, 10, 81

Benjamin, Walter, 95

Benoit, Pierre, 226

Beowulf (character), 16, 126, 199, 229, 241; Christian overtones to, 37–38; as hero, 36, 49; Nietzsche's "overman" and, 212, 213; survival of mother religions in representations of struggles of, 68; Unferth's challenge to, 38–40

Beowulf (poem), 203; Christianity and geography of, 37–38; epic character of, 40–42; survival of mother religions in, 68; Unferth's challenge to Beowulf in, 38–40

Bernis, Abbé de, 162

Bettelheim, Bruno, 70

Biran, Maine de, 155

Birth of Tragedy, The (Nietzsche), 54, 85

Black Elk Speaks (Neihardt), 87

Blake, William, 100

Bloom, Leopold (character, Ulysses), 10, 250

Bloomsbury group, 232

Bond, James (fictional character), 61, 251

Book of Job, 82

Borges, Jorge Luis, 248

Bovary, Emma (character, Madame Bovary), 10

Bragadin (Venetian nobleman), 156

Breca (character, Beowulf), 38, 39

Bremond, Colonel, 231

Briffault, Robert, 80

Brokhaus (German bookseller), 137

Brooke, Rupert, 229

Brown, Homer, 117

Browne, Sir Thomas, 51

Burroughs, Edgar Rice, 4

Burroughs, William, 247, 248

Byron, George, Lord, 171

Index

Index

Index

Index

Mother, Egyptian hieroglyphic representation of, 70

Mother religions, survival of, in stories of heroes, 68, 77–78, 80

Mothers, psychoanalytic theory of literary role of, 78–79

Mothers, The (Briffault), 80

Motion pictures: adventure theme in, 223, 225; heroic qualities of stars in, 35, 229; pirate adventurer theme in, 48

Mountain climbing, 250

Mumford, Lewis, 69–70

Musil, Robert von, 10

Mycenean life, women's place in, 69

Mysteries of Paris, The (Sue), 170, 190

Mysteries of Udolpho, The (Radcliffe), 170

Mythology: adventure as source of meanings in, 6, 223; hero figures in, 43; Joyce's use of themes from, 88; struggle between mother and patristic religions represented in, 77–78, 80; women's image in, 69–70

Naked and the Dead, The (Mailer), 249, 251

Naked Lunch, The (Burroughs), 248

"Name of Odysseus, The" (Dimock), 25

Napoleon, 164, 171, 230

Narrative of Arthur Gordon Pym, The (Poe), 15, 17, 189, 191–193

National Aeronautics and Space Administration (NASA), heroic model of astronauts chosen by, 35

Nausea (Sartre), 171, 238, 242–245

Nausicaa (character, *Odyssey*), 23, 27

Naziism, Nietzsche and, 206

Neihardt, John G., 87

Nerval, Gerard de, 88, 247

Nichta (character, Irish legend), 43

Nietzsche, Friedrich, 17, 85, 100, 167, 238; classical ideal for, 53–54; Homer's clarity admired by, 26, 30, 31; philosophy of adventure of, 204–222

Nisba (goddess), 72

No Exit (Sartre), 171

Nordic mythology, adventurer theme in, 48

North American Indians, soul-journey theme among, 87

Northern mythology, hero figure in, 43

Nova Express (Burroughs), 248

Nrthus (goddess), 78

Occult sciences, Casanova's fascination with, 154, 156-158, 160-161, 163

Odysseus (hero), 6, 16, 19–33, 191, 247; Achilles compared with, 52; as adventurer, 49, 126, 252; Beowulf compared with, 36; Calypso and idleness of, 71; as hero, 34, 36, 49; homecoming of, 26–28, 241; as lover, 159; meaning of name of, 25–26; Nietzsche's "overman" and, 199, 206, 212, 213, 215, 219; Penelope and, 69; recurrence of wanderings of, 221; as

Index

Index

Index

Index